American Government and Politics

American Government and Politics

by

ALLEN M. POTTER

With an introduction by
Professor K. C. Wheare

FABER AND FABER LIMITED
24 Russell Square
London

First published in 1955
by Faber and Faber Limited
24 Russell Square London W.C.1
First published in this edition 1961
Reprinted 1963, 1966 and 1969
Printed in Great Britain by
Lowe and Brydone (Printers) Limited
London

FPCE 571 05581 8
Cloth 571 03950 2

To
M.A.P.

Contents

Preface

M r. Marcus Cunliffe of the Department of American Studies in the University of Manchester suggested that I put on paper what I have been telling British audiences about the government and politics of my country. This book is the result.

I have received permission to quote brief passages of several books and articles from their publishers or authors, to whom acknowledgment is made in footnotes to the text. My wife helped prepare the typescript of this book. Professor Wheare suggested improvements. Mr. David Walker of the Department of Economics at Manchester read the section on the fiscal element of American federalism to-day. I thank them all. I am particularly grateful to Professor Wheare for writing an introduction.

I am solely responsible for the statement of what I believe to be the facts and the opinions I express.

ALLEN M. POTTER

Manchester,
January 1955

Introduction

There is an old belief that books on American government intended for British readers should be written by British authors. As massive and indeed almost conclusive evidence in support of this dogma there stood and stands the great name and work of James Bryce and his *American Commonwealth*. That so extreme an opinion can be recognized as an eternal verity would be accepted by few, if any, in these days, but that it contains or symbolizes an important part of the truth cannot be doubted. He who would explain American government to British readers must himself know almost as much about British government as he docs about American government. He must know what British people expect from government and what they think their political institutions are for and what, explicitly or implicitly, they believe the criteria of good government to be, before he can convey to them adequately the fact that Americans think very differently about these matters, and ask and receive very different things from their own political institutions.

It seems to me that a leading merit of this book is that its American author, Mr. Allen Potter, very obviously understands not only the system of government which he is expounding to his British readers, but also the system of government under which his readers live. He is able to tell us how the functions of government as we understand them in Britain and in the Commonwealth are carried out in the United States usually by different methods and institutions from those which we might expect, but at the same time he can avoid giving us the impression that what the Americans are really trying to do is to work the British constitution and that what they are succeeding in doing is to misunderstand it. This is an extraordinarily difficult task, but I believe that Mr. Potter has accomplished it with complete success.

American political parties are a great mystery to the British reader, and even when he has contrived to understand something of their activities in the choosing of a president, he finds their behaviour in Congress completely and continually baffling. Yet the American Constitution and the American system of government are unintelligible without some understanding of the working of the political parties. In this respect I think that Mr. Potter's plan of exposition is both wise and illuminating. He has combined history and analysis admirably in his chapters on the parties and he has had the good sense to realize that although the reader should have more than a superficial knowledge of parties, there is a limit to what he can be expected to grasp. He strikes the right balance here between the exposition of the law of the Constitution—so essential to an understanding of American government above all others—and the description of the politics and politicians so inextricably mixed up with it.

Here then is a book on American government for British readers written by an American author, and for my part I find it most interesting and illuminating. Had I ever held the doctrine that such books should be written by British authors only, Mr. Potter's book would have caused me to lose my faith.

K. C. W.

All Souls College, Oxford
9 January 1955

Chapter 1

The Constitution

The Constitution of the United States is the second written Constitution of the American national government. The American national government began as a revolutionary Continental Congress, which in June 1776 turned over the drafting of a Declaration of Independence and the drafting of a written Constitution to committees on successive days. The Congress adopted the Declaration of Independence, which was almost entirely the work of Thomas Jefferson, on 4 July 1776; its famous phrases,

'We hold these truths to be self-evident, that all men are created equal, that they are endowed by their Creator with certain unalienable rights, that among these are life, liberty, and the pursuit of happiness. That to secure these rights, governments are instituted among men, deriving their just powers from the consent of the governed,'

have been the inspiration of American democracy. But because of disputes between the advocates of strong and weak national government, the Congress did not adopt the first written Constitution, the Articles of Confederation and perpetual Union, until 15 November 1777; and the last of the thirteen original States of the new nation did not ratify the Articles until 1 March 1781.

The Articles remained in force until 2 April 1789, when the House of Representatives under the second written Constitution, drafted in 1787, was organized. Thus there were two constitutional periods in independent American history prior to the establishment of government under the present Constitution: the first from 1776 to 1781, during which the national government worked without a written definition of powers; and the second from 1781 to 1789, during which it worked under the Articles of Confederation.

The Articles of Confederation did not alter the existing institutions of the national government very much. They provided for a unicameral Congress, composed of delegates from the States, each delegation having one vote. The State legislatures elected the delegates annually, but could recall them at any time. The Articles gave Congress authority to appoint a Committee of the States, composed of one delegate from each State, which could exercise some of the powers of Congress during a recess, and to appoint other committees and civil officers 'as may be necessary for managing the general affairs of the united States' under the direction of Congress. There was no provision for 'separation of powers'.

The Articles represented a victory for the advocates of weak national government. In words, the powers granted to the national Congress seemed considerable, embracing the conduct of foreign affairs, the declaration and conduct of war, dealings with the Indian tribes, the borrowing of money, the emission of bills of credit, the regulation of weights and measures, and the requisition of soldiers and funds from the States. But the powers were vitiated by the lack of any means of compulsion. Congress could not compel the States to meet their obligations, and could not reach past the States to control the people in any effective way. It did not, for example, have the power to tax. Furthermore, the ability of the national government to use what authority it had was weakened by the requirement that nine of the thirteen State delegations must concur in the exercise of the most important powers of Congress.

Many merchants thought that a great weakness of the Articles was the absence of national power to regulate interstate commerce, for they were hampered by tariffs and trade wars among the States. Business and propertied classes generally were dissatisfied with government under the Articles. Land speculators were disturbed by the failure of the national government to protect western lands from the Indian allies of the British in

Canada and the Spanish in Louisiana. Government bond-holders were disturbed by the poor credit of the national government. Private creditors were disturbed by the paper money and debtors laws of several States.

The political spokesmen for the propertied classes wanted a strong national government that would protect mercantile and creditor interests, and the Articles of Confederation did not provide a strong national government. The 'nationalists' tried to get the kind of government they wanted by arguing that the Articles should be interpreted as allowing the national govern-ment to act whenever the general welfare was involved. Their opponents successfully pointed out that the second Article clearly said that each State retained 'every power, jurisdiction and right, which is not by this confederation expressly delegated to the United States, in Congress assembled'. The 'nationalists' tried to amend the Articles. The necessary acquiescence of all thirteen State legislatures could never be obtained. (Two attempts to give Congress some taxing power received the support of twelve States, Rhode Island failing to agree in one case and New York in the other.) Finally, the 'nationalists' sought to replace the Articles, and for this purpose they asked the States to send delegates to a convention in Philadelphia in 1787, purportedly to consider amendments to the Articles, but actually to draft a new Constitution.

In view of the aim of the 'nationalists', to create a strong national government that would protect propertied interests, it is not surprising that the delegates who attended the convention were drawn from the professional and propertied classes. What is surprising is how little attention historians paid to this fact until the beginning of this century, when J. Allen Smith brought out his *The Spirit of American Government* in 1907 and Charles A. Beard his *An Economic Interpretation of the Constitution of the United States* in 1913. A large majority of the 55 delegates who attended the convention were lawyers, 29 were university graduates, at least 14 had acquired land for speculative purposes, at least 24 were loaning money at interest, at least 11 had mercantile and manufacturing connections, at least 15 owned slaves, and perhaps 40 owned public bonds and other public securities. The

B   17

framers of the Constitution of 1787 clearly stood to benefit economically from the kind of constitutional revision they proposed.

Some of the negative evidence is equally important. No delegate was a wage-earner or frontiersman. The one delegate who spoke for small farmers left the convention without signing the draft Constitution and opposed its ratification. In other words, well over nine-tenths of the people of the country were practically unrepresented at Philadelphia. The framers of the Constitution were representatives of a minority of merchants and large land-owners in a country where the overwhelming majority of people were small farmers.

Many of the framers were young. Jonathan Dayton of New Jersey was 27, Charles Pinckney of South Carolina was 29, Alexander Hamilton of New York was 30, Gouverneur Morris of Pennsylvania was 35, and James Madison of Virginia was 36. At the other end of the age scale, Benjamin Franklin of Pennsylvania was 81, but the average of the delegates was only 42. Nevertheless, almost all of them were practised men of affairs. About three-fourths of them were or had been members of the national Congress. Eight of them had signed the Declaration of Independence. Several of them were or had been governors of their States. The framers shaped the details of the Constitution they drafted in the light of their own experience as practical politicians under a variety of governments.

Before Smith's and Beard's books appeared, the fashion of American historians was to emphasize the disagreements among the delegates that had to be compromised, the way in which the convention seemed several times to be almost hopelessly deadlocked, and the fact that only 39 of the 55 delegates who attended the convention signed the final draft. There were important compromises: between States with small and States with large populations; between Southern slave-owners and Northern merchants; and among the individual delegates on the details of organization. But there were also important fundamental agreements. They were often hardly discussed at the convention, because the delegates naturally debated fully the points on which they differed and left largely unsaid the points on which they agreed.

Almost all of the delegates agreed that the new national government must be stronger than the old one. They agreed that it must have compulsive power and be supreme in its sphere, and this meant that it must operate directly on the people and not be dependent on the States. They agreed that the new frame of government must provide protection for property rights and put checks on popular government. These agreements were reached in informal discussions among key delegates who arrived at Philadelphia early and were rarely in danger of being upset during the formal convention that followed.

The convention met in secret. The journal of proceedings, published in 1819, recorded only the votes taken. Present knowledge of what went on is based chiefly on the notes which James Madison wrote out after the sessions and which were published in 1840. In the secrecy of the convention, the delegates spoke freely of their motives and interests. They accepted almost without argument the theory that society divides into classes along economic lines. They saw their task as one of preserving property rights, with which they equated liberty, from the attacks of the poorer classes. They did not want to preserve them, however, at the cost of losing their free institutions.

'In future times', Madison said, 'a great majority of the people will not only be without landed, but any other sort of, property. These will either combine under the influence of their common situation, in which case the rights of property and the public liberty will not be secure;—or which is more probable, they will become tools of opulence and ambition, in which case there will be equal danger on another side.'

Again and again the delegates used phrases like 'the evils we experience flow from the excesses of democracy', though several delegates repeatedly warned that the convention should not 'run to the opposite extreme', if only because the people outside the convention would not ratify their proposals.

The framers of the Constitution sought, in short, a practical solution to the problem of middle-class political theory: how to have a government strong enough to protect property rights and mercantile interests, yet not so strong as to infringe property rights and political liberty. The measure of their success is the status of private property and civil liberty in America to-day.

The solution the framers proposed to the problem of protecting property without tyranny was to establish a strong national government within the federal system, but to distribute its powers according to the principles of separation of powers and checks and balances so that no organ of government, particularly the popularly elected House of Representatives, had unchecked power.[1]

The framers established as strong a national government as they thought the voters would accept. Like the Congress under the Articles of Confederation, the Congress under the new Constitution was granted the power to declare war, regulate dealings with the Indian tribes, borrow money, and regulate weights and measures. The new Congress was also granted the power to regulate commerce among the States and with foreign nations, raise and support armies, lay and collect taxes, and 'to make all laws which shall be necessary and proper for carrying into execution the foregoing powers'. The only important reductions in the powers of Congress were that it now shared the conduct of foreign relations with the President and it was not specifically granted the power to emit bills of credit. The first did not reduce the national share of power, and the second reflected the hostility of the framers to the issuance of paper money. They gave Congress the power only 'to coin money, regulate the value thereof, and of foreign coin'.

The new national government had the means to make its powers effective. It had the power to raise armies, to tax, and to pass enabling legislation. It had its own judicial system. The

---

[1] See the Appendix for a copy of the Constitution and its amendments. In 1953 William Crosskey in his *Politics and the Constitution in the History of the United States* (Volumes I and II) sought to prove that the framers meant the Constitution to establish an extremely strong national government, virtually abolishing the federal system; he set off the most important controversy about the framing of the Constitution since Beard wrote his economic interpretation; most of the historians who have entered the controversy have convincingly challenged the thesis.

Constitution provided that the national courts had jurisdiction over cases arising under the Constitution, laws, and treaties of the United States and over controversies between States and between citizens of different States.

Under the Articles members of Congress, elected by the State legislatures, subject to recall at any time, and required to vote as State delegations, were more like ambassadors than legislators. Under the new Constitution members of the House of Representatives, apportioned among the States on the basis of population, were elected directly by the voters, and while the two Senators from each State were elected by the State legislatures, members of both Houses of Congress were elected for fixed terms and were free to vote as individuals. In sum, under the new Constitution the national government was granted wide powers over foreign affairs, fiscal policy, and commercial intercourse; it acted directly upon its citizens; and it was, in part, directly derived from them.

State and local sentiment was too strong in America to allow the framers to strip the States of all their powers. The States were left free to regulate most of their internal affairs. The structure of local government was left entirely to the States. Local government is not mentioned in the Constitution.

But the framers put restrictions on State action that were designed to protect property rights. The Constitution forbade States to coin money, emit bills of credit, or make 'any thing but gold and silver coin a tender in payment of debts'. It forbade them to pass any 'law impairing the obligation of contracts'. To ensure that these restrictions on State paper money and debtors laws would not be evaded, the framers wrote that 'this Constitution . . . shall be the supreme law of the land; and the judges in every State shall be bound thereby, any thing in the Constitution or laws of any State to the contrary notwithstanding'.

Furthermore, the framers were conscious of the need to compromise among the interests of the different geographical sections of the country. Although they paid scant attention to the requirements of small farmers, they struck several compromises between the plantation interests of the South and the

commercial interests of the North. (They should not be interpreted as compromises between the 'slave' South and 'free'
North, however, for it was not the status of slavery that was at
issue but only the status of property in slaves.) The framers took
over, for example, a well-known formula for counting a slave
as three-fifths of a free person, as the basis for apportioning
representation in the House of Representatives and direct taxes
among the States. In addition, they agreed that slaves who
escaped to free States were to be returned when claimed by
their owners, that the African slave trade could not be prohibited by the national government before 1808, and that no
taxes could be laid on exports. These were safeguards to the
interests of southern planters.

On the other hand, northern merchants were guaranteed
adequate protection abroad and at home. The framers expected that a strong national government would exact more
favourable trade terms from foreign countries than had been
obtained under the Articles of Confederation. They assured
merchants of a free home market by a prohibition of State
taxes on interstate or foreign commerce. Some of the framers
looked upon the provisions of the Constitution that forbade
States to issue paper money and to impair the obligation of
contracts and that gave the national judiciary jurisdiction over
controversies between citizens of different States primarily as
further concessions to northern mercantile interests.

Although they wanted a strong national government, the
framers did not want any organ of it to have inordinate power.
Therefore, they divided the power of the national government
among the three historical branches of government: the legislative, the executive, and the judicial branches. In the debates
that took place during the fight for ratification of the new
Constitution, the framers emphasized how they had thus applied the principle of separation of powers, but of more practical importance was the way they used checks and balances to
intermesh the powers of the three branches.

Thus, while the opening phrase of Article I of the Constitution reads that 'all legislative powers herein granted shall be
vested in a Congress of the United States', the Constitution

granted the President the right to propose measures to Congress and to veto measures that pass. Since a presidential veto can be overridden only by two-thirds majorities of both Houses of Congress, the President obviously was given a substantial share of legislative power. Similarly, though the opening phrase of Article II of the Constitution reads that 'the executive power shall be vested in a President of the United States of America', the Senate was given a share in his appointive and treaty-making powers. Similar examples could be multiplied.

The truth is that the framers' English heritage and experience of Anglo-American governments had more to do with shaping the structure of the new government than political theories. The privileges and immunities of Congress and congressmen set out in Article I—'each House shall be the judge of the elections, returns and qualifications of its own members'; 'the Senators and Representatives . . . shall in all cases, except treason, felony and breach of the peace, be privileged from arrest during their attendance at the session of their respective Houses, and in going to and returning from the same; and for any speech or debate in either House, they shall not be questioned in any other place'—and the restrictions on congressional action in the same Article—'the privilege of the writ of habeas corpus shall not be suspended, unless when in cases of rebellion or invasion the public safety may require it'; and 'no bill of attainder or ex post facto law shall be passed'—bear the hallmark of English and colonial constitutional history. The provision in Article II that 'the President shall, at stated times, receive for his services, a compensation, which shall neither be encreased nor diminished during the period for which he shall have been elected' prohibits practices that were part of executive-legislative relations in colonial days: Benjamin Franklin once told of one Pennsylvania Governor signing bills with one hand and taking a legislative bribe with the other, and royal governors sometimes had to bargain with the colonial assemblies even for their proper salaries. The relations among the States set out in Article IV—'full faith and credit shall be given in each State to the public acts, records, and judicial proceedings of every other State', for example—are based on the relations among them under the Articles of Confederation.

Most important of all, the framers sought to emulate and improve upon the true constitution of Great Britain, before it had been perverted by George III. The American presidency, as conceived by the framers, was an improved model of the British monarchy—and the colonial and State governorship. Like the British king, the American President was to be the representative of the nation above faction. He was to be the commander-in-chief of the army and navy and head of the civil executive. He was to conduct foreign affairs. He was to give Congress 'information of the state of the Union', the republican translation of the speech from the Throne, and to have the power to veto legislation. He was to have the right to grant reprieves and pardons.

But the President was to be subjected to checks that would prevent the equivalent of the 'tyranny' of George III. He was elected for a fixed term. His military and administrative powers were checked by Congress more than the king's by Parliament, most obviously by the power of the Senate to consent to or reject many military and administrative appointments. The Senate also had a large share in treaty-making, and only Congress could declare war. The President's veto could be overridden by two-thirds majorities in Congress; the royal veto, though unexercised since the time of Queen Anne, was absolute. Provision for impeaching the President was carefully described in the Constitution.

It has often been said that the framers of the American Constitution failed to notice how profoundly the British Constitution was being changed by the development of the cabinet system. In fact a few of them saw the fundamental implication: Gouverneur Morris referred in the convention to 'the King of England, . . . the real King, the Minister'; but it is true that most of them did not see it. They were not alone in this. What most of the framers did see was the growth of royal influence in the British constitution after the accession of George III, particularly the use of the appointive power to corrupt members of Parliament with offices; and while wanting a strong executive, they did not want a 'tyrant'. The political acumen of the framers should be judged not by how well they foresaw the evolution of the British Constitution, but by how well they laid the foundations for the sort of executive authority they wanted.

The most important aspect of separation of powers is separation of personnel. In this respect the framers did apply a principle rigidly. No congressman may hold a civil office under the authority of the United States; thus the framers forestalled in America the mischief they saw in Great Britain. Indeed, no congressman may be appointed an elector in the electoral college that elects the President. The framers also kept the organs of government distinct by providing that they should each be elected a different way. Under the original Constitution, the President was elected by the electoral college, the Senate by the State legislatures, the House of Representatives by the voters of the States, and the national judges were appointed by the President with the consent of the Senate.

Moreover, the organs are elected for different periods. The President is elected for four years. The Senators are elected for six years with one-third retiring every two years. The Representatives are elected for two years. And national judges are appointed for life.

In a variety of ways, then, the framers set the organs of the national government against one another and made it difficult for one faction, in particular a majority faction, to take control of the whole machinery of government. The modern view often is that they wrote an antidemocratic Constitution. The short answer is that they did and were proud of it. But the short answer can be misleadingly simple.

In the first place, it is only fair to add that they sought to prevent tyranny from any quarter. If they feared the 'tyranny of the majority' most, they were not blind to other dangers. Secondly, it should be pointed out that they were but on the threshold of the history of democratic party politics. Most of them only dimly foresaw the shape political parties would take. They saw a majority faction, not as an organization with fairly stable membership and views, almost ceaselessly propagandizing among the electorate over a fairly long period of time, but as an almost unorganized gust of opinion, temporarily winning the support of a majority of voters or their representatives. The framers were not the only ones who thought that free institutions needed to be guarded against its evil effects. Thomas Jefferson, for example, the author of the democratic phrases of the Declaration of Independence, believed firmly in the need for separation of powers.

One of the myths of American history has been that the Declaration of Independence and the Constitution represented 'revolution' and 'counter-revolution'. In fact, while the first was more radical than the second, most of the signers of the Declaration were drawn from the same classes as the framers of the Constitution, and the two documents were in spirit twin products of the seventeenth-century English heritage, especially the political theories of John Locke, with which eighteenth-century Americans were imbued. Both the signers and the framers believed that government should rest on consent, that governmental power should be checked, and that individual rights should be protected. The emphasis of the Declaration was on the popular rights of resistance and rebellion when these conditions were not met, and the emphasis of the Constitution was on the sanctity of the social and private contracts when they were, but this was not a fundamental difference. Rather the two documents represented, each at the appropriate time, two strands of Locke's thought.

Finally, because the Constitution did provide a free government, and because moderate men like Thomas Jefferson could accept its principles, it could be interpreted in a more democratic spirit than its framers intended. Indeed, Jefferson began the process of turning the Constitution of 1787 into a democratic document. This process, which has often drawn its inspiration from the words of the Declaration of Independence, has been the most important development in American constitutional history. To-day the Constitution is the palladium of American democracy.

George Washington was the presiding officer at Philadelphia, but James Madison is known as the 'Father of the Constitution'. If his notes of the proceedings do not exaggerate his role, and it appears from other sources that they do not, he played the leading part on the floor of the convention. His personal qualities later made him floor leader of the first House of Representatives, Jefferson's political lieutenant, and President of the United States. In 1787 he also had political opinions particularly useful for constitution-making.

Madison saw the need for protecting property rights that all the delegates saw. He also saw the need for guarding against an oligarchic tyranny, which some of the delegates did not see, though most of them realized that unless they wrote a moderate Constitution it would not be ratified. Similarly, Madison saw the need for a strong national government that almost all the delegates saw. He also saw the need for a measure of State autonomy, which some of the delegates did not see, though again most of them realized that unless they wrote a moderate Constitution it would not be accepted. In short, Madison's views represented roughly what the majority of the convention wanted and could have, and his views combined with his natural talents made him not only a very influential member of the convention but also a persuasive interpreter of its work.

During the struggle for ratification of the Constitution, John Jay, Alexander Hamilton, and James Madison wrote a series of papers explaining and defending its provisions. They, and other proponents of the Constitution, called themselves 'Federalists', thereby assuming a name that had previously connoted opposition to strong national government, and the papers are known as *The Federalist* papers. The papers were printed in New York newspapers from the autumn of 1787 to the spring of 1788, 'at the rate', wrote Madison later, 'during a great part of the time, at least, of four numbers a week'. They were necessarily prepared in great haste. Yet they are excellently written and rank collectively as an outstanding treatise on political institutions. They had a particularly important influence on early constitutional development in the United States, because until the publication of Madison's notes in 1840 they were the chief source for divining the intentions of the framers.

Five were written by Jay, 51 by Hamilton, and 29 by Madison. It is interesting to compare the work of Hamilton and Madison, the former with his complete distrust of the people and faith in extremely strong and independent national government, the latter with the more moderate views that prevailed at Philadelphia. (The differences of emphasis in *The Federalist* foreshadow the break between Hamilton and Madison in interpreting the Constitution and plotting the course of government under it.) Hamilton's constitutional opinions have had a profounder effect on American constitutional law, but in 1787–88 Madison's political opinions were more significant. The concise statement of Madison's political philosophy is found in *The Federalist* No. 10, one of the great essays in the literature of political thought. It is to the Constitution of 1787 what John Locke's second *Treatise on Civil Government* is to the Revolution of 1688.

The Federalist No. 10 is, specifically, a dissertation on how to prevent the evils of faction. A faction is defined by Madison as a 'number of citizens, whether amounting to a majority or minority of the whole, who are united and actuated by some common impulse of passion, or of interest, adverse to the rights of other citizens, or to the permanent and aggregate interests of the community'. (This definition is close to the present British definition of a section. In America, however, sectionalism is always associated with a geographical region.) It would be possible, Madison said, to stamp out faction by stamping out liberty, but the means would be worse than the evils it removed. In a free society there is no way to stamp out faction, and the task of constitution-makers is to control its effects.

Factions, he wrote, arise from different opinions about religion, government, and many other points. Indeed, 'so strong is this propensity of mankind to fall into mutual animosities, that where no substantial occasion presents itself, the most frivolous and fanciful distinctions have been sufficient to kindle their unfriendly passions and excite their most violent conflicts.'

'But', he continued, 'the most common and durable source of factions has been the various and unequal distribution of property. Those who hold and those who are without property have ever formed distinct interests in society. Those who are creditors, and those who are debtors, fall under a like discrimination. A landed interest, a manufacturing interest, a mercantile interest, a moneyed interest, with many lesser interests, grow up of necessity in civilized nations, and divide them into different classes, actuated by different sentiments and views. The regulation of these various and interfering interests forms the principal task of modern legislation, and involves the spirit of party and faction in the necessary and ordinary operations of the government.'

How can one faction be prevented from unduly influencing the course of government? If the faction is a minority, 'relief is supplied by the republican principle, which enables the majority to defeat its sinister views by regular vote'. (The republican principle is incorporated in the Constitution by the direct election of the House of Representatives and the indirect election of the Senate and President.) But if the faction is a majority, the republican principle may not be a safeguard. An assembly of elected officials may afford more protection against majority tyranny than direct democracy. On the other hand, 'the effect may be inverted'.

Elsewhere in *The Federalist* Madison explained that the separation of powers was a barrier to majority tyranny. But in *The Federalist* No. 10 he clearly puts his chief reliance on the great extent of the American nation.

'The smaller the society,' he wrote, 'the fewer probably will be the distinct parties and interests composing it; the fewer the distinct parties and interests, the more frequently will a majority be found of the same party; and the smaller the number of individuals composing a majority, and the smaller the compass within which they are placed, the more easily will they concert and execute their plans of oppression. Extend the sphere, and you take in a greater variety of parties and interests; you make it less probable that a majority of the whole will have a common motive to invade the rights of other citizens; or if such a common motive exists, it will be more difficult for all who feel it to

29

discover their own strength, and to act in unison with each other. . . .

'. . . the extent of the Union gives it the most palpable advantage.

'The influence of factious leaders may kindle a flame within their particular States, but will be unable to spread a general conflagration through the other States. . . . A rage for paper money, for an abolition of debts, for an equal division of property, or for any other improper or wicked project, will be less apt to pervade the whole body of the Union than a particular member of it. . . .'

In Federalist No. 51 Madison put his conclusion in a more positive way: 'In the extended republic of the United States, and among the great variety of interests, parties, and sects which it embraces, a coalition of a majority of the whole society could seldom take place on any other principles than those of justice and the general good. . . .' This was a hopeful forecast. A century and a half of American party history offers evidence for judging whether it has been fulfilled.

The framers knew that they would have difficulty in putting their proposals into effect. The suffrage was much more restricted in America in the late eighteenth century than it is to-day. It has been estimated that less than 5 per cent of the total population of the country voted for members of the State conventions that considered the constitutional proposals. But many more could vote than did, for there was a good deal of apathy among the electorate, especially in States where the elections were rushed; and even though the privilege to vote was very limited by modern standards it was wide enough to include a great many small farmers and artisans.

On the whole, the representatives of the small farmers and artisans viewed the movement for constitutional reform with suspicion and hostility. Patrick Henry, the famous radical leader of Virginia, refused to attend the Philadelphia convention because he 'smelt a rat'. The delegates who represented the political opinions of Governor George Clinton of New York

withdrew from the convention without signing the draft Constitution. It was thought likely that Governor John Hancock of
Massachusetts, the first signer of the Declaration of Independence, would oppose the proposals. The radical government of
Rhode Island, where the 'rage' for paper money and lenient
debtors' laws was strongest, had refused to send any delegates at
all to the convention.

The proponents of the new Constitution won partly because
they used a number of tricks and sharp practices. The movement for the Philadelphia convention had started as a private
venture of the 'nationalists'. The Congress under the Articles of
Confederation had finally sanctioned the meeting by advising
the State governments to send delegates for the purpose of proposing amendments to the Articles. (The twelve States other
than Rhode Island sent delegates.) The delegates drafted an
entirely new Constitution, however, and instead of submitting
their work through the normal amendment process, which required the consent of Congress and the legislatures of all thirteen States, proposed that the Constitution should go into effect
when ratified by the conventions of nine States. Strictly then,
the Constitution of the United States was ratified by an unconstitutional procedure.

In some States the proponents rushed ratification through
before the opponents could concert against them. In other
States, where the proponents were in a minority at the conventions, they delayed action until they could wear their opponents
down by persuasion, by reporting the ratifications of other conventions, and by, it is suspected, sometimes paying the expenses
home of delegates who left the conventions before the final
votes. In Massachusetts the Constitution was carried by a vote
of 187—168 largely because the proponents won over the Hancock faction. They promised not to oppose Hancock's next
gubernatorial campaign and pointed out that if, as seemed not
improbable, Virginia failed to ratify before the first national
elections, Hancock would stand a good chance of becoming the
first President. If Virginia ratified in time, George Washington
would of course be elected.

The records of the Virginia convention are particularly interesting, not only because they give the arguments of men like Patrick Henry, George Mason (the author of the Virginia Declaration of Rights), James Madison, and John Marshall (later Chief Justice of the Supreme Court), but also because they show clearly that in the last analysis the struggle over ratification was less one between believers in conservative and radical principles of government than one between spokesmen for particular interests which were more and less likely to benefit from the specific clauses of the Constitution. The broad generalizations about the division of interests in the country are that the East supported the Constitution and the West opposed it, the merchants and planters supported the Constitution and the small farmers opposed it, the creditors supported the Constitution and the debtors opposed it, and the established or formerly established religious sects supported the Constitution and the dissenting sects opposed it. The Virginia records illustrate how local circumstances helped make these rules and made exceptions to them.

Thus, while on the whole the Anglican tidewater planters of the eastern part of the State supported the Constitution with its clauses favourable to their interests, against the opposition of the non-conformist small farmers of the Piedmont, the fullest support for the Constitution came from the Presbyterian small farmers of the Shenandoah Valley. The trend of the Appalachian Mountain system made it easier for them to trade north and south in Maryland and North Carolina than east and west in their own State, and the new Constitution guaranteed the freedom of interstate commerce. While the majority of delegates from what is now the State of West Virginia, some of whose inhabitants used the Ohio River to trade upstream in Pennsylvania, supported the Constitution partly for the same reason, the great majority of delegates from what is now the State of Kentucky, some of whose inhabitants used the Ohio River to go downstream to the Mississippi River and New Orleans, opposed it. John Jay, a wealthy New Yorker who had conducted American foreign policy under the Articles of Confederation and now supported the new Constitution, had proposed that the United States accept, for a time, the right of

Spain to close the Mississippi River at New Orleans to American trade. Even the provision of the new Constitution requiring the assent of two-thirds of the Senators present to a treaty, which in effect preserved the power of the representatives of five of thirteen States to prevent ratification of a treaty under the Articles, did not overcome the fear of what an eastern dominated administration of a more powerful national government might be able to do. The convention as a whole ratified the Constitution, however, by a vote of 89—79.

The victory of the supporters of the Constitution was so close throughout most of the country that they had to make what appeared to be a major concession to their opponents. The draft Constitution was generally criticized for the absence of a Bill of Rights. The supporters argued, first, that there was an adequate Bill of Rights in the document. Congress could not pass a bill of attainder or ex post facto law. The power to suspend the writ of hcbeas corpus was carefully restricted. A national court could not try any person for a crime except by jury in the State where the crime was committed.

The supporters argued, second, that a more general Bill of Rights was unnecessary, and perhaps would be harmful. The national government was a government of delegated powers. It was understood that all powers not delegated were reserved to the States and people. To go further, to write a denial of certain powers in a Bill of Rights would cast doubt on this principle. The national government might then lay claim to those powers neither granted nor denied. Thus the argument was carried into the States' rights camp.

It became clear, however, that the Constitution was not acceptable without amendments. The proponents averted a call for another general convention to draft a Bill of Rights before the State conventions completed their ratifications only by pledging themselves to introduce amendments to the Constitution as soon as it came in force. The Constitution provided that two-thirds majorities of both Houses of Congress may propose amendments, which must be ratified by the legislatures or conventions of three-fourths of the States. James Madison moved the necessary resolutions in the House of Representatives in

C

June 1789, and ten amendments were ratified by December 1791. They are generally considered part of the original Constitution. (Meanwhile, the two States, North Carolina and Rhode Island, that had not accepted the Constitution by the time it went into effect joined the Union.)

The Bill of Rights, like a good part of the unamended Constitution, is based on the English heritage, particularly the English Puritan heritage, and American experience. It prohibits Congress from establishing a religion and abridging freedom of religion, speech, the press, and assembly. It prohibits infringement of 'the right of the people to keep and bear arms' —an echo of the right of revolution proclaimed in the Declaration of Independence. It regulates the quartering of troops, the use of search warrants, the trial of crimes, and suits at common law. And, as an answer to the arguments against adding a Bill of Rights to the Constitution, it specifies in the Ninth Amendment that 'the enumeration in the Constitution, of certain rights, shall not be construed to deny or disparage others retained by the people' and in the Tenth Amendment that 'the powers not delegated to the United States by the Constitution, nor prohibited by it to the States, are reserved to the States respectively, or to the people'.

The Eleventh Amendment, ratified in 1798, may be conveniently mentioned with the Tenth, since it also resolved an ambiguity in the original wording of the Constitution in favour of States' rights. The Constitution of 1787 gave the national courts jurisdiction in controversies 'between a State and citizens of another State'. The Eleventh Amendment made it clear that this provision did not apply to suits against a State.

The Bill of Rights did not, in fact, alter the basic constitutional system laid down in the draft Constitution. It merely defined some of the liberties and procedural rights of Americans, which most of the framers were as anxious to maintain as their opponents. It was easy therefore for the framers to make a conciliatory gesture. But it was a gesture that has had important consequences for American constitutional law and the judicial protection of private rights.

In the late eighteenth century, then, Americans made two attempts to define the federal division of powers between their national and State governments. The second attempt, the Constitution of 1787, still provides the written constitutional basis of the division. The framers of the Constitution feared majority tyranny and sought safeguards for property and liberty: James Madison, the 'Father of the Constitution', hoped that the necessity for encompassing many interests would make the political parties of the federal Union weak coalitions with moderate programmes; the framers divided the powers of the national government among the legislative, executive, and judicial branches; and they accepted their critics' proposal to protect civil liberties in a Bill of Rights. The remaining chapters of this book deal with subjects suggested by this summary: the federal division of powers (Chapters 2 and 3); the party system of the federal Union (Chapters 4 to 6); the branches of the national government, and the corresponding branches of State and local governments (Chapters 7 to 11); and the protection of private rights (Chapter 12). The next chapter also refers to the eleven amendments to the Constitution that have been adopted in the nineteenth and twentieth centuries.

Chapter 2

The History of Federalism

American federalism is older than the United States of America. Federalism involves civic loyalties to a political whole and its parts that are distinct yet not inconsistent. It involves, too, a constitutional division of powers between the whole and the parts. Almost from the beginning the inhabitants of English America had sentiments that may be called federal. Throughout most of the colonial period Anglo-Americans were genuinely attached to the English Crown, yet almost from the first they formed provincial loyalties to the colonies in which they lived. It was not until the revolutionary period, and even then by no means unanimously, that they came to feel that the two loyalties were incompatible.

The divided yet not inconsistent loyalties—one of the aspects of federalism—were supplemented during the pre-revolutionary period of friction between the homeland and colonies by theories of a constitutional division of powers—the other aspect of federalism. For a time most American spokesmen admitted the right of the English Parliament to control the external affairs of the colonies but denied it the right to control their internal affairs. In other words, in modern terms, they argued that the constitution of the British Empire was or ought to be federal. The argument was not accepted by the British Government, and later the American spokesmen took the more extreme position that Parliament had no right to control the colonies at all.

Meanwhile, Americans created the inchoate institutions of the American national government. Intercolonial Congresses were called to concert opposition to British measures. The one that convened in Philadelphia in May 1775 became the first national assembly of the new republic. The new republic was from the first a federal one. During the decade preceding 1775 the colonists had become increasingly aware of their common Americanism, and they had developed a loyalty to America which ensured that when the imperial connection to the several colonies was severed, a national connection to the new States would take its place. But Americans retained their provincial attachments, which ensured that the new nation would be marked by a large measure of State autonomy.

Sectionalism, an important facet of American federalism, also had its beginnings in the colonial period of American history. Sectionalism is an attachment to the interests of a geographical region. It is thus an intermediate loyalty between that to the nation and that to the State. Its strength in the late eighteenth century was reflected in the compromises between southern planters and northern merchants at the constitutional convention of 1787.

Sectionalism seems often to be a more powerful force than State loyalty, and in the Civil War southern sectionalism was stronger than national patriotism. Although sectionalism has rarely had institutional expression—the only important political organization based on sectional lines was the southern Confederacy—it corresponds to real differences among Americans more than State loyalties. There is only a shade of difference, if that, between the citizens of Rhode Island and Connecticut, Colorado and Wyoming, Kansas and Nebraska, or Georgia and South Carolina. There is a substantial difference between the inhabitants of New England and the West or the Midwest and the South. It is important, however, that the written division of powers in the Constitution is only between the nation and States: in the history of American federalism sectionalism has been inescapably associated with States' rights.

It is also important that the division of powers is written. The fact that federal relations are defined in the Constitution means that American political questions become, in part at least, legal questions. They involve not only whether particular policies should be carried out but also whether they can be carried

37

out. Not only must a policy be shown to be desirable, it must be shown to be constitutionally, that is, legally, proper as well.

The two issues are more distinct in theory than practice. In fact, what is found to be desirable almost invariably ends being found to be constitutional too, though it sometimes takes some time for the identification to be made. The necessity to have legal as well as political sanction for a policy, however, inevitably gives American politics a legal cast. Political controversies are often disguised as conflicts of constitutional construction. Political interests are often concealed by legal arguments. The history of American federalism since the Constitution of 1787 went into effect may be described largely as the history of constitutional interpretations.

The Federalists gave the first interpretation to the Constitution. The first two Presidents of the United States were Federalists: George Washington, who served from 1789 to 1797, and John Adams, who served from 1797 to 1801. During most of Washington's administration, Alexander Hamilton, who was Secretary of the Treasury from 1789 to 1795, was the guiding spirit of the Federalist party. Emulating the younger Pitt, he made himself for a time, as head of the Treasury, the 'prime minister' of American government.

The twin objects of Hamilton's policies were to establish firmly the supremacy of the national government and to ally it with the mercantile classes. He sponsored measures that secured the fiscal credit of the nation, assumed the war debts of the States, thereby turning State creditors into national creditors, and founded a partly-private, partly-governmental national bank. He proposed a system of protective tariffs to encourage infant industries. He gave the powers of the national government a broad or loose construction in order to find the constitutional justification for his programme.

In 1801 the Federalists lost control of the elective branches fo the national government. The presidential election of 1800–1 led to the Twelfth Amendment to the Constitution. Under the original provisions, the presidential electors voted for two persons; the person with the greatest number of votes, if the 'number be a majority of the whole number of electors appointed', became President, and the person with the next greatest number of votes Vice-President. In 1800 all the electors of the Democratic-Republican party, who were a majority of the electoral college, voted for Thomas Jefferson, their leader, and Aaron Burr, who was expected to take the vice-presidency. The tie vote meant that the House of Representatives had to settle the contest, from which Burr refused to withdraw. The House chose Jefferson (who appointed James Madison, for ten years his chief lieutenant against the Federalists, as Secretary of State). The Twelfth Amendment, ratified in 1804, provided that the electors should vote separately for presidential and vice-presidential candidates.

Before Jefferson took office, President Adams appointed Federalists to a number of newly-created judgeships, and John Marshall, the retiring Secretary of State, as Chief Justice of the Supreme Court. The Federalists 'have retired into the judiciary as a stronghold . . .', Jefferson wrote, 'and from that battery all the works of republicanism are to be beaten down and erased.' The first of the struggles between the elected branches of the national government and the national courts, composed of judges appointed for life, took place in the opening years of the new administration. In general the courts won; and until shortly before his death in 1835, despite the appointment of Jeffersonian justices to the Supreme Court, John Marshall succeeded in controlling the interpretation of the Constitution.

Marshall wrote Hamilton's loose construction of the powers of the national government into the law of the land. Many of the principles of Marshall's opinions are clearly taken from Hamilton's public papers. In 1819, for example, in the case of McCulloch v. Maryland, the Supreme Court sustained the action of the national government in chartering a bank to implement its financial powers, though no specific power to charter one appears in the Constitution. 'Let the end be legitimate,' wrote Marshall for the Court, 'let it be within the scope of the Constitution, and all means which are appropriate, which are plainly adapted to that end, which are not prohibited, but consist with the letter and spirit of the Constitution, are constitutional.' In 1791 President Washington had asked Hamilton for his opinion on the constitutionality of chartering a bank: 'If the end be clearly comprehended within any of the specified powers,' Hamilton wrote, 'and if the measure have an obvious relation to that end, and is not forbidden by any particular provision of the Constitution, it may safely be deemed to come within the compass of the national authority.'

Washington had also asked Jefferson for his opinion. On the question of what means are constitutional, Jefferson wrote that 'the Constitution allows only the means which are "necessary", not those which are merely "convenient", for effecting the enumerated powers'. He defined 'necessary means' as 'those means without which the grant of the power would be nugatory'. More generally, he wrote:

'I consider the foundation of the Constitution as laid on this ground—that all powers not delegated to the United States, by the Constitution, nor prohibited by it to the States, are reserved to the States, or to the people. . . . To take a single step beyond the boundaries thus specifically drawn around the powers of Congress, is to take possession of a boundless field of power, no longer susceptible of any definition.'

This rule of strict construction of national powers was specifically rejected by Marshall in 1824: 'Is there one sentence in the Constitution', he wrote in the case of Gibbons *v.* Ogden, 'which gives countenance to this rule? . . . We do not . . . think ourselves justified in adopting it.'

The power involved in Gibbons *v.* Ogden was the power to regulate commerce among the several States, which has provided the main theme of the Court's construction of the powers of Congress ever since. Marshall defined its scope and nature in sweeping terms. 'To what commerce does this power extend?' he asked. ' . . . to that commerce which concerns more States than one,' he answered.

'The genius and character of the whole government seem to be, that its action is to be applied to all the external concerns of the nation, and to those internal concerns which affect the

States generally; but not to those which are completely within a particular State, which do not affect other States, and with which it is not necessary to interfere, for the purpose of executing some of the general powers of the government. The completely internal commerce of a State, then, may be considered as reserved for the State itself.'

It should be noted that it is intrastate rather than interstate commerce that is strictly defined. 'What is this power?' Marshall asked. 'It is the power to regulate; that is, to prescribe the rule by which commerce is to be governed,' he answered.

'This power, like all others vested in Congress, is complete in itself, may be exercised to its utmost extent, and acknowledges no limitations, other than are prescribed in the Constitution. These are expressed in plain terms. . . .'

In sum, Marshall interpreted the Constitution of 1787 not as a mere contract among the States, permitting the federal government to exercise certain enumerated powers within strict limits, but as a broad grant of authority to a nation: '. . . we must never forget', he wrote in McCulloch *v.* Maryland, 'that it is a constitution we are expounding.'

Hamilton's political principles were decisively repudiated by the American electorate, though the effects of much of his work endured. He established the financial stability of the national government, for example, upon which succeeding administrations built. On the other hand, many of Marshall's, and therefore Hamilton's, constitutional principles still form part of the basis of constitutional interpretation by the American courts. Later justices have sometimes narrowed Marshall's broad view of national powers, but they have never denied his doctrines. The result has been that Marshall's loose construction of national powers has provided the precedents for constitutionalizing the great expansion of national power that has taken place in recent years. The constitutional justification for the broad exercise of national power under the New Deal rests on the decisions of John Marshall.

The Jeffersonian Democratic party shaped the political development of American federalism in the first quarter of the nineteenth century. Its successor, the Jacksonian Democratic party, shaped the political and constitutional development during most of the remaining years before the Civil War of 1861–5.

In opposition to Hamilton's mercantilism, Jefferson advocated *laissez-faire*. 'A wise and frugal government,' he explained in his first inaugural address, 'which shall restrain men from injuring one another, shall leave them otherwise free to regulate their own pursuits of industry and improvement, and shall not take from the mouth of labor the bread it has earned. This is the sum of good government. . . .' 'Agriculture, manufactures, commerce and navigation,' he wrote in his first annual message to Congress, 'the four pillars of our prosperity, are the most thriving when left most free to individual enterprise.'

In opposition to Federalist nationalism, Jefferson advocated States' rights. He drafted the Kentucky Resolutions of 1798, which asserted that States could judge the constitutionality of the enactments of the national government. (He thus laid the basis for the later claim that States could nullify acts of the national government, and the ultimate claim that they could secede from the Union.) Shortly before he became President, he wrote: 'The true theory of our Constitution is surely the wisest and best, that the States are independent as to every thing within themselves, and united as to every thing respecting foreign nations. Let the General Government be reduced to foreign concerns only. . . .'

The quotation illustrates not only Jefferson's view that the national government was merely the American department of foreign affairs but also the gloss he gave the Constitution of 1787. Jefferson's 'true theory of our Constitution' was not one with which most of the framers would have agreed. It has always been easier, however, to reinterpret the Constitution than to change it.

In directing the foreign concerns of the government President Jefferson took steps that went, to use his words of 1791, 'beyond the boundaries . . . specifically drawn around the powers of

Congress'. He persuaded Congress to accept and implement the treaty by which the United States acquired the Louisiana Territory in 1803 and to embargo overseas trade in 1807. The Constitution does not enumerate powers to acquire territory and to embargo trade. The Federalists, in opposition, condemned the 'usurpations' of power. After the demise of the Federalist party, however, Chief Justice Marshall held in the case of The American Insurance Company v. 356 Bales of Cotton in 1828, involving the acquisition and governance of the Florida Territory, that the 'Constitution conferred absolutely on the government of the Union the powers of making war, and of making treaties; consequently, that government possesses the power of acquiring territory, either by conquest or by treaty' and referred in Gibbons v. Ogden in 1824 to the 'universally acknowledged power of the government to impose embargoes'. Later constitutional decisions have indeed, as Jefferson predicted, enabled the national government in the conduct of foreign affairs 'to take possession of a boundless field of power'.

But in general the effect of the Jeffersonian political victory was to arrest the mercantilistic and nationalistic trend of government policy. *Laissez-faire* and States' rights were the tenets of the Democratic-Republicans and the agricultural interests they represented. Most activity was left to the people, and most governing was left to the States.

After the second war with Great Britain, the War of 1812, there was a partial resurgence of mercantilistic nationalism. A new national bank was chartered (the charter of the first one had been allowed to expire in 1811), against State resistance that led to the case of McCulloch v. Maryland. Protective tariffs were passed, though against increasing sectional resistance in the South. The faction of the now all-embracing Democratic-Republican party that favoured these policies won a nominal victory in the presidential election of 1824-5. No presidential candidate received a majority of votes in the electoral college, and under the provisions of the Twelfth Amendment of the Constitution the House of Representatives chose the President from among the three candidates with the most electoral votes. Largely owing to the influence of Henry Clay,

Speaker of the House, the Representatives passed over General Andrew Jackson, who had received the greatest number of electoral votes, for John Quincy Adams, the son of John Adams, who had received the next greatest number. Adams chose Clay as his Secretary of State.

Adams and Clay advocated a programme that differed from Hamilton's primarily in its more broadly popular appeal. They wanted the national government to finance internal improvements—roads and canals—in order to develop the country. But Jacksonian propaganda against the 'corrupt bargain' of 1825 kept the administration from having much influence in Congress and the country. In 1828, in a straight contest between Adams and Jackson, in which a new two-party system began to emerge, Jackson won the presidential election decisively. From then until 1860 Jacksonian Democracy was the chief force in American politics. Between 1828 and 1856, for example, the Jacksonian party won six of the eight presidential elections: the chief opposition party—in 1828 and 1832 the National Republican, from 1836 to 1852 the Whig, and in 1856 the Republican—won only in 1840 and 1848.

Jacksonian Democracy differed from Jeffersonian Democracy in several respects. It rested on greater mass participation in government. The suffrage was extended in the first half of the nineteenth century until almost all adult white males could vote. Jacksonian Democracy increased greatly the number of elective offices in State and local governments, and Jackson himself was in a sense the first popularly elected President of the United States. Before 1828 the State legislatures took a much greater part in choosing presidential electors than they have since. In 1828, and thereafter, the presidential election was turned into a popular referendum, for almost all, eventually all, the State legislatures allowed the voters to choose 'rubber stamp' electors pledged to the various candidates.

Jacksonian Democracy developed the spoils system of rotating public offices among partisan supporters. The effect on party structure was to increase the power of the State and local party organizations, which 'got out the vote' and thus earned the spoils.

The westward movement of population gave Jacksonian

Democracy a much larger western contingent than Jeffersonian Democracy, and the larger western contingent largely accounted for the distinctive equalitarianism and nationalism of Jacksonian Democracy. Jefferson had spoken of a 'natural' aristocracy based on virtue and talents, as distinguished from an 'artificial' one based on wealth and birth. Jacksonians were more likely to say that 'one man's as good as another'. It is significant of the difference between the two Democratic movements that while all the Presidents, Federalist and Jeffersonian, before 1829 were Massachussetts and Virginia aristocrats, perhaps 'natural' as well as—by American standards—'artificial', Andrew Jackson was born in the back country of the Carolinas and was not an 'artificial' aristocrat in breeding, upbringing, or behaviour.

Westerners tended to be national minded. Most of them had been Americans before they became citizens of their new States. President Jackson denied the validity of arguments derived from Jefferson's Kentucky Resolutions of 1798 when he made it clear to South Carolinians in 1832–3 that he would meet with force any practical attempt to nullify acts of the national government. 'Our Federal Union,' he had given earlier as a famous toast, 'it must be preserved.'

Two doctrines of the two Democratic movements were the same, however: *laissez-faire* and States' rights. Jacksonian equalitarianism did not require the intervention of the state in private affairs, and Jacksonian nationalism did not require a strong central government. When Jackson vetoed a bill to recharter the second national bank, he wrote: 'There are no necessary evils in government. Its evils exist only in its abuses. If it would confine itself to equal protection, and, as Heaven does its rains, shower its favors alike on the high and the low, the rich and the poor, it would be an unqualified blessing.' Although Jackson said the Union must be preserved against nullifiers, he vetoed a bill giving national aid to a road company of the State of Kentucky on the ground that 'if it be the wish of the people that the construction of roads and canals should be conducted by the Federal Government, it is . . . indispensably necessary, that a previous amendment of the Constitution, delegating the necessary power . . ., should be made.'

Later Democratic Presidents were even more likely to interpret national powers strictly, chiefly because the party fell ever more under the influence of its southern wing. Southerners wanted low tariffs, few internal improvements (southern rivers were natural arteries of commerce), and no interference with slavery. They pushed their sectional advocacy of States' rights to the point, however, where it broke both the Jacksonian party and the Union.

Andrew Jackson also inherited Thomas Jefferson's dispute with Chief Justice Marshall. Both Presidents denied that the Supreme Court had the right to make the final legal interpretation of the Constitution. On this point they lost. But Jackson was able to appoint justices who opposed Marshall's other opinions; and in 1835-6, after Marshall's death, he appointed Roger B. Taney, a staunch Democrat, as the new Chief Justice. During the next forty years the decisions of the Supreme Court reflected the views of Jacksonian Democracy. In general, the decisions construed national power more strictly, construed State power more leniently, and treated privileges granted by any government less favourably than the decisions of John Marshall, though the basic principles of Marshall's opinions were not repudiated.

Anyway, as a result of Jeffersonian and Jacksonian political predominance, the national government exercised little of its constitutional authority over domestic affairs before the Civil War. American federalism was highly decentralized. It should be remembered that in this period the American economy was largely local in character. By present-day standards there was little manufacturing and interstate commerce. Only in the last years before the Civil War was a railway net built that laid the foundation for a truly national economy. Whatever national domestic legislation there was before the Civil War helped the business community rather than regulated it. Hence the Democratic agrarian hostility to national legislation.

Furthermore, because the structure of the national political parties became increasingly decentralized in this period, when the national government did act, debates and votes in Congress tended to follow sectional rather than party lines. This characteristic of pre-Civil War politics still exists to-day, chiefly because the structure of the political parties has not been substantially changed since. Although Marshall's broad definitions of national power have been fully restored by recent decisions of the Supreme Court and the American national government now exercises great power over a national economy, the two major American political parties remain largely as they were in 1850 (though the Republican party has replaced the Whigs): coalitions of State and local organizations.

Two other developments characterized the evolution of American federalism before 1860: the expansion of the continental territory of the United States, with the concomitant growth in the number of States in the Union; and the conflict between slave and free States. The latter led to the Civil War, and to the Thirteenth, Fourteenth, and Fifteenth Amendments to the Constitution.

The present boundaries of the continental United States—the territory on the North American continent including and contiguous with the original nation—were defined by 1853; and the number of States in the Union grew from thirteen to thirty-three by 1860. The Federalists, with their political support concentrated along the eastern seaboard, had often been hostile to the admission of new States with equal rights. The Constitution merely provided that 'new States may be admitted by the Congress into this Union', for Gouverneur Morris, the framer chiefly responsible for the final draft, purposely deleted a reference to equality. But the Democratic parties welcomed new States on equal terms. They thus ensured that the continental Territories (non-States) of the United States would never be treated for long as colonial appendages of the old States of the Union. The continental domain was filled with forty-eight States by 1912.

The Western States and Territories played an important part in the conflict between slave and free States. From 1820 to 1850, as the result of deliberate policy, slave and free States were kept in balance. But by 1850 most of the remaining Territories were unsuited to slavery, and the slave States, as part of the 'Compromise of 1850', gave up their claim to equal representation in the Senate by accepting the admission of California as an unmatched free State. For other reasons southern slaveholders became increasingly alarmed in the decade before the Civil War: anti-slavery sentiment was growing in the North and the population of the North was being swelled by immigration much faster than that of the South. Southerners considered it vital to their interests, as further unmatched free Territories prepared to enter the Union, to redraw the boundary between slave and free soil to their advantage.

On this point westerners joined northerners generally in opposition to the extension of slavery. Frontier farmers did not want to compete with slave labour. When the Civil War came, the western States joined the old northern States to save the Union. The war President was Abraham Lincoln from the then western State of Illinois.

The conflict between slave and free States engendered a great deal of constitutional debate. Could a State nullify acts of the national government? Could a State secede from the Union? Were the States sovereign or was the nation? Neither side convinced the other in the debate. The issue in the nullification controversy of 1832-3 was left unresolved, and an attempt by the Supreme Court in the Dred Scott case of 1857 to settle the question whether the nation could bar slavery from its Territories—it ruled that it could not—merely lowered the prestige of the Court in the North. Finally, the issues were settled by force of arms: secession failed. Looking at the result, the Supreme Court of 1869, only two of whose eight justices had been on the Court in 1857, decided in the case of Texas *v.* White that the Constitution did, after all, look to 'an indestructible Union, composed of indestructible States'.

While States are indestructible, however, governments are not. After the Civil War Congress treated the governments of the States that had joined the Confederacy as the governments of conquered provinces. In Texas *v.* White the Court virtually endorsed congressional power to 'reconstruct' them.

Three Amendments to the Constitution, the first since 1804, are associated with 'reconstruction' policy. One, the Thirteenth, adopted in 1865, prohibited slavery and another, the Fifteenth, adopted in 1870, prohibited the United States or any State from discriminating among otherwise eligible voters 'on account of race, color, or previous condition of servitude'. The longest of the Amendments, the Fourteenth, adopted in 1868, penalized State restrictions on adult male voting in its second section; barred former office-holders who had supported the Confederacy from holding office again, unless amnestied by Congress, in its third section; and invalidated the war debts of the Confederate States in its fourth section. The penalty clause has never been applied, Congress amnestied almost all ex-Confederates fairly quickly, and the debt clause, having served its purpose, has had no after effects.

The first section of the Fourteenth Amendment, however, has had enduring importance as embodying the most important restrictions on State action added to the Constitution of 1787. It begins by 'overruling' a statement in the Dred Scott case that a Negro, even a free one, is not a citizen of the United States. 'All persons', the section reads, 'born or naturalized in the United States, and subject to the jurisdiction thereof, are citizens of the United States and of the State wherein they reside.' It continues: 'No State shall make or enforce any law which shall abridge the privileges or immunities of citizens of the United States. . . .' The drafters of the Amendment meant this wording to apply the restrictions on national action contained in the Bill of Rights to State action as well, but the Supreme Court has never given it this meaning or, except for a very short time, any independent meaning at all.

The Court has given a varying, but usually very important, meaning to the next clause of the section: 'nor shall any State deprive any person of life, liberty, or property, without due process of law. . . .' This due process clause has been the prime basis of national judicial oversight of State action during the last seventy years. Until 1937 the Court interpreted the clause so as to invalidate a great deal of State social and economic legislation, and the due process clause of the Fifth Amendment so as to invalidate some congressional legislation; and since 1925 the Court has used the due process clause of the Fourteenth

D

Amendment, rather than its privileges or immunities clause, to apply parts of the Bill of Rights to the States. Finally, the Court has applied the last clause of the first section of the Fourteenth Amendment, prohibiting a State from denying 'to any person within its jurisdiction the equal protection of the laws', to invalidate unduly discriminatory legislation, especially in recent years legislation against racial minorities.

The constitutional consequences of 'reconstruction' policy have thus been far-reaching. They have gone far beyond the subject of governmental and Negro-white relations in the post-Civil War South. But, until recently, they have fallen far short of granting the Negro real civil equality. Recent attempts by the Supreme Court to apply the Fourteenth and Fifteenth Amendments more rigorously as safeguards of civil liberties and civil rights have made their interpretation one of the most bitterly contested frontiers of contemporary constitutional law.

The Civil War is a milestone in the history of American federalism for several reasons. It marks the end of the great constitutional debate about secession. It marks the rise, from earlier beginnings, of industrial capitalism in America. It marks the passing of political power from the Jacksonian farmers of the West and the South. It marks the rise of a new mercantilistic and nationalistic political party.

The rise of industrial capitalism, which by the end of the nineteenth century gave the United States a commanding lead as the chief industrial producer of the world, nationalized the American economy. Great industrial trusts, national in scope, became in many cases more powerful than the State governments that chartered them. State regulation of the economy, adequate in the days of Jefferson and Jackson, became increasingly inadequate in the days of Carnegie and Rockefeller.

The Republican party, 'the party of the Union', replaced the Democratic party, 'the party of the rebellion', as the predominant party of the nation. It won every presidential election, for example, from 1860 to 1880, all but two presidential elections from 1860 to 1908, and all but four from 1860 to 1928. Whatever it may have been in 1860, the Republican party was by

1870 the party of business men, the inheritor of the principles and interests of the Federalist party and the Whig party, whose northern and western organization it had largely absorbed. The Republican party was usually identified thereafter with a number of policies that restored the Hamiltonian alliance between the national government and the business community: cession of public lands in the West, with railways among the main beneficiaries; high tariffs; monetary policies favourable to Wall Street; and anti-trade union policies.

The nationalism which both the Whigs and dissident Democrats brought into the Republican party in the 1850's was a prenatal influence the party only finally lost in the years of the New Deal. Its 'reconstruction' policy was vigorously nationalistic. Its use of national power to help business was on a Hamiltonian scale. But as the Democratic party re-formed after the Civil War, the opponents of the new mercantilism found that the old slogan of *laissez-faire*, though conveniently forgotten when tariffs were under discussion, was now appropriated by the business community and its political allies as a defence against government regulation. The Republican party helped, but in general did not police, the great trusts. And, since in American politics political arguments are partly constitutional arguments, Republicans rationalized their position by claiming that the national government had power to assist business but not to interfere with it.

The result was that, on the whole, despite the new national character of American society after the Civil War, its regulation remained highly decentralized. 'An American may,' wrote James Bryce, a distinguished British observer of American institutions of the 1880's,

'through a long life, never be reminded of the Federal Government, except when he votes at presidential and congressional elections, lodges a complaint against the post-office, and opens his trunks for a custom-house officer on the pier at New York when he returns from a tour in Europe. His direct taxes are paid to officials acting under State laws. The State, or a local authority constituted by State statutes, registers his birth, appoints his

guardian, pays for his schooling, gives him a share in the estate
of his father deceased, licenses him when he enters a trade (if it
be one needing a licence), marries him, divorces him, entertains
civil actions against him, declares him a bankrupt, hangs him
for murder. The police that guard his house, the local boards
which look after the poor, control highways, impose water rates,
manage schools—all these derive their legal powers from his
State alone.'[1]

In the last decades of the nineteenth century, however, a few
scattered national acts initiated the process of coping with the
new society industrial capitalism was creating. The first steps
were taken toward national regulation of the railways. The
pious words of the Sherman Anti-Trust Act were put on the
statute book. These rivulets of regulation became a stream after
1900. In the administrations of Presidents Theodore Roosevelt,
William Howard Taft, and Woodrow Wilson, act after act was
put on the book, though sometimes to be rendered nugatory by
decisions of the Supreme Court.

Perhaps the reforming surge was related to the apparent dis-
appearance of the frontier 'safety-valve' in the 1890's. It was
certainly derived in part from widespread disgust at corrupting
business men and corrupted politicians. For both major parties
and the country this was the Progressive Era. It was a confused
one. The spiritual descendents of Jefferson and Jackson were
groping for a creed to replace *laissez-faire*. By this time many of
them were able to discard States' rights and to talk of a 'New
Nationalism' that would use 'Hamiltonian means to Jeffersonian ends'; but as individualists they were suspicious of what is
now called the welfare state; and, though they continued to
talk of destroying economic privilege, they could not decide
whether that meant they should destroy giant corporations or
control them. By 1920, when the nation returned to Republican
'normalcy', they had done neither.

But, besides leaving precedents for vigorous national action,
the Progressives of the early twentieth century made one per-

[1] *The American Commonwealth* (London: Macmillan & Co., 1888), II, 20.
Quoted with permission of the publishers.

manent addition to national power that was fraught with enormous consequences: they firmly established the right of the national government to levy income taxes. In the past the fiscal policy of the national government had essentially been tariff policy. Before the Civil War, the Democratic party kept national expenditure at a minimum and relied on the revenue of a mildly protective tariff. After the Civil War, the Republican party raised the tariffs in order to afford more protection and drew about half the national revenue from them. Following the enactment of the Sixteenth Amendment to the Constitution, permitting the national government to levy income taxes, in 1913 and the entry of the United States into the First World War in 1917, income taxes became the most important source of national revenue. In the 1930's and 1940's the share of taxes raised by the national government in taxes raised by all American governments rose sharply. The income tax became the buttress of national fiscal supremacy, and national fiscal supremacy profoundly altered the relation between nation and States.

The political predominance of the Republican party from the 1860's to the 1920's meant that the majority of justices on the Supreme Court were Republican appointees. Although the justices rarely divided along party lines, the majority of them usually applied the constitutional rationalization of the Republican political position to the cases they decided. Since justices are appointed for life, however, there were almost inevitable time-lags at the beginning and end of the period. The one at the end led to a constitutional crisis, whose consequences have determined the present constitutional character of American federalism.

The Supreme Court continued partly to reflect Jacksonian thinking through the 1870's, largely because the original Republican party contained a large Jacksonian element, which had several representatives among the justices appointed by Presidents Abraham Lincoln and Ulysses Grant. It was also largely owing to the use of the appointive power by Grant that a majority of the Court sustained, almost immediately after a decision the other way, the right of the national government to make paper money legal tender. Despite the general deflationary policy of the Republicans, the Grant administration wanted the wartime legislation relating to 'greenbacks' held valid. Grant was able to take advantage of two vacancies on the Court to change its balance, though historians disagree about the extent to which he knew what he was doing. The new majority upheld the wartime legislation in the Legal Tender cases of 1871, on the ground that while the framers had not given Congress the power to issue paper money as legal tender, the power was a 'resulting' power, 'arising from the aggregate powers of the government'. A later Court upheld subsequent peace-time legislation in the case of Juilliard *v.* Greenman in 1884.

From the 1880's the decisions of the Court reflected orthodox Republican views. By increasingly inconsistent lines of precedents national action beneficial to business was justified, while national power to regulate it was often denied. There were important exceptions: the Sherman Anti-Trust Act of 1890 was sustained, for example; but the general trend was to hold that national action that seriously interfered with the freedom of business men either exceeded the powers of Congress or, as in the case of similar State action, took property without due process of law. One effect of the two increasingly contradictory sets of decisions, simultaneously extending and restricting national power, was to expand the discretion of the justices in deciding each case. The importance of the Court in shaping public policy was markedly greater after the Civil War than before.

One example, the doctrine of production for commerce, illustrates the state of constitutional law by 1930. The national government relied primarily on the interstate commerce power to support legislation regulating the economy. The Court held several times that the power did not permit Congress to regulate production for commerce. This rule made it difficult to enforce the Sherman Act until the Court accepted the fact that an undue monopoly in manufacturing could fairly easily be shown to be one in interstate commerce as well. The Court often made it particularly easy to show that a strike or a boycott of 'black goods' by trade unionists unduly restrained commerce.

It also allowed Congress to bar lottery tickets and impure food and drugs from interstate commerce. But when Congress barred the shipment of goods made by child labour, the Court held in the case of Hammer v. Dagenhart in 1918 that the legislation was invalid, because the 'act in its effect does not regulate transportation among the States, but aims to standardize the ages at which children may be employed in mining and manufacturing within the States': '. . . the production of articles intended for interstate commerce is a matter of local regulation'. The words 'in its effect' and 'aims to' are important, for on its surface the act merely regulated interstate commerce, exercising a congressional power that, according to Marshall, 'acknowledges no limitations, other than are prescribed in the Constitution': 'These are expressed in plain terms. . . .' The Constitution says nothing about the effect and aims of the use of the commerce power, and for that matter says nothing about production for commerce. On the other hand, the Court maintained, more properly, that a State could not bar goods made in other States, including perforce goods made by child labour, because the bar would in effect be a trade barrier against interstate commerce. In short, the Court, by narrowing Marshall's definition of the congressional commerce power in some cases, created a 'twilight zone' between national and State authority which neither level of government could effectively regulate.

During the Progressive Era, the Court was widely attacked, particularly for its anti-labour bias. During the period of 'normalcy', the tempers of the Court and the country were more in accord. Then 'normalcy' ended with a depression a good deal more severe than normal, and the electorate's faith in the Republican party and business men was shattered.

In the early 1930's cries for help came from distressed citizens and local governments; the State governments were overwhelmed by the demands put upon them; only the national government had the financial resources to meet the cries for help with effective policies. It met them under the New Deal of President Franklin Roosevelt. National regulatory power was exercised even more than in the brief period of war mobilization in 1917–18. Government regulation of business was incorporated in a flood of acts. The national fiscal power was exercised not only to police the private economy but to save it, and to save local agencies of government as well. New patterns of co-operation were created between the national government and the people and between the nation and its subdivisions. American federalism became far more centralized than in the past.

Faced with an unprecedented degree of national interference with business, the Republican party and its business allies abandoned their national outlook for States' rights as well as *laissez-faire*. The political about-face was now complete. The Democratic party of Franklin Roosevelt was advocating 'Hamiltonian means to Jeffersonian ends,' and the Republican party 'Jeffersonian means to Hamiltonian ends'. The change in party doctrines was accompanied by the most important re-alignment of political forces since the Civil War.

Decisively repudiated at the polls in 1932 and 1936, the Republican party continued in effect to control the Supreme Court, for most of the justices shared its views. In 1935-6 the Court used the line of precedents hostile to national power to strike down some of the key measures of the New Deal. It put further restrictive codicils on the bequests John Marshall had made to the national government. The result was a struggle between the President and the Court reminiscent of the days of Jefferson and Marshall. The Court emerged from the constitutional crisis with its authority preserved, but with its membership sufficiently changed that henceforth New Deal measures were held to be constitutionally proper.

In consequence, constitutional interpretation rather than constitutional amendment has sanctioned the recent expansion of national power. Ironically, the net effect for the federal division of powers of the amendments since the Sixteenth Amendment has been a slight shift of power back to the States. The Seventeenth Amendment, adopted in 1913, provided for the popular election of Senators; the Eighteenth, adopted in 1919, required the prohibition of intoxicating beverages; and the Nineteenth, adopted in 1920, forbade the United States or any State to discriminate among otherwise eligible voters on account of sex. The Twentieth, adopted in 1933, fixed new dates for the presidential inauguration and annual convening of Congress, thereby shortening the period between a presidential election and inauguration and eliminating the 'lame duck' regular session of Congress, which had been held by an old Congress between the times that a new Congress was elected and took office. (Under the original Constitution, the annual convening was in December, and since congressmen were elected in November but did not take office until March, this meant that a 'lame duck' session was held from December to March every second year; under the Twentieth Amendment the annual convening is in January, when congressmen elected in November now take office.) The Twenty-first Amendment, adopted in 1933, repealed the prohibition of intoxicating beverages, but forbade the importation into any State of intoxicating liquors in violation of its laws; and the Twenty-second, adopted in 1951, limited the President to two terms of office. In sum, the effect for the federal division of powers has been, under the provisions of the Twenty-first Amendment, to return to the States the power over the importation of intoxicating liquors that they surrendered under the Constitution of 1787: they are now free to erect trade barriers against out-of-State products.

The Constitution is, however, what the judges say it is. Since 1937 the Supreme Court has applied the sweeping definitions of John Marshall to national powers at a time when most commerce is interstate and national government spending affects all parts of the economy. The definitions have proved adequate to justify the broadest reaches of national power over national affairs in peace and war. But the new centralization has destroyed neither the States nor the sections. Political power in America is still divided along federal lines. American political loyalty is still an amalgam of several levels of patriotism. The United States is still a federal state.

In broadest outline, the history of American federalism since 1789 began with Federalist mercantilism and nationalism, which left a permanent impact on constitutional interpretation favourable to national action. Sixty years of Democratic *laissez-*

faire and political localism followed, in reponse to the demands of a pioneering people to be left alone. In this period American party institutions acquired their basic forms. Then the rise of industrial capitalism nationalized the economy and led in time to demands for the exercise of national regulatory power over the great corporations of private business. These demands have been largely met, especially since great depressions and wars have made the financial strength of the national government a dominant factor in economic and political affairs. As a result, there has been a marked relative shift in power from the States to the nation.

In this history the Civil War is an important turning point. Before the War, observers of American institutions, like Alexis de Tocqueville, who came from France in the 1830's, believed that the Union might disintegrate as the result of growing political localism and sectional conflict. The federal Constitution of the Dominion of Canada, the British North America Act of 1867, was drafted with provisions for a relatively strong national government in order to correct the weaknesses of the federal form of government that had become apparent in the recently divided Union to the south. To-day, though the opinion is sometimes expressed that the division of powers still weakens American government, no one speaks seriously of disruptive tendencies. Many Americans believe that the centralizing tendencies have gone too far. (They have certainly gone much further than in Canada.) American federalism has adapted itself to a world very different from that in which it began. It is, therefore, a very different federalism to-day.

Chapter 3

Federalism To-day

It is useful to distinguish several elements in American federalism to-day, which are products of different stages in its evolution. The present fiscal and administrative elements have been shaped very largely by events since 1933: the New Deal, the Second World War, and the 'cold war'; and the present governmental element, that is, the exercise of power by the nation and States, has been shaped very largely by events of this century: the Progressive Era, the First World War, and events since 1933. On the other hand, the present constitutional element, that is, the relevant provisions of the Constitution and their interpretation by the Supreme Court, is still largely constituted as in the days of John Marshall; and the present political element, that is, the party system, is still largely constituted as in the 1850's. The complexity of the federal system to-day is better comprehended if these differences in development are taken into account.

First, the fiscal element of American federalism to-day. In fiscal 1932, that is, from 1 July 1931 to 30 June 1932, the budget expenditure of the American national government was less than $5,000 million; in fiscal 1939 it was about $9,000 million; in fiscal 1945 it was nearly $100,000 million; in fiscal 1950 it was about $40,000 million; and in fiscal 1953 it was nearly $75,000 million. In January 1954 President Eisenhower submitted to Congress a budget for fiscal 1955 of over $65,000 million.

Fiscal 1945 was the peak year of budget expenditure during the Second World War, and fiscal 1953 the peak year during the 'cold war'. Fiscal 1932, 1939, 1950, and 1955 are perhaps the best years for showing the secular trend in spending; for they have been, respectively, the last fiscal year before the New Deal began, the last fiscal year before the outbreak of the Second World War in Europe, the last fiscal year before the outbreak of the Korean War affected government spending, and the first fiscal year whose budget recommendations were shaped entirely by the Eisenhower administration. The following description of the fiscal element refers mainly to those years, though the information about the last one is tentative and incomplete.

New Deal 'welfare state' measures started the great increase in national government spending since 1933, and the defence and war efforts of the Second World War and 'cold war' sustained it. The latter had, on the whole, the greater effect.

It is difficult to gauge the factors accurately, because of the problems of dealing with trust fund accounts, which play a major part in the financing of American social services, defining 'welfare state' expenditure, and finding comparable figures for different years. But Table A gives a rough idea of the trends. It is based on data about fiscal 1932, 1939, and 1950 in the annual *Statistical Abstract of the United States,* published by the United States Bureau of the Census, and the recommendations for fiscal 1955 in President Eisenhower's budget message of January 1954. Where necessary, the appropriations of the national government to the old-age and survivors' insurance and railroad retirement trust funds are added to budget expenditure to give total expenditure; the expenditure of the Atomic Energy Commission is added to the expenditure of the departments now in the Department of Defense to give defence expenditure; and expenditure other than for defence, interest on the national debt, and foreign aid is listed as general expenditure. Expenditures for interest and aid are shown in order to complete the breakdown of the total figures. The Table indicates the importance of the rise in general spending until 1939 and of the rise in defence spending in recent years in accounting for the rise in national government spending. These changes have taken place in an inflationary period, but the rises have not been merely inflationary: in '1939 dollars' the total expenditure for 1950 was about $23,000 million.

TABLE A

ANALYSIS OF AMERICAN NATIONAL GOVERNMENT SPENDING
(amounts in millions; and percentages of total
expenditure or total increase)

	1932 $	1932 %	1939 $	1939 %	1950 $	1950 %	1955 (recommended) $	1955 (recommended) %
Expenditure:								
Total	4,659	100	9,469	100	42,262	100	71,679	100
Defence	834	18	1,368	14	13,990	33	40,540	57
General	3,226	69	7,160	76	17,950	42	18,939	26
Interest on debt	599	13	941	10	5,750	14	6,800	9
Foreign aid	—	—	—	—	4,572	11	5,400	8
Increase over previous year listed:								
Total	—	—	4,810	100	32,793	100	29,417	100
Defence	—	—	534	11	12,622	39	26,550	90
General	—	—	3,934	82	10,790	33	989	3
Interest on debt	—	—	342	7	4,809	15	1,050	4
Foreign aid	—	—	—	—	4,572	14	828	3

The total effect of defence and war efforts on post-Second World War budgeting has been much greater than that of the defence item of the budget alone. In fiscal 1950 expenditure for veterans' services, included in general expenditure above but perhaps more appropriately considered separately as expenditure for past wars, was about $6,647 million. Expenditure for interest on the national debt, by far the greater part of which has been contracted to meet defence and war expenditures, and expenditure for foreign aid, designed to alleviate the ill effects of past wars and to prevent future ones, accounted for about $10,322 million. All told, in fiscal 1950 expenditure for defence, veterans' services, interest on the debt, and foreign aid amounted to about $30,959 million, that is, about seven-tenths, of national government expenditure. President Eisenhower recommended that in fiscal 1955 expenditure for the four items amount to about $56,932 million, that is, about four-fifths, of national government expenditure.

A large part of the money required to finance the increase in national government spending has been borrowed. In 1932 the national debt was about $19,500 million; in 1939 about $40,400 million; and in 1950 about $257,400 million. On 30 June 1954 it was about $273,000 million.

Another large part of the money has come from national income taxes. In 1913 the national government was granted the constitutional power to levy income taxes. In 1919, at the end of the First World War, income and profits taxes produced well over half its revenue. In fiscal 1932 they brought in about $1,100 million in total receipts of about $2,000 million; in fiscal 1939 about $2,200 million in total receipts of about $5,700 million; and in fiscal 1950 about $28,300 million in total receipts of about $41,300 million. In 1950 individual income taxes raised about one and a half times as much revenue as corporation income and profits taxes. President Eisenhower recommended and estimated for fiscal 1955 individual income tax receipts of about $30,300 million and corporation income and profits tax receipts of about $20,300 million in total receipts of about $71,200 million. Since it is hard to see how the great expansion of the national debt could have been underwritten without the assurance of future income-tax revenues, it is probably fair to say that national income taxation has been the prime instrument of the growth of national fiscal power, which has revolutionized the distribution of fiscal power in American federalism.

The revolution may be partly described in terms of national and State-local government purchases of goods and services. The *Statistical Abstract of the United States* gives figures for some calendar years. The first two lines of Table B show how much greater the growth of national government purchases was from 1933 to 1950.

TABLE B

GOVERNMENT ECONOMIC ACTIVITY IN THE AMERICAN ECONOMY
(amounts in millions; and percentages of the
gross national product)

	1933 $	1933 %	1940 $	1940 %	1950 $	1950 %
National government purchases	2,018	4	6,170	6	22,165	8
State-local government purchases	5,940	11	7,763	8	19,700	7
Gross national product	55,760	100	101,443	100	284,187	100
Government interest, subsidies, and transfers	2,642	—	4,399	—	19,446	—
Total government expenditure	10,600	—	18,332	—	61,311	—

The first two lines of the Table also put government purchases as percentages of the gross national product, the figures for which are given in the third line. They show that while national government purchases grew as a share of the gross national product, total government purchases remained about the same share, the relative increase in national government purchases having been offset by the relative decrease in State-local government purchases. Total government purchases have been a fairly large fraction of the gross national product in years of heavy war and defence spending by the national government: nearly two-fifths in 1945 and well over one-fifth in 1952, for example; but they were approximately the same fraction, about one-seventh, in 1933, 1940, and 1950. Total government-economic activity became permanently more important in the economy as a whole after 1933 because of government interest, subsidy, and transfer payments, figures for which are given in the fourth line of Table B. Transfer payments include social security benefit payments, for example. The figures for total government expenditure, which is the sum of government purchases and payments, are given in the last line of the Table.

Attempts have been made to describe the revolution in fiscal power since 1933 in terms of total government expenditure. It has been estimated that when the New Deal began, the national government spent about one-third, the State and local governments about two-thirds, of all money spent by American governments. In the period between the Second World War and the Korean War the national government spent about two-thirds, the State and local governments about one-third. In less than twenty years the ratio of national to State-local government spending was roughly reversed. The difficulties of allocating and comparing government expenditures make it unwise to consider this estimate as providing more than a suggestion of the change that took place. But it is indisputable that the growth of national fiscal power has tended greatly to centralize the fiscal element of American federalism.

Second, the administrative element of American federalism

to-day. The growth of national fiscal power has centralized this element too, by financing an expansion of national administrative activity. The effect may be suggested by the following figures: in 1932 there were about 620,000 civilian employees of the national government and about 2,670,000 civilian employees of State and local governments; in 1939 about 970,000 and about 3,090,000; and in 1950 about 2,100,000 and about 4,280,000. In addition, in 1932 there were about 240,000 men in the national armed forces; in 1939 about 330,000; and in 1950 about 1,460,000. The figures underestimate the extent of the change, however, because an increasingly large number of State and local employees have been doing work partly, sometimes almost entirely, paid for and controlled by the national government. The growth of national fiscal power has tied levels of administration together, by such devices as grants-in-aid.

Grants-in-aid, first in the form of public land, then in the form of public money, have had a long history in the United States; but their present character is very largely a product of the last twenty years. In 1932 national grants-in-aid to State and local governments amounted to about $240 million. In fiscal 1950 they amounted to about $2,230 million. In 1932 they accounted for about 3 per cent of State and local government revenue. In 1950 they accounted for about 11 per cent of State and local government revenue. The purposes for which grants are made have undergone an important change. In 1932 well over half the grants were for highway construction. In fiscal 1950, though highway construction projects still received more than one-sixth of the money, the public assistance programme, begun by the Social Security Act of 1935, received slightly over half.

The growth of grants-in-aid has not followed a standard pattern. Most grants require matching, but some do not. A few grants equalize conditions, but most do not. The amount of national supervision varies a great deal too. But this may be said: there is some national supervision of every grant, and it concerns itself not only with the particular programme but also with the internal affairs of State public administration. Under the social security scheme, for example, State programmes must conform to certain national standards, State administration must be controlled by a single State agency, the personnel of the State agency must be employed on a merit basis, and applicants whose claims for assistance are denied must be given a fair hearing. In addition, State employees under the programme are regulated by national acts restricting the political activities of national employees, on the ground that part of their work is paid for by the national government.

Not every instance of co-operation between national and State-local administration is accompanied by national grants of money. Even where there is no grant, however, co-operation in civil administration has developed very much in the last twenty years. There has been, for example, a growth of co-operation in law enforcement. The Federal Bureau of Investigation helps the State and local authorities as much as the constitutional powers of the national government permit. That these powers can be stretched very far was illustrated in 1942 when seven dangerous convicts escaped from a State penitentiary. After several days the F.B.I. joined the search for them on the ground that they had not, as required by valid national legislation, registered with their local draft boards. The co-operation works both ways: officials of the Secret Service, charged with such duties as preventing counterfeiting and protecting the President, have long relied on the aid they receive from State and local police.

A development in the administration of American federalism that has occurred almost entirely since 1933 is direct formal co-operation between national and local government agencies, thereby 'short-circuiting' the States, which are the only constitutional subdivisions in the federal system. One reason for the new relations was that the national government became involved in matters previously almost exclusively local: housing and agricultural planning, for example. At the same time, State grants-in-aid to localities and State-local administrative co-operation generally have grown too. Centralization within the nation has been more than matched by centralization within the States.

The examples that have been given illustrate that there has

been something besides centralization, however. There has been more working together lately. A new conception of federal interrelations has developed, often called 'co-operative federalism'. It emphasizes mutual administrative assistance among the levels of governments instead of administrative competition and conflict. The change should not be exaggerated. There has always been a good deal of co-operation, though one of the oldest examples, co-operation in military affairs, was so unsatisfactory that it has been almost entirely replaced by centralization. There is still in practice a great deal of competition and conflict. But administrators, and especially students of administration, are now more conscious of the need for co-operation.

Co-operative federalism proved itself a very useful part of American government in the Second World War, when the national government relied as never before on State and local agencies, in carrying out its rationing programme for example. The vertical co-operation of nation, States, and localities is much more effective in dealing with tasks of government than the horizontal co-operation of equal States. Co-operative federalism may be, as some charge, surreptitious centralization. It may be, as others charge, often less efficient than full centralization. But in view of the fiscal supremacy of the national government on the one hand, and the strength of local political sentiment on the other, it is almost certain to remain one of the most important aspects of the administrative element of American federalism.

Third, the governmental element, that is, the exercise of power by the nation and States, of American federalism to-day. It was pointed out in the last chapter that a trickle of national acts dealing with the new industrial society of the late nineteenth century grew into a stream in the Progressive Era of the early twentieth century and then, after a period of 'normalcy', became a flood under the New Deal. The Progressive acts, such as railways, pure food and drug, banking, and anti-trust legislation, developed the regulatory powers of the national government. On this foundation the largely temporary exercise of war powers in the First World War was built. Railways were temporarily nationalized, food and fuel were controlled under national legislation, and the production of goods was supervised by national boards.

On the Progressive foundation and war experience much of the regulatory legislation of the New Deal was based: the Securities Act, the National Industrial Recovery Act, and the National Labor Relations Act, for example. Far more than in the past, however, the New Deal also used national power to sustain the economy. The fiscal power of the national government was put to work. Acts to revive farming, provide relief and employment for the destitute and out of work, and help the aged, are examples of legislation that raised the level of national government spending.

During the Second World War a further expansion of the exercise of national governmental power took place, less in entirely novel ways than in unusually full use of means of dealing with previous emergencies: rent and price control, rationing, and direction of production, for example. In the second post-war period the extent of the exercise of national power has varied a great deal, but it has never, even under the Republican administration of President Eisenhower, contracted to its pre-war limits. In 1946 Congress passed an act that probably constituted the fullest single exercise of national power in the history of the Republic: the Atomic Energy Act, with its provisions for public monopolies, absolute governmental control, and enormous administrative discretion. (In 1954 Congress amended the Act in order to allow private business a greater part in atomic development.)

One of the ways to indicate the growth of national governmental activity in American society is to compare the expansion of the national civil service with the growth of population in this century. In 1900, in a population of about 76,000,000, there were about 260,000 civilian employees of the national government. In 1930, in a population of about 122,000,000, there were about 610,000. In 1940, in a population of about 132,000,000, there were about 1,080,000. In 1950, in a population of about 151,000,000, there were about 2,100,000. The

population roughly doubled in half a century, and the national
civil service roughly octupled.

The States have expanded their activities in this century, too:
regulatory legislation, labour legislation, public health and welfare services, educational services, public works programmes,
have all grown. Even local governments have found new things
to do: city planning and zoning ordinances, for example, are
virtually twentieth-century forms. There has been, in short, an
increase in governmental activity generally. The total number
of civilian employees of American governments is now more
than one-tenth of the total labour force of the country.

Centralization of American federalism has taken place then,
far less by the withdrawal of the State and local governments
from fields of activity (though within the States some State
governments have taken over functions from local authorities)
than by the entrance of the national government into fields
previously almost exclusively dealt with by the other governments, if dealt with by governments at all. An American is
much more frequently reminded of the national government
to-day than when Bryce wrote in the 1880's: if young, he is
perhaps particularly conscious of national service legislation;
if middle-aged, of the direct taxes he pays to national officials;
if old, of the scale of social security benefits. Moreover, he much
more frequently looks to the national government for guidance
when the impact of social forces disturbs him, even if he believes, in a country where faith in *laissez-faire* is still strong, that
the guidance should usually be passive rather than active. He
wants, at a minimum, a 'fireside chat' from the President. The
national government, in consequence, has increasingly invaded,
but by no means appropriated, the State and private fields of
social and economic control.

The use of national fiscal power has altered Bryce's list of
functions carried out almost exclusively by State and local
authorities. The national government now helps finance some
poor relief and highway construction projects. But the State
and local governments still pay for an American's schooling.
Education is the largest single enterprise of State and local
governments: in 1950 about 1,720,000 of their 4,280,000 em-

ployees were teachers and other school employees. So far it has received only a very small amount of national aid. It is symptomatic of the shift of fiscal power and the need for co-operative federalism in modern America that the burden is proving too much for lesser authorities and that in many places national aid is desperately needed.

Bryce's list is now most apt with respect to functions connected with ordinary civil and criminal law—registration of births, appointment of guardians, regulation of marriage and divorce, and punishment for murder, for example. The most important change is that the nation now declares an American a bankrupt, the congressional act responsible for the change having been passed in 1898. However, though the preservation of State predominance in this field means that part of the governmental element of American federalism remains highly decentralized, it concerns a traditional rather than new and expanding field of regulation. It has not seriously checked the centralizing tendencies of recent years.

Fourth, the constitutional element, that is, the relevant provisions of the Constitution and their interpretation by the Supreme Court, of American federalism to-day. Only one amendment to the Constitution, the income-tax amendment of 1913, has added substantially to the powers of Congress. It may not have been necessary. The Supreme Court of 1895 had departed from precedents in declaring a national income-tax law void; and it is probable that the Supreme Court of a decade later would have held a new national income-tax law valid without a constitutional amendment. Likewise, only one amendment to the Constitution, the Fourteenth Amendment of 1868, and in particular its due process and equal protection of the law's clauses, has restricted substantially the powers of the States. Otherwise, the recent centralization of American federalism has had to rest, constitutionally, on the phrases of 1787 and the Supreme Court's interpretation of them.

Until 1937 the Court did not interpret them broadly enough to allow full scope to the expansion of national power. Thereafter it did, largely by reasserting principles of construction laid down by John Marshall from which later judges had departed. Thus the task of constitutionalizing the growth of national activity hás been fairly easy. It is worth emphasizing that the New Deal and all that has happened since its advent have not required a single amendment increasing national power. The Supreme Court has found the authority for twentieth-century government in the sweeping constitutional generalizations of the early nineteenth-century Court. In 1942 in the case of Wickard v. Filburn the Court ruled unanimously that an Ohio dairy and poultry farmer who raised wheat most of which was consumed on his own farm was subject to the national power to regulate interstate commerce in wheat, even if none of the wheat about which the case had been brought was 'intended for interstate commerce or intermingled with the subjects thereof', on the ground that his activity affected, however minutely, the supply-demand nexus of wheat in the United States. (Since this decision most constitutional lawyers have given up trying to define the limits of the commerce power.) The decision was squarely based on 'a return to the principles first enunciated by Chief Justice Marshall in Gibbons v. Ogden' in 1824.

It is possible in a brief space to make only a few comments about the recent trends of interpretation on questions involving the division of powers. The effect of the broad interpretation of national powers has been to obliterate the 'twilight zone' between national and State powers: the distinction between production and commerce has been done away with. The methods of co-operative federalism have been accepted: the use of national grants-in-aid to bribe, as critics put it, the States into doing certain things in certain ways has been sustained. The troublesome issue of intergovernmental tax immunity, that is, the extent to which one level of government may not tax the instruments of the other, has been dealt with by leaving a large measure of discretion to Congress. The long-standing rule that whenever otherwise valid national and State regulations conflict national law overrides State law has been rigorously enforced. Since 1937, in short, the Court has sustained national action against every claim of impingement on States' rights.

Judicial supervision of State action remains fairly exacting, though some of the criteria used to judge State action have changed radically. One constant criterion, indicated above, is that State action cannot conflict with national policy. It is not always easy to decide, however, whether it does. If the national government sets certain standards for interstate road hauliers, does a State that regulates the size of vehicles and weight of loads on its highways run counter to the will of Congress or the implications of the interstate commerce clause of the Constitution? If the national government specifies certain safety measures for interstate railways, does a State that limits the length of trains as an additional safety measure within its boundaries conflict with the national act or Constitution? There are no simple answers to questions like these, though the Court decided that, in the absence of a clear prohibition of State action by Congress, the Constitution required judicial answers of 'no' to the first—in South Carolina State Highway Dept. *v.* Barnwell Bros. in 1938—and 'yes' to the second—in Southern Pacific Co. *v.* Arizona in 1945. It was influenced by the fact that the States maintain highways but not railways.

The criterion that State taxation may not unduly burden interstate commerce gives rise to even more difficult questions. The answers rest on even nicer distinctions. The Court refused, for example, in the case of McLeod *v.* J. E. Dilworth Co. in 1944 to allow the imposition of an Arkansas 'sales tax' on goods sold in Tennessee but shipped to Arkansas, though it indicated that it would have allowed the imposition if the tax had been called a 'use tax'. The examples cited—and examples of similar complexity could be cited in connection with judicial interpretation of the constitutional provision that each State shall give 'full faith and credit . . . to the public acts, records, and judicial proceedings of every other State'—give some idea of the detail involved in judicial umpiring of the federal system.

In general the Court, imbued with a belief in co-operative federalism, has tended since 1937 to give somewhat wider scope than in the past to State action within the interstices of national law and constitutional restraints. It has required national courts, when dealing with controversies between citizens of different

71

States, to be guided much more than in the past by decisions of the appropriate State courts. It has freed the States as well as the nation from the restrictive effect that the interpretation of the due process of law clauses once had on the content of economic and social legislation. In contrast to these tendencies to respect State action, however, two developments limit State power more than in the past. One is the growth of the national exercise of power; for whatever the Court may allow the States to do when Congress is silent or equivocates, it allows very little when Congress speaks clearly. The other is the growth of the restrictive effect that the interpretation of the due process clause of the Fourteenth Amendment has on State regulation of civil liberties. Judicial review of State action has left one side of due process only to enter more fully the other.

When the Court invalidated a number of State laws on the ground that they abridged personal freedoms, it was said that the Court would be at least as strict with national action in the same field. But when the national government evacuated (and detained) American-born citizens of Japanese descent living on the west coast during the Second World War, the Court, which had denied a State, for example, the right to require that pedlars of religious literature obtain a pedlar's licence, upheld the action. It would be unfair to say that the Court permits the abridgement of civil liberty if the deprivation is on a grand scale. It would be fair to say that it is more impressed by claims that the nation is in danger than by similar claims made by States. In practice the Court is now more lenient to national than State action when dealing with substantive legislation of any kind. The constitutional element of American federalism to-day is in accord with the fiscal, administrative, and governmental elements.

Fifth, the political element, that is, the party system of American federalism to-day. Since the recent centralization of American federalism has largely been associated with Democratic party administrations and with economic and social reform, it is a theme of Republican and business propaganda that it has gone too far. When the Republican party returned to

office in 1953, it established a Commission on Intergovernmental Relations to study the problems, many of them fiscal,
of federalism to-day with a bias towards devolving functions of
the national government on the State and local governments.
The fact is, however, that the necessity or desirability of most
of the specific measures that have centralized American federalism is too generally accepted for the measures to be repealed;
and when the first chairman of the Commission showed that he
took seriously President Eisenhower's homilies against excessive
centralization, he was replaced. (He supported a proposed
amendment to restrict the treaty power of the national government which the President opposed.) The Commission may offer
some useful suggestions for dealing with technical problems and
perhaps some arguments against further centralizing measures,
in effect further social reforms, but it is unlikely to find a way to
turn back the trend.

Nevertheless, the party system itself resists the centralizing
tendencies, and State and local party organizations and the
interests they serve give practical content to the political sentiment for States' rights. Despite the changes of recent years, the
structure of the two major American parties remains nearly as
decentralized to-day as in the days before the Civil War. Compared with the other elements of American federalism, therefore, the political element often appears highly decentralized
indeed. It has been said that there are no truly national parties
in America, that what seem to be such are simply coalitions of
State parties. To some extent the remark understates the case,
for often the State parties are themselves coalitions of local
organizations. On the whole, the county organizations are the
disciplined units of American party politics.

Decentralization affects every aspect of party activity.
National party conventions are composed of delegates chosen
in the States, either by their party organizations in conventions
or by their voters in presidential primary elections. The national
conventions nominate presidential candidates just a few months
before the general elections. National party platforms, drawn
up at these conventions, have usually consisted of vague compromises that represent the lowest common denominators of

73

State and local party views. The platforms carry no binding effect. They have been compared to the platforms of railway stations: useful for getting on the train but not to be taken on the trip.

National party committees have been composed, until a slight modification was made in the Republican party in 1952, of an equal number of delegates from each State regardless of party strength and have almost no powers. National party discipline is extremely weak because a congressman is often safe from defeat so long as he keeps his local fences mended but rarely safe from defeat if he supports national party policy that runs counter to strong local interests. As a result, voting in Congress is largely in terms of local interests, and party lines are disregarded. Many of the customs of American politics, such as the local residence rule and 'senatorial courtesy', strengthen the State and local party organizations.

There have been some changes in recent years. National party leadership has been more vigorous. National party lines have become more meaningful, partly because outside groups with national interests, like organized labour and big business, often exert a unifying influence within the parties. The State and local professional politicians are relatively weaker in national party counsels to-day than they were thirty years ago. But they are still powerful enough to give the party system its markedly decentralized character.

In defence of their power State and local politicians often speak of States' rights and the protection they give to local interests. But it is revealing to discover who benefit most from their position. First of all, they do. They are able to extract patronage and special favours from the national government. The effect is to promote inefficiency and corruption in administration.

Next, wealthy and well-organized pressure groups can secretly buy and openly intimidate the local political organizations and the men they elect, since the national party leaders are not strong enough to control or protect them. A large corporation can, practically speaking, buy a State political organization and through it have powerful friends in Washington. An ex-servicemen's organization can, through local pressure and national lobbying, intimidate a large majority of the 531 Members of Congress into passing legislation it wants, though significantly it often fails to intimidate the one President of the United States, who often vetoes the legislation.

It follows that the State and local politicians often give protection, sometimes inordinate protection, to special local interests. But generally these interests fall into two categories: those that are so special that it is politically inadvisable even within a State to admit how much they are being helped; and those that are special, not to a State, but to a region. In the first category are, for example, the interest a drug concern may have in avoiding the operation of a pure drug act and the interest a local labour racketeer has in preventing an investigation of trade union practices; these are things that local politicians 'fix' locally, in the State capitals, and in Washington. In the second category are, for example, the interests of cotton, corn, wool, textile, and steel producers and the interest the South has in preserving its pattern of race relations. State lines do not define the geographical bounds of either category of interests.

The partial identity of States' rights and regional interests is, however, a very old one. The pre-Civil War debate between North and South, for example, was superficially largely a constitutional debate about States' rights. It was in fact a sectional disagreement channelled, in the absence of sectional political organization, through the nation-State structure of American federalism.

Indeed, the only valid historical generalization about 'States' rights' is that it has been a useful political slogan and constitutional interpretation for those sections, pressure groups, and political parties that have wanted to resist the contemporary trend of national governmental action. Its use has, however, inculcated the belief that undue centralization is dangerous and that the federal system with a fair measure of States' rights is, like the separation of powers, an indispensable safeguard against tyranny. This is a belief held more in the abstract than in the concrete: it is appealed to more effectively against centralization in general than against specific measures, such as the national social security acts. But if it embodies a correct political theory, one of the chief beneficiaries of the power of the State and local political leaders is, finally, free government in America.

The practical meaning of States' rights to-day is, then, the privileges of State and local politicians in the national political parties, the excessive and often hidden influence of wealthy and well-organized pressure groups in the political system, the protection accorded to local interests that seek to evade effective national regulation, the protection accorded to regional interests, and the belief that decentralization is necessary to free government. This is a powerful combination, and political sentiment prevents American federalism from becoming as centralized as the present distribution of fiscal power might seem to impel and the present interpretation of the Constitution permits. On the whole, the defenders of political decentralization, in particular of the decentralized party system, are only frank about the last two items in the list. The reasoned argument for the preservation of political decentralization, as compared with administrative devolution in a politically centralized state, rests on the protection it gives regional interests and the safeguard it provides against tyranny. These are not, of course, minor points.

Finally, a few concluding remarks. Centralizing tendencies have been important in almost every democratic society in this century. Central governments have taken an increasing share of national resources for their traditional function of defence. Central governments have also acquired new functions, as government regulation of and intervention in the economy has grown, as the central governments have proved more effective regulators than the local ones, and, not least important, as the central governments have proved much more effective tax-collectors. What is happening in America is happening nearly everywhere: strands of functional union are crossing lines of geographical subdivision in increasing numbers, knitting national societies closer together.

In every society the pattern is different, and even within a society the development is rarely uniform. Knots of resistance arrest and modify the centralizing tendencies, and a confused pattern emerges. In America the party system and sectionalism, especially that of the South, provide the most effective political resistance to national centralization; and the States, which are constitutionally protected from destruction or remodelling, provide its focal points. Within the States local government units, though lacking such strong constitutional protection, serve similarly as points of resistance against State centralization. Anything like complete political and constitutional consolidation in America seems impossible.

The fundamental weakness of decentralizing forces in American politics, however, is that the party organizations are necessarily divided along State lines, which do not correspond to the sectional divisions in the country. Thus the two chief sources of resistance to national consolidation remain imperfectly allied. The difficulty of co-operation among independent and equal local authorities, even when controlled by the same political party, is almost a rule of local government relations; it is certainly true of the relations among the American States. Consequently, when anything of great importance to a region has to be dealt with, the national government is usually called in. It is significant that the Tennessee Valley Authority, the most important governmental development along regional lines in this century, is an example of national administrative devolution, not of interstate regional co-operation.

If political systems are to be judged by the neatness of their arrangements, the present American federal system rates rather badly. States and State party organizations prevent uniform centralization, but are incapable of maintaining really effective governmental decentralization. The result is an unusually confused variety of often inconsistent administrative and political compromises. There is hope for some order in the devices of co-operative federalism. There is hope for further order in some recent unifying trends in the party system. But government in the United States will always be relatively complicated compared with that in a unitary state like Great Britain. This is the price paid for the nation-State federal system created in the late eighteenth century.

What was obtained was a unity that might not have been possible otherwise. What is still obtained is a greater measure of local autonomy from Washington in the United States than from London in Great Britain. These are important gains, and such considerations have made federalism a common form of government for larger units created from the association of smaller ones: Switzerland, Canada, Australia, for example, and possibly some day Western Europe and the world. The hard part of the bargain is that if the time comes for closer association—it is not clear, however, despite the great changes of the last twenty years, that the time has come in America—the rigidity of a federal constitution prevents evolution into a unitary state. Hitler turned a federal republic into a unitary one very quickly, but the task is probably beyond the competence of democratic statesmen. Federalism is like a heavy mortgage: it makes it possible to build a house, but it is very difficult to pay off.

Chapter 4

The Electoral System

The American electoral system is perhaps most usefully described in terms of its interaction with the American party system. The topics dealt with below are the magnitude of the electoral system, the American two-party system, the effects of the electoral system on Presidential campaigning and the composition of American legislatures, electoral regulations, and nominating elections. These illustrate the connection between electoral arrangements and party organization and activity.

It has been estimated that the American electorate is called upon to elect more than three-quarters of a million public officials: the President and Vice-President of the United States, members of the national Congress, State officers and legislators, county officers, city and town officers, and school district and other local government officers. Since most terms of public office are fairly short—from one to four years—the voters choose a large number of officials every year.

In almost all States, moreover, the electorate is asked to take part in two elections, both State regulated, for some or all elective offices: a nominating party primary and a general election. The voters in the first choose the party nominees who run in the second. In many States and localities they also elect party officials. In about one-fourth of the States the electorate has the right to petition for the inclusion of amendments to the State Constitution on the ballot; and in almost all the States the voters in a general election vote on amendments, however initiated. In about a score of States they vote on legislative proposals under similar provisions for 'initiative and referendum' or referendum alone.

Several factors account for the great magnitude of the American electoral system. One is the enormous number of local government units, partly the result of federalism and localism, partly the result of geography and the pre-automobile age of transportation, and chiefly the result of the use of special local authorities to deal with particular activities. A great many school districts, the most numerous units, have been abolished and consolidated in recent years, but the number of government units in the United States is still very large: in 1952, according to the Bureau of the Census, 116,743. One nation, 48 States, about 3,000 counties, about 17,000 municipalities, about 17,000 towns and townships, about 67,000 school districts, and about 12,000 other districts require a proportionately large number of officials.

In fact, they have a disproportionately large number of elective officials because of other factors. The New England town-meeting tradition of short-term elected executive officers has helped determine the structure of local government units except in the South. Separation of powers has also led to the direct election of executive as well as legislative officials. The belief, based on the New England town-meeting tradition and associated especially with Jacksonian Democracy, that a large number of elective officials, including judges, is part of democratic government has had more to do than anything else in multiplying the number of elective offices.

The desire of the Progressives, carrying Jacksonian ideas a step further, to make the internal organization of the political parties democratic led to laws regulating party structure and nominating processes. The belief that a Constitution should be ratified directly by the people was acted upon during the Revolution: the Massachusetts Constitution of 1780 was ratified by a State-wide election—and a doubtful count. The Progressives carried this idea further too, by providing that constitutional amendments and ordinary legislation might be initiated by the voters and submitted to them in referendum.

The national Constitution, drafted by anti-democratic politicians of the late eighteenth century, provided only for the direct election of the House of Representatives. The presidential election became in effect almost a direct one in the early nineteenth century, but despite some agitation in Jacksonian times the Senate was not made directly elective until 1913. Even to-day, there are only 533 elected officials in the national government, hardly a disproportionately large number for the size of the country, and providing only a very small fraction of the 50, 75, 100, or more officials whom the voters of a particular electoral district may be asked to elect in one election. Jacksonian Democrats and their spiritual descendants, the Progressives, in their activities in State and local government rather than the framers of the Constitution of 1787 in their provision for national government have been responsible for the great size of the American electoral process.

The terms of the various officials of a unit of government frequently differ and the terms of holders of the same office, United States Senators for example, are sometimes staggered. The result is staggered elections. A large number of elective offices, two elections for most offices, and staggered elections make it necessary for American party organizations to be elaborate and well-disciplined if they are to exercise an integrated control over governmental organs. American party organizations are elaborate, and often at the local level and sometimes at the State level well-disciplined. They sometimes exercise a fairly integrated control over governmental organs. But local party leaders concentrate so much on manipulating an overcomplicated electoral system that they usually dispense with formulating a binding party programme. Discipline on matters of campaign support and patronage is often very strong, but discipline on matters of policy is usually weak.

An elaborate and in some respects well-disciplined party organization functioning primarily at the State or local level is called a party machine. It sometimes has one acknowledged leader known as a party boss or several leaders known as a party ring.

American party organizations receive help from voluntary workers, especially in national elections, but for the steady work

F

required by the complex electoral system, the machines buy help with the patronage system. Estimates of the number of professional party workers differ a great deal; for some are full- and some are part-time workers; some are maintained as patronage appointees on the public payroll and some receive only petty patronage, such as appointments as polling-station clerks for an election, and special favours; and there is no way of collecting reliable statistics in any case. In the 1880's Bryce estimated that there were well over 200,000; at the turn of the century M. Ostrogorski estimated that there were about 900,000. In the 1930's James Farley, Democratic national committee chairman, estimated that there were over 150,000 Democratic workers, which may be converted into a figure of over 300,000 for the two major parties, since despite the Democratic predominance in the 'solid South' the party is probably not better organized than the Republicans in the country as a whole. In the 1940's two textbook writers put the figure at about 800,000.

Party machines are indeed highly professional. They gain power in order to sell its fruits to the highest bidders. They are less interested in policy than office, and barter governmental action for money and electoral support. Consequently, they often work closely with wealthy, well-organized, and criminal minority groups that are interested in governmental action. The cost to the public at large of machine politics is beyond reckoning, but some of the city machines have been known to plunder the public treasury directly for tens of millions of dollars, and in proportion to their opportunities they are probably no more corrupt than hundreds of powerful rural county rings. The cost of criminal racketeering, which could be reduced very much by honest law enforcement, is put on terms of several thousand-million dollars a year.

Party machines and bosses have been common in America partly because, contrary to the expectations of the democratic reformers, the unorganized voters have been incapable of operating the electoral system created for them and the party machines have been the most efficient organizations for operating it in their stead. The American electoral system has furnished an excellent environment for breeding machines. The frequency and scope of elections put too great a burden on the voters; and voter participation, especially in most nominating elections, is usually low. As a result, comparatively small but well-organized groups of voters usually control nominations and, partly through them, general elections.

Occasionally a burst of righteous indignation among the voters at large may defeat a party machine in one election, but staggered elections and the diffusion of power in American government protect the machine from being destroyed by one defeat. The righteous indignation fades, partly as a result of disappointment at the failure to accomplish any real reform, and the machine survives. The fact that, though a machine is usually primarily local in operation, it controls or influences elections at all three levels of government—local, State, and national—increases the difficulty of defeating it permanently. It may be defeated at the local level, but it may still receive patronage and other help from its supporters in the State capital and Washington.

In short, party machines are local geographically but national in their political strength. There is a political co-operative federalism as well as an administrative one. But power in political federalism is concentrated near the bottom, and the holders of it are often not the local voters but the party bosses and rings.

The two major American parties have a near monopoly of American elective offices. Between them the Democratic and Republican parties always elect the President and Vice-President of the United States and nearly all the members of Congress. The combined vote of the Democratic and Republican presidential candidates is usually about nineteen-twentieths of the popular vote. Minor parties and independents occasionally win some State offices, but except for the third parties of a few midwestern States in the past and of New York State at the present, minor parties have hardly been more important in the States in this century than in the nation as a whole. (The Liberal party of New York, an anti-Communist offshoot of the American Labor Party, which it has now replaced as the largest

minor party of the State, has for some time commanded sufficient support to be an important factor in the closely fought
competition between the two major parties.) Only at the local
level is the normal major party monopoly of elective offices substantially broken: 'non-partisan' elections are common, particularly in small and medium-sized municipalities. Since party
politicians often stand as 'independents' in 'non-partisan'
elections, however, the exception is more apparent than real.

There are several reasons why the two-party system is so
effectively maintained. Except in 'non-partisan' elections,
American ballots consist of party-tickets, that is, lists of candidates with their party affiliations, and perhaps the names of a
few independent candidates. State laws, which apply to national
as well as State and local elections, often make it extremely
difficult for a minor party, especially a new one, to put its
candidates on the ballot. The supporters of Henry Wallace's
'Progressive' presidential candidacy in 1948, for example, were
unable to put electoral college candidates pledged to him
before the voters of several States. In Illinois, where the supporters were concentrated in Chicago, they were unable to
meet the requirement that the enabling petition of a new party
had to be signed by 200 registered voters in each of fifty
counties. In Oklahoma the laws set so early a date for submitting petitions that both the supporters of Wallace and the
supporters of the 'Dixiecrat' presidential candidate, J. Strom
Thurmond, failed to gain a place on the ballot.

Such laws are usually passed less to hamper true third parties, which the party bosses rarely fear, than anti-machine
independent candidacies. In 1953, for example, Mayor Vincent
Impellitteri of New York City, a dissident Democrat who had
been elected as an 'Experience party' candidate in 1950, was unable to get his name on the ballot when he sought to stand for re-
election—after unsuccessfully contesting the Democratic party
nominating primary—because the Board of Elections disquali-
fied many of the signatures on the enabling petition required of
an independent candidate. Among the grounds for disqualification were that the signature on the petition did not exactly
correspond to the signer's registered name, including middle

initials, and that a signature, though valid when made, had been rendered invalid by subsequent changes in the boundaries of polling-station districts. The effect of the restrictive laws and their administration is to strengthen the 'regular' candidates of the two major parties against all other candidates.

The American presidency also strengthens two-party politics. Its effect may be illustrated by a comparison with French multiparty politics. There are many diverse political interests in each country. In France the interests have sometimes divided into two main factions, which have been coalitions of distinct national parties. The parties of the predominant coalition share cabinet offices, and therefore executive policy-making.

In the United States the political interests usually divide into two national factions: one for, one against the incumbent President. The fact that he alone is the effective chief executive, however, makes it difficult for the two factions to be coalitions of distinct national parties. To share cabinet offices in America is not to share executive policy-making. Thus the American national parties tend to be two vertical coalitions of national, State, and local organizations rather than horizontal coalitions of several national organizations. The presidential prize usually ensures at least a superficial duality at the top of the political system.

The American electoral system helps maintain the two-party system by distorting election results. The basic American electoral unit is the single-member district. There are many nominally multiple-member districts: for example, each State elects two United States Senators and usually several State officials on a State-wide basis, and most counties elect several county officials on a county-wide basis. But staggered elections and the absence, except in a very few places, of any form of proportional representation give almost all multiple-member districts the characteristics of single-member constituencies, and they may be regarded as such.

The usual rule for determining the victorious candidate is that the candidate with the most votes wins. In some nominating elections, however, he must also receive an absolute majority of votes cast for all candidates, and there are provisions for run-off elections if needed. This unusual requirement is found in southern States, where the nominating primaries of the Democratic party are or have been the only real elections and several strong factions in the party often put up candidates. In most nominating elections and almost all general elections the winning candidate needs only a simple majority or, as it is called in America, plurality of votes cast. Thus the typical American electoral arrangement consists of essentially single-member units and simple-majority requirements. This arrangement, as British Liberals are well aware, markedly reduces the representation of third parties.

The method of electing the American President distorts the election results in the same way as the single-member district system but to a much greater degree. Constitutionally, each State legislature determines how the presidential electors of the State are chosen and the electors, meeting in the State (thus the electors of all the States never meet together), vote for whom they please in the electoral college. In practice, the State legislature allows the voters of the State to choose the electors and the electoral college candidates pledge themselves to vote for particular presidential and vice-presidential candidates. Traditionally, their pledges have been political rather than legal undertakings, though legal provisions have not been altogether absent. Recently, the split among southern Democrats, which has focused on attempts to use the electoral votes of southern States to bargain between the two major national parties, has led to efforts to give the pledges firm legal status. In 1952 the United States Supreme Court held in Ray v. Blair that the State of Alabama can authorize a State party committee to require a pledge from an electoral college candidate to support the presidential and vice-presidential candidates of the national party, even before they are chosen, but left undetermined whether the State can provide for legal sanctions in case the pledge is broken.

In practice, too, the State legislature allows or requires the voters to vote for a single slate of electors, who almost always pledge themselves to the same men, with the result that the slate which receives a plurality of popular votes in the State almost always casts all the electoral votes of the State for one pair of presidential and vice-presidential candidates. In a few States only the names of the electoral college candidates appear on the ballot. In other States the names of the presidential and vice-presidential candidates appear with the names of the electoral college candidates pledged to them printed beneath. But in most States, which have all told the great majority of electoral votes, only the names of the presidential and vice-presidential candidates appear, usually in accordance with State laws that provide that a voter's mark beside the name of one pair is legally a vote for the electors pledged to them. The fusion of constitutional provisions, legal requirements, and political customs in the operation of the American electoral college is worthy of a nation with an English political heritage.

The presidential election in each State works then on the principle of all or nothing. Regardless of the size of his popular plurality, the winning candidate takes all the electoral votes of the State. In 1948, for example, President Truman carried Illinois by about 34,000 votes in nearly 4,000,000 cast and received all 28 electoral votes of the State, California by about 18,000 votes in over 4,000,000 cast and received all 25 electoral votes, and Ohio by about 7,000 votes in nearly 3,000,000 cast and received all 25 electoral votes. In the country as a whole Truman received 303 electoral votes and Governor Dewey 189. Had about 30,000 voters in the three States mentioned, properly distributed among them, voted for Dewey instead of Truman, Dewey would have received their 78 electoral votes and won the election. (In 1952 General Eisenhower's popular majorities were much more substantial.)

The all-or-nothing arrangement usually protects the two major parties against third parties. A third party must have its support highly concentrated in one or a few States if it is to receive any electoral votes. In 1948, for example, Henry Wallace received about 2·4 per cent of the popular presidential vote but since he received no more than about 8 per cent of the popular vote in any one State, he won no electoral votes. On the other hand, J. Strom Thurmond also received about 2·4 per cent of the popular presidential vote, but since almost all of his support was in the South, he won the 38 electoral votes of four States. In addition, an elector of Tennessee, elected on the Truman slate, voted for Thurmond, making Thurmond's total electoral vote 39. However, a third party whose support is highly concentrated in one section cannot hope to become a major national party and its supporters soon come to terms with one of the two major parties, at least in presidential elections. It is symptomatic of the pressure the electoral college system puts on the party system that since 1860 the major party monopoly of electoral votes for President has never been broken in two successive elections.

Between the two major parties the electoral college arrangements usually benefit the one that receives the more popular votes. In 1932, for example, Franklin Roosevelt received about 57·4 per cent of the popular presidential vote and President Herbert Hoover about 39·7 per cent. Roosevelt received about 88·9 per cent of the electoral votes and Hoover about 11·1 per cent. In 1952 General Eisenhower received about 55 per cent of the popular presidential vote and Governor Adlai Stevenson about 44·4 per cent. Eisenhower received about 83·2 per cent of the electoral votes and Stevenson about 16·8 per cent. A victorious presidential candidate must receive an absolute majority of all the electoral votes. The arrangements for electing the electors distort the reflection of the popular votes in the States so much that since 1828 one candidate has always received an absolute majority in the electoral college, though on twelve occasions he failed to receive an absolute majority of all popular votes cast.

In extremely close elections, however, the distortion may turn against the most popular candidate. On two of the twelve occasions just referred to the candidate elected received fewer popular votes than another candidate: in 1876 Rutherford Hayes was elected though he received fewer votes than Samuel Tilden; and in 1888 Benjamin Harrison was elected though he received fewer votes than incumbent President Grover Cleveland. This sort of result can also occur in the single-member district system: in the 1951 British general election the Conservative party and its allies received fewer votes than the Labour party but won a majority in the House of Commons. In each system it is the exception to the rule.

The working of the electoral college greatly affects the conduct of presidential campaigns. Each State has one electoral vote for every member it has in Congress. Since there are 435 Representatives, apportioned according to population, and 96 Senators, apportioned two to a State, there are 531 electoral votes, their distribution somewhat favouring the least populous States. The all-or-nothing principle, however, puts an enormous premium on winning the most populous States. It promotes a concentration of national electioneering efforts in large marginal States like New York, California, Pennsylvania, Illinois, and Ohio. These five States now have 161 of the 266 electoral votes needed to win an election.

It is often said that minority groups in the large pivotal States have an inordinate influence on national party policy. It has been unofficially estimated, for example, that in 1950 the Jewish population of New York State was over 2,200,000 in a total population of about 14,800,000. President Roosevelt carried New York in 1944 by a plurality of about 316,000 votes in over 6,300,000 cast, Governor Dewey carried it in 1948 by about 61,000 votes in nearly 6,300,000 cast, and General Eisenhower carried it in 1952 by about 948,000 votes in over 7,100,000 cast. The policy of the national parties towards the Arabs-Israeli conflict has sometimes been demonstrably influenced by awareness of such facts. According to the 1950 census, the Negro population of New York, California, Pennsylvania, Illinois, and Ohio was a larger percentage of the total population in each State than the plurality of Governor Dewey or President Truman in the 1948 election was of the vote cast for the two candidates in it. The policy of the national parties towards Negro demands for equal rights has often been demonstrably influenced by awareness of the importance of northern Negro votes.

In a democracy groups of voters ought to have some influence on public policy, a principle which critics of concessions to 'New York Jews' frequently overlook. Whether in a given case the influence is inordinate must be a matter of opinion. But the extent of the influence should not be exaggerated. Jewish influence on American Middle Eastern policy has frequently met hard resistance in the State and Defense Departments. American Negroes gain far less by their influence in northern elections than they lose by their lack of due influence in the South, where over three-fifths of them live. They are badly represented in Congress, and they receive far more in party promises than in party performances.

What is most important is the influence the working of the electoral college gives the urban majority of the country in selecting the President. The Bureau of the Census called 64 per cent of the American population of 1950 urban. The key States are more urban than the country as a whole: New York is 85·5 per cent, California 80·7 per cent, Pennsylvania 70·5 per cent, Illinois 77·6 per cent, and Ohio 70·2 per cent urban. Facts like these have largely determined the selection of presidential candidates and presidential campaign issues in the last four elections.

The converse of concentration of presidential campaigning in pivotal States is neglect of safe States. On the whole, despite spectacular Republican victories in 1928 and 1952, the southern States have been safely Democratic throughout this century. There has been almost no incentive for Republican activity in the South: to raise the normal Republican vote of a deep southern State from, say, one-fifth to one-third of the total vote would not in itself win any electoral votes, elect any Senators, or, probably, elect more than one or two Representatives. The present Republican parties in the South have usually discouraged the growth of the party there. They are organized primarily to distribute national patronage when the Republican party is in power in Washington; and the fewer the party members, the less the spoils have to be divided. The efforts of 'regular' Republicans in States like Texas to keep recruits out of the party received national prominence in 1952 when the 'regulars' supported Senator Robert Taft for the Republican presidential nomination and those seeking admission to the party supported General Eisenhower. The 'solid South' has been the greatest block of safe territory, but States in other parts of the country have sometimes been safe for one party for a fairly long time, and the effect on the other party organization has been about the same as in the South.

Since the party in control of a safe State is usually not hard pressed by its opponents, the national committees of both major parties pay relatively little attention to it during a national campaign. Democratic neglect of southern white sentiment when bidding for northern Negro votes so angered southern congressmen that they helped sponsor a constitutional amendment in 1950 providing for apportionment of electoral votes in an election according to the distribution of popular votes in each State. (The winning candidate would be required to receive only two-fifths instead of an absolute majority of electoral votes.) Such a change would indeed have a striking effect on the American party system. It would make popular votes as much sought after in safe as in pivotal States; and since the amendment proposed to keep the present distribution of electoral votes that favours States with small populations, it would induce the parties to strengthen particularly their organizations in and appeals to the now safe rural States of the South and conversely to concentrate less on the marginal urban States of the North. The Senate passed the proposal by more than the two-thirds majority required to send it to the States. The House of Representatives rejected it, 210 to 134.

It is useful to describe at this point another important American electoral arrangement: the gerrymander. Strictly, the word 'gerrymander' is applied to the drawing of election district boundaries in order to give undue advantage to one party. This can be done, and still not violate the principle of having districts of equal population, by setting up a good many districts in which one party has small but fairly secure majorities and a few districts in which the other party has very large, and therefore largely 'wasted', majorities. It usually requires, however, creating some oddly-shaped constituencies. The supporters of Elbridge Gerry, an early nineteenth-century Governor of Massachussetts, created one that looked like a salamander: hence the name 'gerrymander'. Other famous examples have been a 'shoe-string' district in Mississippi and a 'saddle-bag' district in Illinois.

Broadly, the word 'gerrymander' is applied to any misapportionment of legislative seats, either deliberately created or deliberately maintained, in order to benefit a particular political interest. The electoral system of almost every American State legislature is gerrymandered in this sense in order to benefit the rural and small town political interest, sometimes enormously so. Forty-seven States have bicameral legislatures. In most States at least one of the Houses of the legislature is elected under a system of apportionment that makes some departure from apportionment by population in favour of units of local government with small populations. In a few States one House is elected under a system that completely equalizes the representation of each county or town. Even a House supposedly elected under a system of apportionment based on population may contain an undue proportion of rural and small town delegates who prevent a reapportionment to meet changes in the distribution of population. Since State legislatures apportion congressional districts within their States, the rural and small-town members of them gerrymander national representation too, so that both the national House of Representatives, supposedly elected on the basis of population, and the national Senate, elected on the basis of the equality of the States, over-represent rural and small town areas.

In the present House of Representatives, for example, according to the 1950 census, the member from the Twelfth District of Michigan, predominantly a rural and small town district, represents about 178,000 people and the member from the Sixteenth District of Michigan, in the Detroit metropolitan area, represents about 525,000. The member from the Seventeenth District of Texas, containing the city of Abilene with a population of about 46,000, represents about 227,000 people, and the member from the Eighth District of Texas, containing the city of Houston with a population of about 596,000, represents about 807,000.

Rural overrepresentation in the composition of American legislatures naturally means that the rural political interest has an influence in American politics disproportionate to the size of the rural population. It also means that while presidential campaigning usually stresses the appeal to urban voters, congressional campaigning is more likely to stress the appeal to rural and small town voters. The consequences of this difference in electioneering for presidential-congressional relations receive a great deal of attention. But there is surprisingly little discussion of the 'rotten borough' system itself.

Electoral regulations may be put in four categories: suffrage, registration, campaign, and balloting regulations.

The Constitution of the United States and the national government give no one directly the privilege to vote in the States, even for national offices. The original clauses of the Constitution require that the United States guarantee to every State a republican form of government, which implies that every State must give the suffrage to some of its inhabitants, and that the voters for members of the national House of Representatives 'in each State shall have the qualifications requisite for electors of the most numerous branch of the State legislature'. The Seventeenth Amendment sets the same requirement for voters for members of the Senate. Other amendments bar certain forms of discrimination: the Supreme Court has construed the equal protection of the laws clause of the Fourteenth Amendment as forbidding a State to discriminate on account of race; the Fifteenth Amendment specifically prohibits the United States or any State from denying the right to vote on account of race, colour, or previous condition of servitude; and the Nineteenth Amendment prohibits the United States or any State from denying the right on account of sex. Finally, the second section of the Fourteenth Amendment permits Congress to reduce the representation in the House of Representatives of any State that denies the right to vote to any male inhabitants, 'being twenty-one years of age, and citizens of the United States . . . except for participation in rebellion, or other crime'. (This section, if enforced, would virtually create a national suffrage, since the States would almost certainly avoid incurring its penalty; but Congress has never tried to enforce it.) Although some of these provisions put important restrictions on State action, all of them leave the positive definition of the suffrage to the States.

State suffrage regulations vary a great deal. But all States now require that a voter be a citizen, though at one time at least twenty-two States and Territories permitted certain classes of aliens to vote; that he reside in the State a certain length of time, varying from six months to two years; that he be at least twenty-one years of age, except in Georgia, where the voting age is eighteen; and that he meet various qualifications relating to sanity and non-criminal behaviour. About one-third of the States also have some form of literacy test. The most complex suffrage requirements are in the South, where under the guise of disfranchising the Negro, conservative groups have sometimes disfranchised a large part of the white population as well. The most famous device, still used in five or six southern States in 1952, is a poll tax. Many of the devices aimed solely at disfranchising the Negro, in nominating primaries as well as general elections, have now been swept aside by the Supreme Court of the United States. Probably political apathy and social intimidation rather than statutes keep most southern Negroes from the polls.

Registration regulations vary more than suffrage regulations. In most States registration is permanent, in some States permanent in some areas and periodic in others, and in two States periodic. In most States voters must take the initiative in registering, and in some States officials prepare lists. Almost all States have laws providing for the registration and voting of absent military personnel, and most States for the voting of absent civilians. All States have laws designed to prevent fraudulent registration and voting. Unfortunately, enforcement of the laws is usually in the hands of election officials put in office by the party machines. Fraudulent registration and voting, therefore, are not uncommon.

Campaign regulations show even greater variety than registration regulations. Most campaign regulations deal with campaign funds. For example, most States prohibit contributions from certain sources, such as corporations and public office

94

holders. Almost all States require a candidate to report his disbursements, and most States require him to report his receipts. Most States require a party to report its disbursements and receipts. Most States limit the amount of money a candidate may spend, though only about a third of the States limit the amount of money others may spend in his behalf. Most States put some restrictions on the way money may be spent.

Congress has passed the same kind of legislation covering campaigns for national offices and, where national authority can reach them, State and local offices. The Taft-Hartley Labor-Management Relations Act of 1947, which extended the scope of similar earlier legislation, prohibits a corporation or trade union from making 'a contribution or expenditure in connection with' any general election, primary election, political convention, or caucus held to elect or nominate anyone to a national office. It prohibits certain classes of corporations governed by national authority from spending money in connection with any election or nominating process for any office, national, State, or local. An earlier act prohibits contractors with the national government from contributing money or anything of value in support of anyone seeking nomination or election to any office. Other legislation prohibits one employee from assessing another for political purposes among national civil servants and among State and local civil servants whose work is partly paid for by national funds.

Congress requires 'political committees' that support candidates in two or more States or that are branches of national organizations to make financial reports, including the names and addresses of all contributors of more than $100. It limits individual contributions to a committee to $5,000 a year. It limits the amount a committee may receive or spend to $3,000,000 a year. It limits the amount a candidate may spend in a general election campaign for the Senate or House of Representatives on a scale based on the number of votes cast in the last election for the office. Subject to the right of the States to set lower limits, the scale runs from $10,000 to $25,000 for the Senate and $2,500 to $5,000 for the House, but the law exempts several important types of expenditures: for travelling,

95

stationery, postage, the printing and distributing of letters and circulars, and telephone service, for example.

Many of the State and national laws are patently unworkable. Some of the loopholes in the congressional acts illustrate the shortcomings. Individual contributions of $5,000 may be made to an unlimited number of committees with the same object. Similarly an unlimited number of committees with the same object may receive or spend $3,000,000 a year. The supporters of the major party presidential candidates now collect and spend, through a variety of committees, amounts of money that must be reckoned, especially for the Republican candidate, in tens of millions of dollars; yet after the presidential election of 1944 the Republican national committee reported, with well-justified mockery, that its annual receipts had been $2,999,999 and 48 cents. In congressional campaigns a candidate is restricted (though not very effectively) in his expenditure, but anyone else may spend an unlimited amount of money in his behalf. Committees that supported Senator Taft for re-election in 1950 reported to the State of Ohio that they had spent about $250,000; it has been unofficially estimated that all told his supporters spent about $1,800,000; he himself reported an expenditure of less than $2,000 under national law.

The Supreme Court has put loopholes for corporate and trade union campaign expenditure in the Taft-Hartley Act by its construction of it. In this way the majority of justices have avoided the question whether the full prohibition of expenditure in the Act abridges freedom of expression as guaranteed by the Bill of Rights.

When the State and national regulatory acts are well drawn and sympathetically construed, they are usually poorly enforced. Some of the acts protecting civil servants from assessment are fairly effective, but less on their own merits than because there are some effective civil service systems, including the national system, that protect employees from partisan pressures generally. On the whole, campaigning in America would probably not be markedly different, were most campaign regulations repealed.

Balloting regulations comprise State laws governing the form of ballot. In all States the ballot, whether by printed papers or by voting machines, is secret. Usually the most important issue about its form is whether it should be easy for a voter to vote 'a straight party ticket'. A party with a popular programme or a strong candidate for an important office benefits if it is possible for a voter to put one mark at the top of a party column, or pull one lever on a voting machine, thereby voting for all the candidates of the party who are running for the various offices at stake in the election. From 1930 to 1950 the Democratic party generally benefited most from straight voting because of the appeal of its national programme and leading candidates. In 1952 the Republican party benefited from the popularity of General Eisenhower, though the poorer showing of most other Republican candidates indicated that many voters, even where it was easy to vote straight, 'split their tickets'.

Provision for a one-mark vote normally not only reduces split voting but also increases the number of votes cast for minor offices. If a voter must put a separate mark for every office, he often ignores the minor posts. In one election in California, for example, of those who went to the polls, about 99 per cent voted for candidates for Governor, about 95 per cent for candidates for Lieutenant Governor, about 89 per cent for candidates for State Secretary of State, and so on, down to about 81 per cent for candidates for State Assemblymen and about 55 per cent for a technical question among twenty-three constitutional and legislative proposals put on the ballot under the provisions of 'initiative and referendum'. The tendency illustrated is known as voter fatigue. It is a proof that the American electoral system requires too much of the voters.

Balloting regulations also comprise State laws prohibiting any unorthodox marking or folding of ballots, as safeguards against bribed voting. There are other elaborate laws governing the counting of ballots. But again, unfortunately, enforcement of the laws is usually in the hands of State and local machine politicians and fraudulent counting is not uncommon. The national administration may protect general elections for national offices from frauds; and in 1941 the national Department of Justice convinced the Supreme Court in the case of

G 97

United States *v.* Classic that under legislation enacted in the 'reconstruction' period the national administration may also protect nominating primary elections for national offices, at least in some circumstances. But the national powers are rarely invoked. On the whole the State governments have the task of improving the administration of elections. At present electoral administration is probably the worst-managed phase of American public administration.

American machine politics is as old as the Republic. Tammany Hall was a political machine in New York City before the end of the eighteenth century. But the evils of machine politics did not bring a nation-wide reaction to them until after the Civil War, when the party bosses and rings of rapidly expanding urban centres, like the infamous 'Tweed Ring' of New York City, raised corruption and plunder to new heights. At first those who attacked the machines had no other programme than 'throw the rascals out'. By the Progressive Era, however, they were substantially agreed on a programme of political reforms. The measures that struck most directly at machine control of politics were those regulating the internal concerns, especially the nominating methods, of the parties.

At that time local meetings of party members and local and State party conventions made party nominations in the States; and party meetings, conventions, and committees chose the delegates to the national party conventions that nominated the presidential candidates. These methods are still partly used, especially in the presidential nominating system, but the Progressives initiated widespread changes. As was mentioned earlier, in almost all the States there are now two sets of elections, one set in which the voters nominate party candidates and one set in which they choose among party candidates and independents who reach the ballot on enabling petitions. The nominating elections are called direct primaries and are used to nominate most local, State, and congressional candidates. In addition, elections called presidential primaries, in which the voters indicate their preferences among presidential aspirants, choose the delegates to the national party conventions, or do both, were held in 1952 in seventeen States whose delegates had about half the votes at the conventions.

The passage of legislation providing for primary elections in Great Britain would be a great departure from existing practice, but the legislation establishing the direct and presidential primaries in America was a natural development from legislation introducing the secret ballot. Before the introduction of the secret ballot in the last years of the nineteenth century, the parties printed their own ballots, listing their candidates for all the offices at stake in an election. A voter took one of the party tickets, modified it if he wished by scratching out some names and writing in others, and slipped it in the ballot box. When the States produced their secret ballot, they put all the party tickets on a single sheet of paper or on the face of a voting machine, which the voter marked or manipulated. They had to define in law, therefore, a party with a right to have its ticket appear. (Great Britain, by using a candidate rather than a party ticket form of ballot, merely had to define in law a candidate with a right to have his name appear.) How the laws of the American States help the two major parties, which usually have virtually prescriptive rights to put their candidates on the ballot, has already been described.

Furthermore, the States soon had to define which of several factions in a party dispute had the right to submit the official list of party candidates. They had to define, in other words, what constituted a valid party nomination. By the time they had done that, the camel's nose of State control was well inside the party tent. When the Progressives passed legislation to take the nominating process 'from the party bosses' and give it 'to the voters', they simply changed the method of arriving at a legally valid nomination. The principle of State control had already been established. In some States the order of reforms differed from that described: South Carolina, to cite the extreme example, did not provide a State-produced secret ballot until 1950, nearly sixty years after it passed primary legislation —and six years after it repealed it. But the general trend in the country as a whole guided reformers in passing the primary laws.

The degree to which Americans have now been conditioned into thinking that party nominating procedures are public functions is illustrated by the way the Supreme Court has dealt with recent southern attempts to preserve the 'white primary'. The constitutional issue involved is that the Fourteenth and Fifteenth Amendments prohibit a State, but not private persons, from discriminating against voters on account of colour. The attempts have all been based on the argument that the Democratic party primary, almost always the only real election in the States concerned, is not a public election and discrimination in it is not 'State action'. By 1944 the Court had made it clear that if a State had any legislation dealing with a primary, the primary was a public election and discrimination in it was 'State action' within the meaning of the constitutional prohibitions.

It was for this reason that South Carolina, for example, repealed its direct primary legislation with the assurance that the Democratic party would continue to hold a direct primary, but in its new capacity as a 'private club'. The Supreme Court had also said, however, in United States v. Classic that it would consider a primary a public election 'where in fact the primary effectively controls the choice' of elected officials. When lower national courts held that the South Carolina primary was in fact still a public election and the action of the Democratic party in 'blackballing' Negroes was, even in the complete absence of relevant State laws, 'State action' and therefore unconstitutional, the Supreme Court refused to hear an appeal. In 1953 in the case of Terry v. Adams the Court carried constitutional interpretation further, though it is not clear on what grounds. White Democrats of a Texas county had long held a pre-primary primary to select local candidates who then entered the Democratic primary and almost invariably won it without opposition. The Supreme Court ruled, the justices dividing eight to one, that the activities of those taking part in this obvious device for depriving Negroes of any real political influence involved unconstitutional 'State action', though none of the justices found a legal reasoning for the decision upon which a majority could agree. Whether the justices would be willing to interfere so far in the nominating procedures of a two-party area is a moot point.

An important issue generally of nominating election rules is who among the qualified voters of the States are qualified to vote in the primary of a particular party. Primaries are either 'closed' or 'open'. In 'closed' primary States there is a separate ballot for each party. In most of them a voter must register as a party member some time before the primary is held in order to receive one of the ballots. In some of them he must meet trivial tests on polling day: he may be asked, for example, to pledge himself to vote in the general election for the nominees of the party in whose primary he takes part; since the general election is by secret ballot, the test is unenforceable. In no State is he required, for example, to contribute to party funds.

In 'open' primary States the voter either marks a comprehensive primary ballot that resembles a general election ballot or secretly selects and marks one of the separate party primary ballots. Either way he votes in the primary of any party he chooses without meeting any requirements at all. In the State of Washington he may even vote in two or more primaries in the same election, provided he does not vote for candidates for the same office in more than one. There are also many variations in the rules regulating how candidates may enter primary elections. In a few States candidates sometimes win the primaries of two or more parties.

The primary rules sometimes make party lines less meaningful than ever in a country where they have often seemed to mean very little in any case. In the South and other one-party areas the nominating elections, being the only real elections, give the electorate some choice. In other areas, too, they often appear to stimulate intraparty competition. Primary legislation has, therefore, had some effect on the party system. But the result the Progressives sought, freedom from boss rule, has not been achieved. Except in one-party areas, voter participation is usually lower in primaries than in general elections, and the professional politicians often have little difficulty in controlling the results.

Other Progressive legislation designed to regulate the internal processes of the parties, such as laws providing for the popular election of party committees, has also been unsuccessful in accomplishing the purpose of destroying the party machines. It is clear that burdening an already overburdened electorate with more tasks helps as much as hinders the party bosses. As a result, there has been a reaction against the theory of Jacksonian Democracy that the more elected offices, the more democracy. Even in the Progressive Era, there were attempts to reduce the long ballot; and since then, further efforts have been made, involving in some instances the abandonment of Progressive reforms.

The Progressives were right, however, in striking at machine control of nominations, even if their methods failed. Control of nominations is vital to a party machine. Most party machines are destroyed, not by reformers, but by other party machines that capture party nominations. Thus a machine prefers losing a general election to losing a primary. 'I don't care', said Boss Tweed, 'who does the electing, just so I do the nominating.'

There are several reasons why. First, a party out of office still has a certain amount of patronage and power. There are a great many bipartisan commissions in American government, especially in electoral administration, and a great deal of legislative activity is bipartisan too. The machine in control of the nominating process of the minority party thus still gets some of the 'spoils of office', but a party faction defeated in the nominating primary of either major party gets nothing.

Second, the faction in control of the local nominating machinery receives patronage and other help from the State and national parties. It exacts this help because as long as it controls nominations it decides not only who is picked for local elections but also, partly at least, who is picked for State and national elections. Herein lies the importance of the local residence rule, by which in law or custom American elected officials must be inhabitants of the districts they represent. For most of them this means that they must co-operate with the local party machines and county rings.

Finally, and above all, the faction in control of the party nominating process lives to fight again. In a two-party area the outs are sure to be the ins sometime; and while they are outs, they receive the support of those dissatisfied with the party in power. A machine out of office still has the aura of power. A machine out of the primary has lost the aura.

These are the hard facts of the political business in which the party machines are engaged. They lead to the significant conclusion that the party machines are not, after all, very partisan. They are less interested in winning elections for their party than holding power in it. That is why American parties sometimes lose elections because of internal divisions over spoils. That is why party machines of supposedly opposing parties often work together, especially against reform elements, until in cases where one is much stronger than the other the more powerful one may in fact control the other. That is partly why American parties have often failed to offer clear-cut alternatives of policy and to mobilize their supporters behind them. American party machines are not designed to bring people into policy-making but to keep them out.

Chapter 5

Party Politics before 1933

Have there been any real differences between the two major American national parties? James Bryce gave an answer for the parties of his time that expresses a typical British point of view. 'Neither party', he wrote in 1888,

'has any principles, any distinctive tenets. Both have traditions. Both claim to have tendencies. Both have certainly war-cries, organizations, interests enlisted in their support. But those interests are in the main the interests of getting or keeping the patronage of the government. Tenets and policies, points of political doctrine and points of political practice, have all but vanished. . . . All has been lost, except office or the hope of it.'

Later he quoted an American journalist as saying 'that the two great parties were like two bottles. Each bore a label denoting the kind of liquor it contained, but each was empty.'[1]

Differences between parties may be of four kinds: differences in social composition among their supporters, differences in general policy when campaigning, differences in social composition among their elected representatives, and differences in general policy when in office. The first two kinds of differences may be said to characterize the parties in the country, and the last two the parties in the capital. The American national parties have in fact been much less like empty bottles outside than in Washington. It is possible to trace a fairly consistent line

[1] *The American Commonwealth* (London: Macmillan & Co., 1888), II, 344–5, and (New York: Macmillan & Co., 1914), II, 29. Quoted with permission of Macmillan & Co., Ltd., London, and The Macmillan Company, New York.

through American party divisions from the beginning of government under the Constitution to 1933. The following account of the differences in social composition and policy describes tendencies only; no social group, for example, ever identified itself completely with one of the political parties; but the tendencies were marked enough to be significant.

In broadest terms, from the beginning until 1933, one of the major American parties represented the established or dominant people in America, with a few minority groups attached, and the other major party represented people seeking greater equality for themselves as compared with the established people. The first party usually advocated mercantilistic measures, and the second *laissez-faire*. The first party went under different names: Federalist, National Republican, Whig, and Republican party. The second was always called, in part at least, the Democratic party.

One of the ways some people became the established people in America was to get there first. Thus in the port cities in the late eighteenth and early nineteenth centuries the Anglo-Saxons were the established people and the Irish were the most noticeable new stock, poor, discriminated against, and not fully accepted as Americans. The wealthier Anglo-Saxons were Federalists. The Irish became strong Democrats as early as the 1790's. The Naturalization, Alien, and Sedition Acts of 1798, passed by the Federalist party at a time when the United States was almost at war with France, were drafted with the different social compositions of the two major parties in mind. In the guise of countering Jacobin influence, one of the Acts lengthened the time it took aliens to become citizens, thus in fact making it more difficult for recent immigrants to become Democratic voters.

The Anglo-Saxons were Protestants and the Irish Roman Catholics. The racial difference between the parties gave rise then to a religious difference between them in the northeastern ports. But Protestant Scotch-Irish farmers of the South and West were Democrats during the first half of the nineteenth century. The religious difference between the parties was not important in the country as a whole.

After the Civil War, however, a great many western Protestants supported the Republican party and a great many more
immigrants entered the United States. The diverse immigrant
races tended to align themselves with the two major parties
along religious lines. Outside the South, Protestants were
usually Republicans, and Catholics Democrats.

The explanation of the alignment of the late nineteenth and
early twentieth centuries is fundamentally the same as that of
the Anglo-Saxon and Irish alignment earlier. Protestants were
largely assimilated in the old stock, and therefore were established as full Americans, much more rapidly than Catholics.
Protestant immigrant groups, like the North Germans and
Scandinavians, thus became Republicans, though they were
often independent-minded. Catholic immigrant groups, like the
Poles, became Democrats. Moreover, some Catholic racial
groups, notably the Irish, remained Democrats even after they
had been in America a long time, partly because they retained
the religious difference that prevented full assimilation with the
dominant old-stock strain and partly because they held influential positions in the anti-old-stock political and social coalition.

The dominant stock received political support from some
minority groups. A few Catholic immigrant groups, for example, were largely Republican in some cities, at least for a
time, partly owing to their resentment of Irish domination of
urban Democratic professional politics. The perennially most underprivileged of American races, the Negroes, if permitted to
vote, tended to be Federalist, then Whig, then Republican. One
reason was that in the North, where Negroes were more likely to
vote, many of them were domestic servants, who voted as their
employers requested as long as the ballot was open. Another
reason was that Negroes found themselves in economic competition with the Irish, and as a result of bad feeling between
the two races, the Negroes stayed away from the Democratic
party. After the Civil War the strongest reason was that the
Republican party had freed the slaves. The adherence of the
Negroes to the Republican party was consistent in any case
with the alignment outside the South of Protestant Republicans
and Catholic Democrats.

Geographical divisions cut across the racial and religious divisions. Despite the influx of immigrants into the northeastern ports, people were on the whole more established in the East, and after the Civil War in the Northeast and Midwest, than in other parts of the country. There has been, for example, an economic colonialism within America with the imperial centre in Wall Street. The Federalist-Whig-Republican party, as the party of established people, was the party of the East, later the Northeast and Midwest, more than the Democratic party. The Democratic party was the party of the West and South.

The pre- and post-Civil War sectional alignments were separated, however, by an important transitional period. The old Jacksonian Democratic alliance of southern and western agricultural interests against eastern mercantile interests was broken in the years before the War, when the Democratic party became more than ever the party of the South, but lost its identification with the farmers of what was then the West and is now the Midwest. The question of slave and free territory in the West, as was pointed out in an earlier chapter, united westerners and northerners in support of the Republican policy of limiting slavery. After the Civil War the Republicans tried to keep the allegiance of Protestant western farmers by granting free homesteads and liberal veterans' disability pensions, 'waving the bloody shirt', and labelling the Democratic party the party of 'Rum, Romanism, and Rebellion'. The tactics succeeded so well that the first post-Civil War agrarian protests against Republican business policy took the form of third-party movements instead of reunion with the Democratic party; and when the Democratic party again became the party of the West in the 'free silver' election of 1896, it was as the party of the Great Plains and Rocky Mountain States rather than the midwestern corn belt that had been the West of Andrew Jackson. (The most famous use of the phrase 'Rum, Romanism, and Rebellion', though, at a welcome to the Republican presidential candidate in New York City during the campaign of 1884, is usually deemed to have cost the Republican party New York State and with it, for the first time since the Civil War, the presidential election.)

The racial and sectional alignments that have been described may be put in part simply as economic alignments: old stock tended to be better off than new, Protestants better off than Catholics, and easterners had more money than westerners. Furthermore, in agricultural areas sectional party alignments after the Civil War may be put in terms of economic activity: the Republican party was strong in the hay-and-pasture, corn, and part of the corn-and-winter-wheat belts; the Democratic party was strong in the cotton, subtropical farming, and part of the corn-and-winter wheat belts. In industrial areas polling-district party alignments may often be put in terms of economic class: the Republican party was usually strong in districts where business men lived; the Democratic party was often strong in districts where white workers lived. But it should be emphasized that the economic class division were not in general the most pronounced. It was often much easier to guess a man's party allegiance if one knew his religion, for example, than if one knew his income.

The general policy of the Federalist-Whig-Republican party was mercantilism, that is, government aid to business. The general policy of the Democratic party was *laissez-faire*, that is, abolition of special government aid to business. The mercantilistic party supported, for example, high tariffs, a foreign policy that opened and protected overseas markets, and easy bankruptcy laws. The *laissez-faire* party advocated low tariffs, an isolationist foreign policy, and strict bankruptcy laws. Some of the key issues of American presidential elections illustrate the continuity of the differences between the parties: Hamiltonian fiscal policies that allied the business community to the national government divided Federalists and Jeffersonian Democrats, the status of the second national bank divided Whigs and Jacksonian Democrats, and tariff policy divided Republicans and Cleveland Democrats (Grover Cleveland was President from 1885 to 1889 and 1893 to 1897), in each case the first party supporting and the second party opposing government aid to business.

In other ways, too, the Federalist-Whig-Republican party was the party of governmental action and the Democratic party

the party of *laissez-faire*. The former sought to control immigration, first by proposing to restrict it, then by encouraging the
importation of cheap labour, then by erecting barriers against
entry partly in response to anti-immigration pressure from
organized labour, and finally by establishing restrictive racial
quotas. The latter, though sometimes also responsive to the
pressure from organized labour after the Civil War, was more
willing to let the movement of peoples as well as goods take its
natural course. In one form or another the immigration issue
has distinguished the policies of the two parties, in a fundamentally similar way, from the time of the Alien and Sedition
Acts to the days of 'D.P.'s'. The Republicans also favoured laws
restricting or prohibiting the sale of intoxicating beverages
more than the Democrats. The Federalist-Whig-Republican
party was, finally, the party of nationalism, the Democratic
party the party of States' rights or geographical *laissez-faire*.
After the Civil War, for example, the Republican party, at first
in practice and later only in theory, sought to protect the
southern Negro by national action. The Democratic party
wanted the white South left alone.

The presidency of Woodrow Wilson, from 1913 to 1921,
marked an important shift in the attitude of a Democratic
administration to economic policies. Wilson used the national
regulatory power even more than Theodore Roosevelt, the
more vigorous of the two Republican presidents of the Progressive Era. But Wilson continued to stress that the Democratic party was primarily against special privileges granted by
government rather than for what would now be called welfare
state measures. Tariff reform remained a major issue with the
parties aligned as in the time of Hamilton and Jefferson. Furthermore, the Democratic party of the 1920's was, in contrast
to the Republican party, still the party of the Roman Catholic
Church, which opposed centralization in a predominantly Protestant country; of the 'wets', who opposed prohibition; of the
white South, whose dogma was States' rights; and of the West
(though the Progressive Republicans were strong in this part of
the country), which opposed the financial alliance between
Washington and Wall Street.

The history of American party alignments before 1933 may be summarized then as follows: The party finally called the Republican party received most support from old-stock citizens, Protestants, Negroes, easterners, and business men, and advocated mercantilism and nationalism. The Democratic party received most support from immigrants, Catholics, white southerners, westerners, and urban workers and advocated *laissez-faire* and States' rights. Non-southern farmers were less constant in their political allegiance than other groups. Most of them were first Jacksonian Democrats; then Republicans; and finally, though still normally Republican, a divided and usually decisive 'floating vote'.

One important characteristic of the social alignments was that the Republican party had a greater natural cohesion than the Democratic party. The Republican party was based on a strong core of established people. The Democratic party was a mixture of those opposed to the established people. It contained urban Catholic workers and evangelical southern farmers, immigrants and people suspicious of foreigners. As long as the policy of the Democratic party was *laissez-faire*, that is, an essentially negative policy, party unity of a sort was usually possible. Adoption of a policy of positive action would almost inevitably lead, however, to increasingly bitter intraparty strife.

Differences in social composition between the two major parties were much more marked among their supporters than among their elected representatives, and differences in policy were much more marked in elections than in office. Except for the early years, when the presidents and many congressmen were from southern planter and northern merchant families, the elected members of the national government in both major parties were predominantly middle class. Most numerous were those who belonged to perhaps the most middle class of occupations, the legal profession. In the 1830's Alexis de Tocqueville wrote about the dominance of lawyers in American politics. It was increased when the remnant of southern planter politicians virtually disappeared after the Civil War. Although there were enough wealthy men in the United States Senate at the end of the century to give point to attacks on the 'rich man's club', James Bryce had to explain the general absence of upper class leadership in American as compared to British politics in a chapter entitled 'Why the Best Men Do Not Go into Politics'. Most of the wealthy men left after the Senate became directly elected in 1913.

Some of the social differences between the parties in the country were reflected in their congressional delegations simply because the local residence rule and the strong tendency to send a member of the largest racial group of a district to Congress meant that if the Democratic party won more southern votes than the Republican, it had more southerners in Congress, and if it won more Catholic votes, it had more Catholics in Congress. But the economic differences between most Democrats and most Republicans in the country were not reproduced. The great majority of congressmen of both parties were or had been lawyers, small-town newspaper editors, farmers, and small business men. The economic class division was not sharp in the country. It was very dull indeed in Washington.

Between the voters and the congressmen were the men who 'delivered the votes': the machine workers, precinct captains, district leaders, members of the county rings, and city bosses. In both parties they were usually members of the most numerous racial and economic groups of their districts. Even though the American middle class may be defined very broadly, this meant that many more of them than congressmen were working class. Perhaps especially for them politics was 'nothing more than a means of rising in the world'. They were the truly professional politicians of American politics.

They sought power in order to get jobs and sell favours. They spent their energies in putting men in office rather than putting programmes across. Those who paid for their services named the policies. Raymond Moley, one of Franklin Roosevelt's original 'brains trust', described a bargain he made in 1932 with James Farley, Democratic national campaign manager for Roosevelt and a professional politician: 'I just want you to know', he quoted Farley as saying, 'that I'm interested in getting him the votes—nothing else. Issues aren't my business. They're yours and his. You keep out of mine, and I'll keep out of yours.' Moley and Farley shook hands on that, and 'there was never the slightest suggestion', Moley wrote, 'of interference on policy matters from Jim Farley'.[1]

The attitude expressed by Farley in that bargain helps explain why the American parties failed to implement many of their campaign pledges when in office. Professional politicians put great stress on party loyalty, but they meant loyalty to the campaign ticket and personalities rather than loyalty to programmes of public policies. American party machines have been compared to feudal baronies: the political vassals swore fealty to their lords and promised to follow them wherever they led. Sometimes they rebelled, not because they disagreed over public policy, but because their chiefs failed to support them adequately or others offered better spoils. Machine politicians, in sum, were interested in public policy mainly as a means of winning elections, not in winning elections as a means of carrying out public policy.

American national party organization accorded with this order of priority. It was chiefly an intermittent organization that sprang to life every four years as a coalition of State and local parties which tried to capture the American presidency. It was not designed to put a programme of public policies into effect.

For one thing, the working of the national nominating conventions deprived the parties of the strong, permanent national party leadership required for such a task. Congressional party caucuses nominated the presidential candidates of the Democratic-Republican party until 1824, when the break-up of the one-party system in that year led most members of the party to oppose the caucus nominee. After a brief period when State legislatures, party caucuses, and conventions made nominations, in most cases merely endorsing the obvious leaders of the two major factions that replaced the all-embracing Jeffersonian party, national conventions were convened. The substitution of the national convention for 'King Caucus' completed the

---

[1] Excerpt from *After Seven Years*, published by Harper & Brothers, New York. Copyright, 1939, by Raymond Moley, pp. 36–7.

destruction of the relatively centralized national party organization of Jefferson's presidency. The convention usually nominated a different type of man.

All the presidents before 1824 had been distinguished national politicians: Washington had been the 'Father of his Country'; John Adams and Jefferson had been revolutionary leaders and vice-presidents when the Vice-President was the second choice of the electors for the presidency; and Madison and James Monroe had stepped from the secretaryship of State to the presidency. In 1824-5 John Quincy Adams, one of the opponents of the caucus nominee, followed Madison's and Monroe's example. Thereafter presidential candidates might be national politicians: some like William Howard Taft, successful Republican candidate in 1908 (and unsuccessful candidate for reelection in 1912), with careers of national service comparable to those of the early presidents; others like William Jennings Bryan, unsuccessful Democratic candidate in 1896, 1900, and 1908, with great followings in the country; and others like Senator Warren G. Harding, successful Republican candidate in 1920, undistinguished candidates of machine politicians. They might be popular generals: some like Jackson with a good deal of previous political experience; others like Grant with almost none. Or they might be State governors: some like Alfred E. Smith of New York, unsuccessful Democratic candidate in 1928, of outstanding ability; others like James M. Cox of Ohio, unsuccessful Democratic candidate in 1920, apparently of only mediocre ability.

A nominee to oppose or replace the incumbent President usually had to gain the support of the State and local party leaders. Sometimes one of the most popular aspirants won a nomination quickly. But more often enough State delegations put forth 'favourite son' candidates to make it impossible for any candidate to be nominated on the first ballot. The votes of 'favourite sons' might be traded on later ballots for a promise of a cabinet post, a promise of an appointment to the Supreme Court if a vacancy occurred, or the vice-presidential nomination, which usually went as a consolation prize to a faction and geographical section of the party that had been defeated in the main contest. The winning candidate thus bought the support of rival candidates and the State and local machines. Sometimes a 'favourite son' or 'dark horse' won the presidential nomination. Franklin Pierce, for example, the successful Democratic candidate in 1852, was nominated on the 49th ballot, having received no votes at all until the 35th; Harding was nominated on the 10th ballot in 1920, having received less than a tenth of the votes on the first; and John W. Davis, the unsuccessful Democratic candidate in 1924, was nominated on the 103rd ballot, after an extremely bitter struggle between the supporters of the two leading contenders, William McAdoo and Alfred E. Smith.

The Democratic party had the longest fights, because it contained more diverse elements than the Republican party, and because it required that the winning candidate receive two-thirds of the votes cast on a ballot and the Republican party required only an absolute majority. The two-thirds rule gave the southern Democrats virtually a veto power over the presidential nomination, which partly compensated after the Civil War for the fact that it was inexpedient to nominate a southern politician. The rule made more obvious, moreover, the need often to win the approval of most party bosses.

Franklin Roosevelt was the first President to serve more than two terms. The anti-third-term tradition assured the party bosses that they would have the chance to be king-makers not less frequently than every eight years. Indeed, a President might even be denied one renomination, though in fact—counting the nominations of Theodore Roosevelt in 1904, Calvin Coolidge in 1924, and Harry Truman in 1948, that is, of vice-presidents who had succeeded to the presidency, as renominations—the President has always received it since 1888. A defeated presidential candidate was infrequently renominated. Since he had no prior claim on the next nomination, his titular party leadership meant nothing and his views often carried little weight. The next presidential candidate might have quite different opinions. Consequently, a good deal of opposition party policy awaited the nomination of a presidential candidate just a few months before an election. The customs of the nominating conventions precluded effective long-term policy-making.

It is true that the nominating conventions also drafted party programmes. But they drafted the programmes before nominating the candidates. Occasionally one faction of the party had predominant influence over drafting the party platform and another succeeded in nominating the presidential candidate, with the result that the candidate promptly repudiated a major plank of the platform. In 1928, for example, the Democratic convention pledged 'its nominees to an honest effort to enforce the Eighteenth Amendment' prohibiting the manufacture and sale of intoxicating beverages, then nominated Alfred E. Smith, who wired the convention that it was 'well known that I believe there should be fundamental changes in the present provisions for national prohibition' and that he intended 'to point the way . . . to a sane, sensible solution of a condition which . . . is entirely unsatisfactory to the great mass of our people'. Obviously a programme that did not bind the presidential candidate endorsed by the same convention did not bind anyone else.

These arrangements suited the professional politicians. The structure of national party organization made it possible for them to fight the presidential elections and, when they won, obtain patronage and other special favours from the national government. But it did not make it possible for the national party leaders to reduce them to mere agents of the central party. The local machine politicians could still sell their services to the local highest bidders, even though they went against the policy of their national leaders in doing so. In other words, the success with which the local bosses played local politics depended partly on the autonomy they possessed within the national party organization.

Similarly, congressmen, often working with the local bosses and rings, took advantage of weak national discipline to vote according to local pressures instead of national party policy. It was sometimes almost impossible to distinguish party attitudes in Congress. It is not surprising, then, that observers of American politics sometimes found little real difference between the two major political parties. Although alleged differences were often lively campaign issues, the lack of party discipline seemed to reduce the differences a great deal when actual governing was to be done.

However, critics of the American party system—not Bryce so much as some who read him—were too ready to apply British standards to American institutions. They overlooked, for example, the extent to which the decentralized American party machinery was adequate to the tasks put upon it before 1933. Neither major party needed a strongly organized national machine capable of putting across a sustained programme of national action.

It is not much of an exaggeration to say that before 1933 only Alexander Hamilton tried to put such a programme into effect. He failed, after some initial successes, because he failed to hold the support of the majority of the voters. When latter-day Federalists, the Republicans, took over many of his policies, they found that by the second half of the nineteenth century the policies required only intermittent legislative action. Once a high tariff was passed and land grants made, for example, Republican politicians could relax their efforts while their business friends reaped the harvest. It was to their advantage that legislative action was often difficult, for it was harder to undo governmental action and destroy vested interests in legislation than to act and create interests in the first place. Furthermore, Republicans could help their friends simply by weak administration of regulatory laws. A complex government without clear lines of responsibility concealed a great deal of this help from the public.

Most Democrats were for States' rights and *laissez-faire*. It did not take strong action to leave the South alone, let immigrants come into the country, and withhold privileges from business. It is true that the Democrats had, as indicated above, great difficulty in repealing mercantilistic measures. Tariff reform became an almost impossible task. But until 1933 sustained positive action was a small part of their programme. The major policies of both parties could be carried out moderately

well without well-disciplined organizations and clearly defined
congressional alignments.

Indeed, the nature of American society and the provisions of
the American Constitution made it necessary for American
national parties to be loosely organized. James Madison had
been right. The political alignments of a nation of continental
proportions were not neatly drawn, particularly along 'the
most common and durable' divisions arising from 'the various
and unequal distribution of property'. The strongest 'class con-
sciousness' in America before 1933 was sectional and racial,
and a diversity of geographical areas and immigrant races
made American political parties, especially the Democratic
party, coalitions of social groups as well as coalitions of political
machines. The complex mixtures of social groups provided the
basis for party organizations containing, however illogically in
terms of principle, relatively liberal and conservative wings.
The social basis for integrated national party organizations
simply did not exist.

The framers of the Constitution, by providing for various
modes of election, systems of apportionment, and terms of
office, had deliberately made government by one faction difficult. Strong governmental action in America was usually possible only when popular pressure succeeded in inducing large
groups in both major parties to support it. The history of
American party politics is as much the history of great swings
of opinion in both parties as the history of 'swings of the pen-
dulum' between them. From the Civil War to the First World
War, for example, the two parties usually maintained, in theory
at least, their distinctive tariff policies, symbolic of the traditional distinction between advocacy of mercantilism and of
laissez-faire; but in their hostility to what would now be called
welfare state measures the two parties were almost indistin-
guishable during most of the late nineteenth century; and in
their advocacy of some social and political reform they were
only slightly more distinguishable during most of the Progressive Era of the early twentieth century. Perhaps it was fortunate
that while the Constitution was fairly rigid, the party organizations were fairly loose. If the Constitution made partisan policy-

making difficult, there was much to be said for party organizations that made bipartisanship easy.

Thus similies about the parties being like empty bottles were misleading, if they implied that American party politics was without meaning. The American political parties, even when in office, were at least slightly different. And to the extent that they did agree at any time, they were less like empty bottles than ones filled with the same liquor. When the parties agreed, in other words, they were less likely to thwart the expression of majority opinion than both to represent it. (The temporary appearance of strong third-party movements almost always resulted from failures on the part of the major parties to represent particular minority opinions rather than failures to represent current majority opinion.) American party politics was never entirely meaningless.

But what would happen if the demands on the party machinery and the social basis of American politics changed? Woodrow Wilson foresaw the need to adapt the customs of the parties and the Constitution. Traditionally, a strong President put sufficient intermittent political pressure on congressmen of both parties to have his few legislative proposals passed by bipartisan majorities, though he usually worked closely with some of his partisan supporters and almost invariably took partisan credit for his successes. When Wilson became President in 1913, he wanted a number of reform measures passed rather quickly. Influenced by British comparisons of American and British political institutions, he thought that he must become 'prime minister' of his party in pushing his programme through Congress. He believed that by exercising frankly partisan leadership he could overcome the difficulties the Constitution seemed to impose on more continuous presidential control of congressional action than in the past.

He was successful in his early efforts, as strong presidents not infrequently were in any case. The Republican delegation in his first Congress had enough progressive members to make bipartisan co-operation possible, even if the Democratic President talked in unusually partisan terms. But Wilson lost his hold on Congress after the American entry into the First World

War. The decisive turning point in his fortunes came in the congressional election of 1918, when in accordance with his ideas about party leadership he asked the voters to return a Democratic majority so that he might carry on the war effort effectively. The voters, perhaps aroused by the apparent slur on the patriotism of the Republicans, elected a Republican majority. Wilson was broken, politically and personally, in his efforts to win ratification of the Treaty of Versailles.

Wilson had exaggerated the need for change in his time. The conditions for stronger party leadership and more distinct party lines did not yet exist. What is most important is that his experience was taken as a caution by Franklin Roosevelt, Wilson's Assistant Secretary of the Navy, who was never fully convinced that Wilson's conception of presidential leadership was practicable at any time in the American system, despite the difficulties the traditional conception later put in his own way. For the real test of the adaptability of American political institutions to new conditions came in the administration of Franklin Roosevelt, after 1933.

On the basis of presidential elections the political history of the United States until 1933 falls into these periods of party rule: 1789–1801, 1801–61, 1861–85, 1885–1921, and 1921–33. From 1789 to 1801 the Federalist party was in office. From 1801 to 1861 the Democratic party was usually in office. From 1861 to 1885 the Republican party was in office. From 1885 to 1921 the parties shared office fairly evenly: Democratic Presidents held office from 1885 to 1889, 1893 to 1897, and 1913 to 1921; Republican Presidents held office from 1889 to 1893 and from 1897 to 1913. From 1921 to 1933 the Republican party was in office. In broadest terms 1861 may be taken as the year in which power passed from the western and southern agrarian alliance of the Democratic party to the western agrarian and northern business alliance of the Republican party. From 1885 to 1933 the Democratic party was occasionally able to join far-western and southern farmers with eastern and midwestern workers and farmers to win the presidency, but the Republicans were able to hold their alliance together more often and, consequently, win more elections.

When the traditional policies of the two major parties are taken into account, it may be said that from 1801 to 1861 American politics was dominated by a States' rights party, which eventually became partly a secessionist party; and from 1861 to 1933, despite the growing need of the urban working class for governmental action in its behalf, power was shared by a party that remained primarily the mercantilistic party of the business community and a party that remained largely the party of *laissez-faire*, though both parties passed some economic and social reform legislation in the Progressive Era. In these circumstances the professional politicians who ran the local party machines carried out two important tasks. Until 1861 they helped keep the nation together. Until 1933 they furnished some social justice for the urban poor. The part party machines have played in American party politics cannot be properly appreciated unless those two services are recognized.

The State and local party organizations seem to decentralize American party politics to-day, but they tied the national party organizations together in the States' rights era before the Civil War. As sectional differences increased other national organizations split apart. The Baptist and Methodist Churches, for example, split into northern and southern wings about 1845 over the question whether the Bible condemned or sanctioned slavery. The parties held together a few years more, as professional politicians tried desperately to find the formulae that would save their national coalitions. They sought often to minimize sectional differences.

In return for their services they extracted a large amount of patronage from the national government. But even the interests created by the patronage system played a part in keeping the Union together. For patronage attached large numbers of office-holders and would-be office-holders to the national government in the way that Hamilton's policies had earlier attached the business community. John C. Calhoun, the chief spokesman of southern sectionalism, noted with disgust how the 'devotion to party, where the spoils are the paramount object' led to 'the unwillingness of the two wings of the respective parties, in the different sections, to separate, and their desire to hold together'. In the end the party politicians failed to prevent the break, but they helped delay the Civil War long enough to permit the North to become far stronger than the South (though that was not their purpose). After the Civil War, too, the Democratic party organizations, by reuniting almost immediately, sewed one of the first threads of union between the North and South. The Baptist Church is still divided, and the Methodist Church reunited only in 1938–9.

The party machines always provided some social services. But their social work became much more important after the Civil War, when increased industrialization and immigration rapidly expanded the population of the cities. Industrialization led to the growth of great urban slums, huddling the workers in compact hovels. Immigration poured diverse races into the great ports, particularly New York City, filling the American 'melting pot'. The two major parties provided very little in their national programmes for the urban poor. The Republican party was the party of the old stock and the wealthy. The Democratic party was the party of *laissez-faire*.

After years of endorsing social policies scarcely less conservative than their opponents', the Democrats identified themselves in 1896 with the comparative radicalism of William Jennings Bryan, who usually dominated the party from then until 1913. He electrified the Democratic national convention of 1896 by telling the wealthy: 'You shall not press down upon the brow of labor this crown of thorns, you shall not crucify mankind upon a cross of gold.' He struck such terror in the business community that the Republican national party chairman raised a record amount of money for the presidential campaign. But Bryan did not press for what would now be recognized as welfare state measures. He wanted silver coined as well as gold so that Plains States farmers would benefit from the resulting inflation. American radicalism before 1933 was mainly agrarian radicalism.

The professional politicians seemed to be the only politicians who cared for the inhabitants of the urban slums. In return the machines received, often quite honestly, their votes.

In the ports the party workers met immigrants as they came off the ships, found them jobs and places to live, and invited them to political clubs and party picnics. They also, of course, helped them get naturalized and on the voting register, though not always in that order. For all the poor the precinct captains ran an employment exchange, a housing bureau, a quick loan office, and an advice bureau. If a local boy needed a job, the precinct captain went to an employer who knew that the taxable value of his property varied inversely with his readiness occasionally to hire someone recommended. If a family needed a larger flat or could not pay the rent for a while, the precinct captain found a flat or persuaded the landlord not to press for the rent. The landlord understood that in return his tenement was not inspected too carefully by fire inspectors.

If the tenement burned down, the precinct captain had the money on the spot to buy new clothes for the tenants. 'I've got a regular system for this,' one Tammany district leader told a reporter.

'If there's a fire in Ninth, Tenth, or Eleventh Avenue, for example, any hour of the day or night, I'm usually there with some of my election district captains as soon as the fire-engines. If a family is burned out I don't ask whether they are Republicans or Democrats, and I don't refer them to the Charity Organization Society, which would investigate their case in a month or two and decide they were worthy of help about the time they are dead from starvation. I just get quarters for them, buy clothes for them if their clothes were burned up, and fix them up till they get things runnin' again. It's philanthropy, but it's politics, too—mighty good politics. Who can tell how many votes one of these fires brings me?'[1]

A precinct captain often received the money for his philanthropy from the local bookmaker or prostitute.

As much as anything, the precinct captain was a friend. He

[1] From: *Plunkitt of Tammany Hall*, by William L. Riordon. Copyright 1905 by Doubleday & Company, Inc. (New York: McClure, Phillips & Co.), pp. 51–2.

was someone to talk over a problem with. And he 'knew the ropes'.

The cost of machine politics was enormous. Public administration was riddled with patronage and graft. Countless millions of dollars and countless lives were lost in fires and accidents that could have been prevented by honest inspection and in criminal activities that could have been suppressed by honest law enforcement, to mention only two of many ways. The precinct captain paid the burial expenses of the man who died in an industrial accident honest factory inspection could have prevented. He helped the family whose claim for damages was disallowed because of a legal technicality the machine was paid to enact. In return the machine received the votes of all concerned. The price of machine services was exorbitant, but before 1933 only the machines provided many of the services at all. The development of official social services might seriously impair the popularity of professional politicians.

In November 1932 Franklin Delano Roosevelt was elected President of the United States in the midst of the worst depression and one of the worst moral panics in American history. His record seemed somewhat less vigorously liberal than that of Al Smith, his predecessor as Democratic presidential candidate. His campaign speeches were mild. Although Roosevelt reassured the country in his inaugural address by saying that 'the only thing we have to fear is fear itself', he seemed to have little new to offer.

The first legislative measures of his administration made a hodge-podge. There were acts to revive and reform the banking system. There was an act cutting government expenditure on pay-rolls and veterans' pensions. There was an act limiting agricultural production. There was an act that helped large businesses to revive and squeeze out some of their smaller competitors. There were acts providing money for unemployment relief.

Then, as time went on, the pieces began to fall together into a pattern of strong governmental action, based largely on the fiscal resources of the national government. It was action designed to help the whole economy, including almost for the first time the underprivileged people in it, the 'forgotten men'. One of the ways to help was to reform. Here resistance was encountered from the business community. The resistance became increasingly bitter.

It seems that about the time he entered office in 1933, Franklin Roosevelt was converted to the programme he had already named without knowing what it was going to be: the New Deal. He adopted a programme of positive governmental action, a programme of social justice, and a programme of reform that struck at interests supported for well over half a century by mercantilistic policies. His conversion set in motion major changes in American party politics.

Chapter 6

Party Politics since 1933

Before 1933 the Democratic party was considered the party of States' rights and *laissez-faire* and the Republican party the party of loose construction of national constitutional powers, though in the twentieth century the distinction became more one in theory than practice. Since 1933 the national Democratic party has been recognized as the party of loose construction and the Republican party as the party of States' rights and *laissez-faire*. This apparent exchange of party principles, which had been foreshadowed whenever regulation of business was a political issue, is explained by the fact that though some of the traditional partisan differences over policies remain—those over tariff reform and immigration control, for example—the New Deal programme of social reform has made the Democratic party clearly the party of national government intervention in the economy and the Republican party the party of opposition to it. Before 1933 the Democratic party was the more isolationist of the two major parties. From the late 1930's it has been the less isolationist (or 'unilateralist'). This change in attitude toward foreign entanglements, which had been foreshadowed in the last years of Wilson's presidency, is explained chiefly by the change in what a non-isolationist policy means. Isolationists used to oppose dollar imperialism, and now oppose dollar aid to other democracies.

The Democratic policies in domestic affairs, both before and after 1933, have been called liberal and the Republican policies conservative. The New Deal changed, therefore, the meaning of liberalism and conservatism in American politics. It also made the difference between the parties more pronounced. After 1933 the Democratic party lost a good part of its conservative wing outside the South, especially in industrial areas where the party has become associated with organized labour, and kept only the nominal allegiance of a good part of its conservative wing in the South. The great majority of northern Democrats, and perhaps of loyal southern Democrats, are now 'left of centre'.

The Republican party lost virtually all its liberal wing. The great progressive Republican tradition of the civil service reformers, Theodore Roosevelt, the elder Robert LaFollette, and George Norris is now almost unrepresented in the party. Wayne Morse was perhaps the last senatorial 'son of the wild jackass', and he broke with the party in the 1952 election. The distinction between 'liberal' and 'conservative' Republicans to-day is one based primarily on foreign policy: liberal' Republicans, chiefly from the East, maintain the internationalist traditions of the party; and 'conservative' Republicans, chiefly from the Midwest, have inherited the isolationism of many of the old Republican progressives, but not their progressivism. It is true that the foreign policy 'liberals' tend to be less conservative on domestic questions than the foreign policy 'conservatives'; for the former must court more support in great poly-racial urban areas, the centres of current American liberalism, than the latter, who reflect the fact that agrarian radicalism, the impulse of the old progressivism, is now almost a spent force. The difference, however, is neither very great nor clear-cut. Almost all Republicans are now 'right of centre'.

The chief cause of the more distinct alignment is that the New Deal led to a greater class division between the two major parties. The tendency for low income, particularly urban working class, voters to be Democrats and well-to-do voters to be Republicans has been more marked since 1933 than before.

The religious and racial aspects of voting behaviour are now less significant apart from the economic aspect than they were. Despite Democratic gains among Protestant workers and recent Republican gains among Catholics, possibly on the anti-Communist issue, Catholics are still more likely to be Democrats than Protestants are. Differences in cultural assimilation and the entrenchment of the Irish, French Canadians, and Italians in city and State Democratic organizations help maintain traditional party loyalties. But the fact that Catholics are, on the whole, less well-off than Protestants in the predominantly urban States where the great majority of Catholics live is now perhaps the main reason for the religious division between the parties.

The most dramatic change in racial politics since 1933 has been the change in the voting behaviour of Negroes. By 1936 northern Negroes were as solidly Democratic as they had previously been Republican. Since Negroes suffered most in the great depression, usually being the first fired and the last rehired, they benefited most from the relief programmes of the New Deal. As a result they left the party of Abraham Lincoln for that of Franklin Roosevelt. After 1936 assiduous wooing of Negro voters by Republican candidates, who pointed out that the Democratic party was also the party of the southern Senators, won some Negroes back. But in the presidential elections of 1948 and 1952 they were again one of the most solid Democratic voting blocks, having apparently decided that both their economic and racial interests are now best represented by northern Democrats.

The most important effect of the greater class division in American social politics, however, has been the breaking of sectional party loyalties. The national rather than sectional character of New Deal politics was demonstrated in 1936 when President Roosevelt, standing for re-election, received more popular votes than his Republican opponent in all but two States. In the closer elections of 1940, 1944, and particularly 1948, sectional alignments appeared, but they varied from election to election, showing that the traditional attachment of sections to one party has now largely ended.

In the 1940 and 1944 presidential elections the Democratic party, supported most outside the 'solid South' by urban working class and lower middle class voters, was slightly stronger than the Republican party in most of the great industrial States of the Northeast and Midwest, which had often been Republican strongholds before 1932. Only the rural non-southern areas returned, less in 1940 than in 1944, to their old Republican allegiance. Within a great belt of States the old sectional division was replaced by an urban-rural one (the change had, in fact, begun before 1933 but it was now much more evident), with the Democratic party the party of the great cities and the Republican party the party of the country districts and small towns.

The Democratic majorities of popular presidential votes in the industrial States made the Northeast particularly seem a new Democratic section in the electoral college results. In 1940 and 1944 President Roosevelt received the electoral votes of Connecticut, Massachusetts, New Hampshire, New Jersey, New York, Pennsylvania, and Rhode Island: 132 votes in 1940 and 130 votes in 1944. His Republican opponent received the electoral votes of the two most rural States of the region, Maine and Vermont: eight votes in each year. The Republican majorities of popular presidential votes in the rural Plains States made them seem a Republican section. In 1940 and 1944 the Republican candidate received the electoral votes of Kansas, Nebraska, North Dakota, and South Dakota: 24 votes in 1940 and 22 votes in 1944.

But the electoral votes of presidential elections partly concealed the most significant non-southern geographical division. The distribution of votes for major offices in the 435 congressional districts clearly revealed the urban-rural pattern. In 1944, for example, in 329 congressional districts outside the southern and 'border' States the Democratic party was the most important party in 81 metropolitan, 31 small city and suburban, and 30 predominantly rural and rural-small-town districts and the Republican party was the most important party in 41 metropolitan, 64 small city and suburban, and 82 rural and rural-small-town districts. In 106 southern and 'border' congressional districts, although most of them were rural, the Democratic party was the most important party.

This geographical division of support—non-southern large city and southern country, Democratic; and non-southern small city and country, Republican—had been recognized by political observers as one of the most important divisions of American politics when President Truman won his surprising Democratic victory in 1948 in a surprising way. He lost most of the industrial States of the Northeast, which Roosevelt had carried, and without which it is supposed to be nearly impossible to win the election. He lost four States in the South to the 'Dixiecrat' party rebels. He lost ground, compared to Roosevelt, in most of the large midwestern cities, but he carried most of the midwestern States because he greatly reduced, and sometimes overcame, the 'normal' Republican majorities in farming and small-town districts. This unusual distribution of rural votes was apparently due to a sudden fear on the part of midwestern farmers that their prosperity might be threatened by a change of administration. That it did not represent a profound political change was shown in the voting for other major offices in the congressional districts, which generally followed the urban-rural pattern of 1944.

In its way, Truman's unusually close victory in 1948 illustrates the new national character of American party politics almost as much as Roosevelt's unusually sweeping victory in 1936. Although Truman won and lost regional groups of States —he carried all the Rocky Mountain States and lost all the Middle Atlantic States, for example—he did not win or lose all the States in the Northeast, the Midwest, the South, or the West, that is, in any of the great subdivisions of the country. It was not uncommon for a candidate to do one or the other in the past. What is more important, Truman's margin of victory or defeat in many States was small. He found few 'safe' or 'hopeless' States in 1948. He received more than 60 per cent of the vote only in Arkansas, Georgia, Oklahoma, and Texas. He received less than 40 per cent of the vote only in Louisiana, Mississippi, South Carolina, and Vermont. (He had no slate of electors on the ballot in Alabama.)

President Eisenhower's victory in 1952 was another national landslide. Eisenhower carried most of the country, including States in every section. All told, only seven of the forty-eight States of the Union have been in the same national party column in the last five elections (1936–52): Maine and Vermont have been consistently Republican; Arkansas, Georgia, Kentucky, North Carolina, and West Virginia have been consistently

Democratic. Obviously not much is left of firm sectional attachments in presidential elections.

Indeed, the most constant geographical division in the last twenty years has been at the level where geographical and class divisions coincide. In large metropolitan areas people of different classes tend to live in different election districts. An analysis of voting behaviour in the great American cities shows that the urban voters who give the most support to the Democratic party live in the poorest districts; the urban voters—usually suburban voters—who give the most support to the Republican party live in the richest districts; and the urban voters who are most doubtful in their political allegiance live in the districts intermediate in the social scale. These generalizations had some validity before 1933, but the growth of Democratic strength among Protestant, especially Negro, working class voters has made them much more valid since. The residents of the doubtful districts are small shopkeepers, white-collar workers on modest salaries, and semi-skilled wage-earners. They have largely replaced the rural middle class, the 1948 presidential election results notwithstanding, as the marginal electorate of national elections.

Before 1933 the Republican party had been the dominant party for seventy years. It had held the presidency, for example, for fifty-six of seventy-two years. After 1933 the normal Republican majority disappeared. The new Democratic predominance, which lasted at least until 1952 and may not yet be destroyed, was, however, necessarily more precarious than the old Republican predominance. It rested on classes rather than sections. This meant that in almost every large State there were two fairly evenly balanced parties and a small shift (or of course a large shift) of popular votes across the country could produce a presidential victory of landslide proportions in the electoral college for either side. Practically speaking, neither party can win to-day without carrying some of the most urbanized States, though, as the 1948 results showed, the rural votes in those States may have a decisive influence in a close election. In general, the change since 1933 from sectional to class politics has been a change from rural to urban politics, and the decisive 'floating vote' is usually the urban lower middle class.

The new Democratic predominance was also precarious because the change from a negative policy of *laissez-faire* to a positive policy of social reform made it much more difficult to keep the diverse elements of the Democratic coalition together. In the early 1790's Thomas Jefferson joined southern planters to Tammany Hall to create the national Democratic-Republican party. Southern whites and northern machine bosses were thenceforth main elements in the Democratic national coalition. But since 1933 their positions in the party have been threatened by the growing importance to the party of organized labour. In particular, the New Deal and Fair Deal programmes, which have increasingly reflected the thinking of trade union leaders, have disturbed a great many southern Democrats. Perhaps the most interesting question of American politics today is what is going to happen to the 'solid South'.

There is a southern liberal element that can fairly easily remain in the national Democratic party. Senator Estes Kefauver of Tennessee is at present the best known southern liberal politician. But the majority of leading southern Democrats are closer to the Republicans in their thinking on domestic social and economic policies than to northern Democrats. Traditionally the strongest advocates of *laissez-faire* and States' rights, they find their relations with a party identified with a national welfare state and 'civil rights' programme increasingly anomalous. Conservative southern Democrats want to remain a major force in the national Democratic party, but they are unwilling to accept the policies with which it is now associated. The efforts of conservative southern politicians in recent presidential elections both to influence the choice of Democratic presidential candidates from within the party and to oppose the candidates from without are symptoms of a conflict between political expediency and political opinions that is not yet resolved.

There are good reasons why conservative southern Democrats are reluctant to leave the Democratic party. It is very doubtful, in the first place, whether they could change parties, at all levels of government, without losing some of their power in State and local politics. At present southern conservative factions, like that of Senator Harry Byrd in Virginia, are strongly entrenched in the Democratic organizations of several southern States. So far, conservative southern Democratic leaders have remained neutral or 'bolted' from the national party only in presidential elections. (One group of 'bolters' supported the 'Dixiecrat' third-party candidate in 1948 and another group, consisting of some of the 1948 'bolters' and many other southern conservatives, supported General Eisenhower in 1952.) Otherwise they claim to be good Democrats. If they abandoned the Democratic party at all levels, however, the liberal Democrats would take over the party machinery from them and thus establish a two-party system. In a two-party system the liberal Democratic factions would almost certainly score more victories than they do now in State and local politics, especially when the national party had a strong presidential candidate to help the ticket; they would, in other words, almost certainly reduce conservative influence.

Moreover, the rationale of the present one-party system is that it keeps Negroes from voting. Even though the Supreme Court has now banned the 'white primary', it is probably still true that two-party contests would bring out more Negro voters than the present factional contests in the Democratic party primaries, if for no other reason than were the South a marginal two-party region, political activity and competition in it would be much more intense in presidential years. A heavier southern Negro poll would chiefly be a heavier poll for liberal candidates. Perhaps conservative candidates would win enough additional white votes to offset Negro votes, but perhaps not. It is natural that the present holders of political power in the South view changes whose results are uncertain with a great deal of caution.

Finally, one result of conservative southerners leaving the Democratic party would be certain: they would have less influence than now in Congress. The virtual monopolies of power conservative Democrats possess in a few southern States and many southern congressional districts mean that southern members of Congress are, on the whole, the senior Democrats in Congress—that is, those with the longest continuous service. They therefore receive a disproportionately large number of congressional committee chairmanships, key positions of congressional influence, when the Democrats have a congressional majority. Turning the South into a two-party area would probably reduce the number of senior southern congressmen. The conservative southerners who joined the Republican party would have to compete in seniority with Republicans from traditionally safe Republican seats. And most important of all, the conservative element in Congress would lose the most important brake it has on liberal policies when the Democratic party is in power: southern conservative influence through Democratic committee chairmanships.

The Republicans have not pressed southern Democrats to join their party. For a very short time after the election of 1928, when Herbert Hoover won several southern States, the Republicans had the choice either to try to organize their growing support in the South within local Republican parties or to work with conservative southern Democrats across party lines. There was a good deal of talk then of a real southern Republican party, but it came to nought. In 1952 Eisenhower's popularity in the South revived the choice; but there was much less talk than in the 1920's of a new southern Republicanism, and apparently the national party did nothing to foster it. Republican leaders discouraged Republicans who sought to enter congressional and State elections in some of the States where conservative southern Democratic leaders were openly supporting Eisenhower; and when the party took office in 1953 the chairman of the Republican national committee distributed national patronage in South Carolina, for example, through 'Eisenhower Democrats'. Although national Republican leaders continue to give some lip-service support to the regular Republican southern organizations, because there are enough Negroes in them to make them good subjects for Republican propaganda among northern Negroes, they avoid doing anything that might seriously split conservative political forces in the south.

The business interests that support the Republican party nationally continue, in the main, to put their faith and money in the conservative Democratic organizations of the South. For them a conservative 'fifth column' in the Democratic party is worth a good deal.

But in parts of the South the Republican party grows despite the lack of encouragement. Outside the 'black belt' the two-party class politics of the nation is gradually displacing the one-party sectional politics of the 'solid South'. In other words, the change is taking place in the kind of States that the Republicans carried in the 1952 presidential election—Florida, Tennessee, Texas, and Virginia—rather than the kind of States that the 'Dixiecrats' carried in the 1948 presidential election—Alabama, Louisiana, Mississippi, and South Carolina. (In essence the 'Dixiecrats' were a faction within the one-party system.) In the 1954 congressional elections the Republican party had a net loss of seats in the country but a net gain of a seat in the South. In the eleven States that joined the Confederacy in the Civil War the Republicans retained five seats—one in North Carolina, two in Tennessee, and two in Virginia—most of which are in traditional Republican oases of strength, lost one seat—in Virginia—and gained two seats—one in Florida and one in Texas. The Democrats carried ninety-nine districts.

Non-southern Democrats have not pressed southern Democrats to join the Republican party either. The issue of how much loyalty the national party should exact from its State organizations was raised at the 1952 national convention, but soon dropped. The so-called 'loyalty pledge' that occupied a good part of the time of the convention was designed merely to ensure that no delegation would be seated at the convention which intended to prevent the voters of its State from voting for Democratic electors pledged to the national party candidates. The Alabama Democratic party had prevented voters from voting for electors pledged to Truman in 1948 and other southern State parties seemed ready to follow its example in 1952. Although the Truman and Stevenson leaders at the convention ultimately forced the seating of all southern conservative delegations, regardless of the extent to which they 'took the pledge', voters in all States did in fact have the chance to vote for electors for Stevenson in the ensuing election. The 'bolt' of southern conservative Democrats like Governor James Byrnes of South Carolina and Governor Allan Shivers of Texas in the election, however, makes it likely that the direct issue of party loyalty will be raised again in 1956.

There are a number of arguments for continuing a lenient policy. The Democratic party does, in the main, receive southern electoral votes. It does maintain a nominal majority in Congress more often than it would if it expelled southern conservatives, and though party loyalty in itself does not mean much in Congress it does mean something. Moreover, party loyalty means a good deal when coupled with questions about which northern and southern Democrats are in general agreement: tariff policy and many aspects of foreign policy, for example. Internationalist southern Democrats in Congress were less likely than internationalist Republicans, for example, to use incidents like the dismissal of General MacArthur to discredit the Truman administration; in other words, men who held the same general views on foreign policy reacted differently to specific events because of their different party labels.

The Democratic (and Republican) task is the task James Madison foresaw: the party must embrace a wide variety of interests in the American subcontinent in order to be the 'majority faction'. The Democratic choice seems at present to be between continuing to attempt to reconcile conservative, or at least moderate, southerners and liberal northerners and ejecting the conservative southerners while moderating its northern liberalism to make up the losses. The difficulties of the first course are obvious because it is the course that has been followed. The difficulties of the second course are indicated by the failure of several radical attempts in the past three-quarters of a century to unite workers and farmers in a permanent alliance against business men, and it is unlikely that an attempt to unite urban industrial workers with suburban middle class white-collar and professional men would be much easier.

Still, there is a limit to what the non-southern part of the party will stand. Although there is practically no tradition for enforcing party discipline on matters of policy, there is a tradition for insisting that members do not 'scratch the ticket'. So far, southern 'bolts' have not mattered: in 1948 the Democratic presidential candidate won anyway, and in 1952 he would still have lost had he carried every southern State. If a 'bolt' costs the party an election, intraparty feeling will be much more bitter, though when in opposition the party naturally finds it easier to cover over its internal differences than when in power. The real test will come if the party returns to power, perhaps after losing an earlier election because of a southern 'bolt', with the kind of liberal impulse behind it that produced the New Deal. Another instalment of a positive policy of reform will probably make it impossible for conservative southerners to remain in the national Democratic party.

By that time liberal and moderate southern Democrats may already have done much to weaken the conservative hold on the South. For the complementary development to the growth of southern Republicanism outside the 'black belt' is the growth of southern liberalism. Increases in the number of industrial workers, trade unionists, and Negro voters strengthen its social base. Southern conservative Democracy is under strong pressure from within as well as without.

It follows from what has been said, however, that the transfer of southern conservatives from the liberal Democratic to the conservative Republican party will not necessarily increase markedly the differences of policy between the two national parties. An American 'majority faction' must be moderate whether based on sections or classes, and changes in southern politics must be compensated for elsewhere. But a more consistent alignment of political forces would make it easier for the parties to carry their policies out, and it has been in that respect that they have sometimes seemed like 'empty bottles'.

The changes since 1933 have in fact already created the conditions for more centralized political parties than America has had. The new marginal voters, for example, affect the conduct of party politics differently from the old. Before 1933 the marginal voters in presidential elections were usually farmers and small-town people closely attached to non-southern farming interests. Their chief interest in national economic policy was as producers. They gained influence not only by being bid for by both major parties but also by organizing producers' pressure groups to lobby for them between elections. They preferred a political system in which congressmen were more subject to local pressures than national party discipline. Congressmen were looked upon primarily as spokesmen for local crops and industries.

The chief weakness of farming interests was lack of economic organization. Farmers were unable to control production and fix prices as effectively as big business. The New Deal filled the gap by governmental production and price regulation, so that farmers have fared better than ever before. But farmers have never been allied for long with urban labour since the Civil War, and the orientation of New Deal policy to the needs of urban labour has meant that in general non-southern farmers have tended to return to their Republican allegiance. Between them and business men on the one hand and urban labour on the other come the members of the urban lower middle class as the new 'floating voters'.

These voters are primarily interested in national economic policy as consumers. Except for semi-skilled workers, members of the lower middle class are poorly organized economically and badly represented among political pressure groups. The chief way their point of view is given organized expression is through the national parties that bid for their votes in presidential elections. Squeezed, as they see it, between organized farming and big business on the one hand and organized labour on the other, they want government at least strong enough, and nationally-minded enough, to protect consumer interests against inflationary and other pressures from producer groups.

Thus the changes wrought in group alignments by New Deal policies provided the political environment for stronger national party leadership and bolder national programmes. Franklin Roosevelt made a great deal personally of the opportunity offered him. He knew how to dramatize the issues of government and to make people feel that the issues were important to them. Even more, he persuaded people that he cared for them. His popularity, within the context of the new class-urban or national politics had startling effects on American electioneering.

Roosevelt was able to win elections, for himself and his party, in States and counties where Democrats had hardly ever won since the Civil War. He carried some areas despite the absence of Democratic organizations. He carried other areas despite the presence of Democratic organizations. In New York City, for example, Mayor Fiorello LaGuardia, a Republican with New Deal sympathies and support, was re-elected in 1937 and 1941 against the Democratic candidate of Tammany Hall. He was the first reform mayor to be re-elected, and the first mayor to be elected to three successive terms, in the history of the city. Yet Roosevelt carried New York City, despite the unusual unpopularity of the regular Democratic organization, in every presidential election.

General Eisenhower's success in 1952 was equally independent of State and local party organizations. Instead of a record of political achievements, which Roosevelt had in his campaigns for re-election, Eisenhower had a reputation built up extremely effectively by an advertising campaign, which indicated that a presidential candidate, provided the material seems to have some self-evident merits, may be sold like soap. But if the 1952 election was a hucksters' victory, it was not a bosses' victory. Other Republican candidates of 1952 fared, on the whole, less well than Eisenhower.

It is now clear, indeed, that the kind of mediocre men who were sometimes nominated for the presidency in the past will no longer do. It is now recognized that the 1936 Republican candidate, Alfred M. Landon, though the leading contender nominated on the first ballot, did not have the stature the people expect a presidential candidate to have. The next Republican nominee was Wendell Willkie, borne to victory by a short but intense preview of the 'Eisenhower boom' advertising techniques and by the fall of France, in whom the regular party politicians grudgingly recognized the necessary qualifications. In 1944 the Republicans nominated Thomas Dewey, nationally-known Governor of the largest State, and in 1948 they broke party precedents against renominating a defeated candidate by nominating him again. In 1952 they nominated General Eisenhower, who could probably have had the nomination of either party in 1948 had he not resolutely refused to run at that time, and who had been the most popular potential presidential candidate thereafter.

The Democrats broke the anti-third-term tradition by renominating, and re-electing, Roosevelt for a third term in 1940 and a fourth term in 1944. There was some popular dismay in April 1945 when Harry Truman, 'a Boss Pendergast man' (the notorious Pendergast machine of Kansas City, Missouri, led by Thomas J. Pendergast at the time of Truman's career in Missouri politics, had supported Truman), became President; but though delegates to a national convention are usually nonchalant, or perhaps just exhausted, when voting for vice-presidential running mates, Truman had been picked by the party leaders with some care as the vice-presidential candidate in 1944. Although his popularity was at an ebb in the spring and summer of 1948, he was nominated by the Democratic convention that summer and elected by the people that autumn. In 1952 the Democratic party 'compromised' on Adlai Stevenson, Governor of Illinois, who had in fact, once Truman announced his intention to retire, been the strongest potential nominee, though not an active candidate. It has been said that a major factor in Stevenson's success was that, unlike the leading active contenders, he was not resolutely opposed by any major group in the party. A similar explanation accounts for the success of several of the 'dark horse' nominees of the past. It is a measure of the extent of the change in American presidential politics since 1933 that 'dark horses' were once men like Warren Harding and John W. Davis and are now men like Wendell Willkie and Adlai Stevenson.

The change has not, however, been institutionalized. The most important formal modification in national party machinery since 1933 has been the abolition of the Democratic two-thirds rule. Since 1936 a successful Democratic candidate for the presidential or vice-presidential nomination, like a successful Republican candidate, has had to have only an absolute majority of votes cast on a ballot. Roosevelt's managers proposed that the two-thirds rule be abolished at the 1932 convention, when they feared that his opponents might be able to hold more than a third of the votes from him, and they cited their earlier statements when abolishing the rule in 1936. Probably the chief reason for the change, however, was that it would make it easier for Roosevelt to name his successor in 1940. As things turned out, he was himself renominated then without much opposition. The abolition of the two-thirds rule deprived the South of its practical veto power over a nomination, though as a matter of strict arithmetic it had not had for a long time the third of the votes necessary to block a nomination without some outside help.

There have been modifications in the apportionment of votes in the national party conventions. The fundamental basis of apportionment in both parties is that each State delegation has twice as many votes in a convention as the State has members in Congress. (Non-States—Alaska, the District of Columbia, Hawaii, Puerto Rico, and the Virgin Islands in both parties and the Canal Zone in the Democratic party—have a few votes.) Following the abolition of the two-thirds rule, the Democratic party awarded two, then four, bonus votes to each State casting its electoral votes for the Democratic presidential candidate in the preceding election. Since 1912 the Republican party has frequently altered the apportionment of votes: for the 1944, 1952, and 1956 conventions, for example; each time it has departed further from the fundamental basis of apportionment. In 1956 a State will lose one vote for each congressional district in which the Republican poll is below 10,000 and another vote for each district in which it is below 2,000. It will gain six bonus votes if in a preceding election it casts its electoral votes for the Republican presidential candidate, elects a Republican Governor, or elects a Republican Senator.

The prime purpose for introducing the Democratic bonuses was to compensate the South slightly for the abolition of the two-thirds rule. The prime purpose for introducing the Republican penalties and bonuses was to reduce the influence of southern 'patronage Republicans' in the convention. In 1952 the Republicans altered the apportionment of membership on their national committee in order to reduce southern influence there, too. Previously both parties had allowed each State two members, one man and one woman, on their committees. Now the Republican party gives each State casting its electoral votes for the Republican presidential candidate, electing a Republican Governor, or electing a Republican majority in its congressional delegation, a third member, its State party chairman. The sweeping Eisenhower victory of 1952, with its heavy southern Republican poll, has made most of the modifications of the basic formulae comparatively unimportant for the 1956 conventions.

Since the bonus systems tend to favour the small safe States over the large marginal ones, the changes run counter to recent trends that make the selection of candidates who appeal to the large marginal States more necessary than ever. Since the southern 'patronage Republicans' usually support an incumbent President's wishes at the national convention and the Republican State party chairmen are more likely to be representatives of the governors than of the congressmen of their States, the Republican changes run counter to recent trends that provide the basis for stronger national party leadership. But since the bonus systems do not make a great deal of difference (nor will the Republican penalty system if the South becomes a two-party area) and the national committees of the parties have little power, the changes will probably not have profound effects.

What is missing in the developments of the last two decades is any indication that there ought now to be a recognized ladder of promotion to the presidency. It is a measure of the limit of the change in American presidential politics since 1933 that a man like Willkie, who never held a public office, should be nominated and governors and generals should have a better chance of reaching the White House directly than Senators and cabinet officers. (Senators are often chosen as vice-presidential candidates: Republican Senators Charles McNary and Richard Nixon were chosen in 1940 and 1952 respectively; and Democratic Senators Harry Truman, Alben Barkley, and John Sparkman in 1944, 1948, and 1952. A cabinet officer, Secretary of Agriculture Henry Wallace, became Roosevelt's vice-presidential running mate in 1940.)

The American Congress and cabinet have a much smaller share of the experienced political talent of the nation than the British Parliament. A Governor of a large State like New York or Illinois may not, in that capacity, gain much knowledge of foreign and defence affairs, but he has training in administrative management and executive-legislative relations. General Eisenhower, on the other hand, may have had inadequate experience in fields governors know well, but he had as war-time allied commander, post-war chief of staff, and 'cold-war' allied commander the opportunity to become well trained in foreign and defence policy-making. But without some sort of recognized ladder of promotion in American national party politics, stability and continuity of leadership, and therefore of policy, cannot be reasonably ensured. These results may not have been important before 1933, but the development of 'big government' in the United States and of the United States as an active great power in the world has made them important since. The American presidency is now an office for which men ought to be groomed.

The Democrats failed in their years in office to establish a system of advancement. Roosevelt met the need for continuity personally by serving as President for slightly more than twelve years. But he had little interest in reforming institutions. His skill was in making existing institutions work. The abolition of the two-thirds rule in 1936 and the care taken in selecting Harry Truman as vice-presidential candidate in 1944 were not parts of a grand design to reform American party politics, though Roosevelt sometimes liked to talk of one, but typically opportunistic measures to prepare for or meet specific situations in his own career. His failure to groom a successor was demonstrated by his failure to take Truman into his confidence. Truman's successor as Democratic presidential candidate, Stevenson, was picked from outside the administration.

Meanwhile, Congress proposed an amendment to the Constitution providing that 'no person shall be elected to the office of the President more than twice, and no person who has held the office of President, or acted as President, for more than two years of a term to which some other person was elected President shall be elected to the office of the President more than once'. It was ratified as the Twenty-second Amendment in 1951. Although the amending process is frequently described as difficult, in this instance it was easy. There was almost no public interest in the Amendment. Republican politicians, over-represented in the rural-gerrymandered State legislatures, were eager to vote against the memory of Roosevelt; and not a few Democratic politicians realized that Roosevelt's long tenure of office had cut down the spoils to the State and local organizations, since his renominations and re-elections did not depend on buying the support of the party machines.

Thus, shortly after the voters had twice accepted the need to allow a President to serve longer than any of his predecessors, congressmen and State legislators deprived them of the right to do so again. It would be extremely difficult to repeal the Amendment, because an attempt to repeal it would almost certainly be made with a particular President in mind, and his opponents would naturally oppose it. The Twenty-second Amendment makes more necessary than ever some institutional recognition of the need for grooming successors, since a President may never again serve for more than eight (or ten) years.

When in office in this century the Republicans have had a better record of providing for the succession than the Democrats, probably because they have usually been a tighter coalition. President Theodore Roosevelt had his Secretary of War, William Howard Taft, nominated to succeed him in 1908; and Republican national leaders, though not President Coolidge, supported the candidacy of the Secretary of Commerce, Herbert Hoover, in 1928. Perhaps the present Republican administration, at the appropriate time, will follow those precedents.

The absence of adequate institutional changes, however, should not obscure the fact that the presidential aspect of national party politics has changed much more than the congressional aspect since 1933. Congressmen are elected in much the same way, are much the same men, and act in much the same way when elected, as twenty years ago. The reluctance with which President Eisenhower intervened in the congressional mid-term election campaign of 1954 indicates how little the tradition that congressional contests are primarily local contests—until the victorious national party interprets the results—has been weakened. (Yet his intervention was considered the most direct in the history of the nation, exceeding in practice Wilson's intervention in 1918.) The differences between the two national American parties may now be of the kind that make party government in the British sense feasible; but congressional politics and congressional-presidential relations are still characterized by weak party discipline, subservience to local pressures, and bipartisanship in enacting legislation. In these respects American national party politics to-day is very much like it was at least half a century ago.

The changes in national politics have inevitably had their effects on machine politics, especially in the Democratic party. Before 1933 the urban Democratic machines were chiefly responsible for getting out the urban Democratic vote. After 1933 their influence with urban working class voters was seriously impaired by the New Deal programme. National social services largely replaced the services party machines rendered the poor. The poor learned that votes given a national leader with a programme of social reform brought better results than votes given to a party machine for special favours. Consequently, their loyalty to professional politicians was undermined.

The Democratic machines were weakened in other ways after 1933. Previously, despite their identification with the more liberal of the two major national parties, the Democratic bosses had been able to obtain a great deal of money from local business men in return for local policies and favours. The machine of Mayor Frank Hague of Jersey City, New Jersey, for example, had become noted for its anti-trade union policy. The popularity of the New Deal among urban voters, however, forced the bosses to go along with the national Democratic social policies. Frank Hague made peace with the Congress of Industrial Organizations in 1939. And money from business men, except for corrupt favours, often proved hard to get.

Furthermore, though the expansion of the national administrative service in the early days of the New Deal had given the local machines more national patronage than they had ever had before, patronage was drastically reduced as time went on. President Roosevelt helped extend the merit system of appointment as he became convinced that his influence in his party did not rest on party patronage; and the fact that he stayed in office over twelve years nearly eliminated the quadrennial or octennial turnover of patronage that had usually been associated with a new President, even of the same party as the old. Patronage is a fertile field for producing recurrent crops of political gratitude only if it is ploughed regularly. A true spoils system is distinguished from ordinary party patronage by regular rotation in office. The spoils system became much less important in American national administration in the last years of Roosevelt's presidency.

The bases of machine power have been changed to much less secure kinds. Instead of controlling a large lower class vote, the party machines often have to rely on voter apathy and splits among their opponents. In the absence of money from superficially respectable sources, they are perhaps forced to rely more than in the past on money from criminal elements. (Machine politics has usually been associated with organized vice, but in the past some bosses boasted that they kept their cities 'clean'.) Nothing has been substituted for large amounts of patronage— State and local as well as national patronage has been reduced —except more emphasis than ever on special favours. As a result party machines are now, on the whole, comparatively loosely organized both in their internal arrangements and in their control of the governments of their communities; they lack the power necessary to maintain the tightly disciplined organizations of the past.

As long as machines are the only year-in-year-out vote-getting organizations of the party, however, they are rarely in mortal danger. Popular presidents and anti-machine reform waves have come and gone before in American history—notably in the Progessive Era—and the machines have survived. Presidents run every four years, but American elections take place every year; reform candidates win once, perhaps even twice or thrice, but once the rascals have been thrown out, spontaneous voting declines and organized voting brings old or new rascals back. The most serious threat to urban Democratic machines since 1933 has come then from the prospect that the local branches of trade unions might become alternative organizations for getting out the Democratic vote in working class areas.

Under the New Deal a much larger share of the working class became organized in trade unions, most of which supported the Democratic party. Trade unions became so important as contributors to Democratic funds and vote-getting organization that by 1944 President Roosevelt reportedly told Democratic leaders that the choice of a vice-presidential running mate for his fourth-term campaign must be 'cleared with' Sidney Hillman, head of the Political Action Committee of the C.I.O. (Whether Roosevelt said that or not, it is known that Hillman opposed the candidacy of James Byrnes of South Carolina, the conservatives in the party vetoed the renomination of Henry Wallace, and both accepted Harry Truman from a short list consisting of Truman and William Douglas suggested by the President.) The growth of trade union influence posed so serious a threat to the Democratic machine bosses that they spent the next few years fighting the infiltration of the trade unions into the party machinery harder than they fought the Republicans.

President Truman, who succeeded Roosevelt in April 1945, sided at first with the bosses. But the results of the 1946 congressional election, when the bosses 'helped' and the trade union leaders sulked, and the Republicans won their first national election since 1928, and of the 1948 presidential election, when the trade union leaders helped and the bosses sulked, and the Democrats won, pointed obvious morals. By 1952 many of the urban Democratic machines had accepted trade unions as partners in organization as well as policy; and what is perhaps more important, the trade union leaders, having found it difficult to maintain the political effectiveness of their own organizations, had accepted the help of the bosses. The bosses seem to have successfully applied, at least for a time, the political adage of professional politicians, 'if you can't beat 'em, join 'em'.

The effects of recent political developments on Republican machine politics have been much less dramatic. Although the influence of urban Republican machines on working class voting was also weakened, if not destroyed, by New Deal policies and political realignments, the Republican party had depended less on urban machines than the Democratic party; and thus the change, though electorally important, was less significant for the intraparty balance of power. Republican rural rings—and southern Democratic rural rings—have not been affected very much by what has happened in the last twenty years.

The most important change has been the rise of suburban Republican machines like that of Bergen County, New Jersey, or State Republican machines largely dependent on suburban organization like those in Connecticut and New York. The development is most obvious in the greater New York metropolitan area because it is the largest suburban area in the country. It is perhaps of great significance for the future of American national party politics: some political observers believe that the rapid growth of suburban population presages a new normal Republican majority to replace that destroyed in the 1930's. The change has already produced what seems to be, on the whole, a new species of party machine. For while some of the new suburban organizations have the characteristics of the old Republican city machines and rural rings—the recent exposure of connections between Bergen County Republicans and criminal racketeers has revealed the usual pattern—many of them seem to be taking advantage of the fact that by far the greater part of business money now helps the Republicans, locally as well as nationally, to limit their acceptance of financial contributions to those from respectable sources for respectable purposes.

It is not considered corrupt to contribute money in return for favourable policies in America any more than in Great Britain. Thus it is considered corrupt to contribute to a party that administers a pure food and drug law laxly but not considered corrupt to contribute to a party that refuses to pass an effective law in the first place. There is obviously a good deal of scope in America as in Britain, especially in the business party, for raising money without resort to 'corruption'. The traditions of generations are not, of course, easily overcome: it is difficult, for example, to keep individual office-holders from supplementing their pay in the usual ways. Governor Dewey of New York sought to keep his machine 'clean', but found it a hard job. In 1953 he had to force the Republican majority leader in the State Senate to resign when it transpired the latter had visited a convicted labour racketeer in gaol, and in 1953-4 he had to deal generally with the corrupt practices of leading Republican politicians in connection with harness racing in the State. Still, the cautious policy may prevail if, on the whole, it pays political dividends.

Nationally, the 'Dewey wing' of the Republican party has won the last three presidential nominations over the wing of the party that was led by Senator Taft and that has been supported by the 'old time' type of professional political leaders. The success of the 'Dewey wing' in 1952 was due to its ability to make the contest appear to be one between the 'people's candidate', General Eisenhower, and the 'machines' candidate', Senator Taft, at a time when the 'Kefauver Committee' investigations of the relations between racketeers and politicians and Republican propaganda about corruption in the Truman administration had put the political profession in even lower repute than usual. The real test, however, is in State and local government. Despite the constant references to scandals in Republican—that is, almost all—newspapers and periodicals, there was very little corruption, at least by past standards, in the Democratic national administration. The trouble was that President Truman never dealt firmly with it. Organized partisan corruption is probably important now only at the State and local levels. If Republican State and local administrations prove less corrupt than Democratic administrations, they may be able to profit thereby in elections and force Democratic organizations to improve too, though there was certainly no sign in the 1954 gubernatorial elections that this process had begun.

In any case, given the endemic character of corruption in American local politics, permanent improvement must be slow. The improvement in the standards of national administration in the last half-century suggests that improvement in State and local administration is also possible. The changes in American politics in the last two decades may even make it fairly likely. But in view of the error of previous announcements that a recently deceased or defeated politician was 'the last of the old time bosses', it would be unwise to expect spectacular results. The 'old time bosses' are a tough breed.

Chapter 7

Congress

The first thing to know about the American Congress is what congressmen are like. The minimum qualifications for being a congressman are set forth in Article I of the Constitution. A member of the House of Representatives must be at least twenty-five years of age, seven years a citizen, and an inhabitant of the State in which he is chosen. A member of the Senate must be at least thirty, nine years a citizen, and an inhabitant of the State in which he is chosen. No person holding any office under the United States may be a member of either House during his continuance in office.

Each House is the judge of the eligibility of its own members, however, and in practice ignores or adds to the constitutional qualifications as occasions arise. On the one hand, in 1806 the Senate admitted Henry Clay of Kentucky when he was less than thirty. On the other hand, in 1900 the House of Representatives excluded Brigham Roberts of Utah on the ground that he was a polygamist. In 1927–9 the Senate excluded William Vare of Pennsylvania for allowing too much money to be spent on behalf of his candidacy.

What is important anyway is not who may serve in Congress but who does serve. Congressmen supply biographies of themselves for the *Congressional Directory*:

'DEAN PARK TAYLOR, Republican, of Troy, N.Y.; born in Troy, N Y , January 1, 1902; educated in the public schools of Troy; attended Colgate University and was graduated from Union University Department of Law with LL.B. degree; appointed assistant United States attorney, northern district of

New York in 1927 and served in that capacity until 1930; now engaged in the practice of law at Troy, N.Y.; New York member Republican Congressional Committee; delegate to Republican National Convention; married Mary Hayford, of Newton, N.H.; one child, Peter; member Phi Kappa Psi fraternity, Sons American Revolution; director Union National Bank of Troy; trustee Russell Sage College and Vanderhyden Hall; elected to the Seventy-eighth Congress on November 3, 1942; re-elected to the Seventy-ninth, Eightieth, Eighty-first, Eighty-second, Eighty-third and Eighty-fourth Congresses.'

'SPESSARD LINDSEY HOLLAND, Democrat, of Bartow, Fla.; born Bartow, Fla., July 10, 1892; son of Benjamin Franklin and Fannie V. (Spessard) Holland; married Mary Agnes Groover, of Lakeland, Fla., February 8, 1919; four children—S.L., Jr., Mary Groover, William B., and Ivanhoe; graduated, Bartow public schools; Ph. B. (magna cum laude), Emory College, 1912; LL.B., University of Florida, 1916; honorary LL.D., Rollins College, Florida Southern College, Emory University; D.C.L., University of Florida; taught in public schools, Warrenton, Ga., 1912–14; practised law in Bartow, Fla., since 1916; prosecuting attorney, Polk County, Fla., 1919–20; county judge, Polk County, Fla., two terms 1921–29; member Florida State Senate two terms, 1932–40; Governor of Florida, 1941–45; served with Coast Artillery Corps in all grades through captain, United States Army, World War I; served as aerial observer Twenty-fourth Squadron, Army Air Corps, in France; awarded Distinguished Service Cross, 1918; Methodist, member of American Legion, Veterans of Foreign Wars; a Kiwanian, Mason, Shriner, Elk; member of Phi Beta Kappa, Phi Kappa Phi, Alpha Tau Omega, Phi Delta Phi; trustee, Emory University, and former trustee, Southern College; member, Florida State and American Bar Associations; member, Executive Council University of Florida Alumni Association since 1924 (president, 1931); Democratic nominee to United States Senate from Florida, May 7, 1946; appointed September 25, 1946, by Governor Caldwell to succeed the late Charles O. Andrews in the United States Senate for the term ending January 3, 1947;

elected November 5, 1946, for full term ending January 3, 1953;
elected November 4, 1952, for term ending January 3, 1959.'

These are typical examples, as the following composite 'biography' of congressmen shows.

In January 1953, when the Eighty-third Congress elected in November 1952 took office, the average age of members of the House of Representatives was in the early 50's. The average age of Senators was in the late 50's. The average length of service of Representatives was between seven and eight years. The average length of service of Senators was about seven years. (The Representative who has served longest is Sam Rayburn, Democrat, of Texas, who has served continuously since 4 March 1913. The Senator who has served longest is Walter George, Democrat, of Georgia, who has served continuously since 8 November 1922.)

Since a Representative's term of office is only one-third as long as a Senator's, the rough equality of average length of service in the two Houses may seem surprising. Part of the explanation is that there are a large number of essentially one-party congressional districts, in which Representatives are elected, within marginal States, in which Senators are elected. In January 1953, for example, slightly over three-fifths of the Representatives had received more than 60 per cent of the votes cast in their districts in their last elections. Only two-fifths of the Senators had received more than 60 per cent of the votes cast in their States in their last elections. Despite the fact that members of both Houses from safe areas usually face competition in nominating elections, members from safe areas tend to be re-elected more regularly than members from marginal areas. Thus the higher fraction of House seats that are safe helps raise the average length of service of Representatives to be slightly more than that of Senators.

About three-quarters of the members of the 1953 Congress had served in State and local offices before coming to Washington. They had been members of State legislatures, governors, administrators, prosecuting attorneys, and judges. Twenty-nine Senators and one Representative, for example, had been governors of their States. Leading congressmen served their apprenticeship along with the rest. William Knowland, Republican, Senate majority leader in 1953 (and, as a result of the Democratic gains in the November 1954 congressional election, Senate minority leader in 1955), served in both Houses of the California legislature; Lyndon Johnson, Democrat, Senate minority leader in 1953 (and Senate majority leader in 1955), served as a secretary to a Texas congressman and State director of the National Youth Administration of Texas before his election, first to the House of Representatives, and then to the Senate. Joseph Martin, Republican, Speaker of the House in 1953 (and House minority leader in 1955), served in both Houses of the Massachusetts legislature and as a State party official; Sam Rayburn, Democrat, House minority leader in 1953 (and Speaker of the House in 1955), served in the Texas House of Representatives, part of the time as its Speaker.

Usually over two-thirds of the members of Congress were born in the States they represent; and many of those who were not moved to the States at an early age. Apart from the fact that congressional service itself takes a man away from his home State, American congressmen are parochial rather than cosmopolitan in background. They are rooted deeply in the States they represent.

Only about one in ten Americans over twenty-five years of age has attended a course of study leading to a bachelor's degree. But usually three-fourths or more of the congressmen have at least a bachelor's degree, most often a law degree. Law is by far the most common previous or alternative occupation of congressmen. About three-fifths of them have been lawyers. Most of the rest have been business men, journalists, teachers, real-estate and insurance agents, farmers, and bankers. Very few of them have been factory workers or regular members of trade unions. Before World War II, about two-fifths of the congressmen had seen military service. In 1953 the fraction was about three-fifths.

Congress is more Protestant than the country as a whole. In 1953 the National Council of the Churches of Christ in the United States estimated that Protestant Church members outnumbered Catholic Church members by less than two to one. But usually more than 70 per cent of the congressmen are known to be Protestant, less than 20 per cent Catholic, and about 1 per cent Jewish. The religious affiliations of about 10 per cent are usually unknown. When the *New York Times* asked congressmen in 1948 about their churches, two Representatives, with more political than religious fervour, answered that they 'get around to them all'.[1]

Precise information about the racial and national backgrounds of congressmen is unobtainable, but one important racial group obviously has little direct representation. About one in ten Americans is a Negro; yet in recent years only from one to three Negroes, representing 'Negro districts' in New York City and Chicago and—in the Eighty-fourth Congress elected in 1954—a predominantly white district in Detroit, have served in the House of Representatives. No Negro has served in the Senate since 'reconstruction' days. Women are also poorly represented. In the most recent Congresses about ten to fifteen have served in the House of Representatives and one or two in the Senate. (The total memberships of the two Houses are 435 and 96 respectively.)

Finally, here are a few random facts from the *New York Times'* survey of the 1948 Congress: Almost all congressmen had married and stayed married. They had an average of slightly more than two children. About 85 per cent of the members were home-owners. Most-read magazines were *Time, United States News, Life, Newsweek, Reader's Digest*, and the *Saturday Evening Post*, all of them Republican periodicals. About one-fifth of the congressmen played a musical instrument, usually the piano. And two Senators, it was alleged, wore toupees.

Congressmen are, in sum, middle-aged middle and upper-middle class Americans with strong local ties. Political activity has been a part- or full-time occupation for most of them for a long time. This political experience often tempers the natural

[1] John M. Willig, 'Portrait of the Average Congressman', *The New York Times Magazine*, 23 May 1948, pp. 13, 34, and 38, at p. 34. Most of the other facts in this chapter about the 1948 Congress are taken from this article. Quoted with permission of the *New York Times*.

conservatism and parochialism of their thinking but also tempts them to protect themselves, politically and financially, from the whims of the electorate by selling their services to well-organized and wealthy pressure groups. Perhaps the most remarkable thing about American congressmen, compared with British M.P.s, is the lack of social differences between members of the two major parties. They come from the same occupations, have had the same education, and, despite partisan differences, think in much the same way. Nothing provides more direct proof of middle class influence in American politics than the membership, both Republican and Democratic, of Congress.

The most important fact about the constitutional organization of Congress is that it is bicameral, with two Houses of different size, method of apportionment, frequency of election, method of election, qualifications for membership, and powers. The House of Representatives has always been larger than the Senate. The first Congress had 65 Representatives and 26 Senators. The present Congress has 435 Representatives and 96 Senators. Representatives are apportioned among the States according to population; Senators are apportioned two to a State. All Representatives serve coincident two-year terms; Senators serve six-year terms, with one-third of them retiring every two years.

Originally, Representatives were elected by popular vote, Senators by State legislatures. Since 1913 Senators have been elected by popular vote, too, but State legislatures may empower governors to make temporary appointments to fill vacancies that occur between general elections. Thus, when Senator Taft, Republican, of Ohio, died in 1953, the Democratic Governor of Ohio appointed Thomas Burke, Democrat, to fill the vacancy until after the November 1954 general election. (George Bender, Republican, who defeated Burke in the election, will serve until January 1957 when the six-year term for which Taft was elected in 1950 expires.) Representatives can never be appointed. The qualifications for membership in the two Houses have already been given.

There are several differences in powers. The House of Representatives chooses its own Speaker; the Senate is presided over by the Vice-President of the United States, who votes only to break a tie. The House of Representatives has sole power of impeachment, the Senate the sole power to try impeachments. The House of Representatives, voting by State delegations, chooses the President of the United States when no candidate receives an electoral college majority, a power it has exercised only in 1801 and 1825. The Senate, voting by individual members, chooses the Vice-President under the same circumstances, a power it has exercised only in 1837. All revenue bills must originate in the House of Representatives.

The most important differences in powers are that treaties and a large number of presidential appointments are submitted to the Senate but not to the House. 'Two-thirds of the Senators present' must concur in making a treaty (on 13 June 1952 three treaties were ratified when the Senator acting as presiding officer voted 'aye' and the only other Senator in the chamber remained silent); and a majority of Senators present must concur in making an appointment. The one fundamental similarity of power, however, is more important than all the differences. All bills, including financial bills, to become law, must ultimately pass through both chambers in the same form.

The framers of the Constitution had three reasons for organizing the Senate differently from the House. They thought that the Senate might serve partly as an advisory council to the executive. They wanted the Senate to protect the States with small populations. And they wanted the Senate to act as a conservative check on the popularly-elected House.

The hope that the Senate might act as an advisory council to the executive was frustrated by the mutual sensitivity of the President and Senate. The Senate has grown too large to act as an executive council anyway, but even when it was a small body it failed to advise as the framers intended. President Washington tried to carry out their intention when negotiating an Indian treaty. He appeared in the Senate chamber and asked the Senators' advice. The experiment failed, the President leaving the chamber on the second day of consultation muttering, according to William Crawford's account, that 'he would be

damned if he ever went there again'. Written consultation between the President and Senate broke down in 1794 during the
negotiations leading to Jay's Treaty with Great Britain. Since
then the President has usually sent a treaty to the Senate only
after the negotiations have ended.

The framers of the Constitution defended the power of the
Senate to advise on and consent to appointments as a salutary
check on the President, but the check soon developed into the
system of organized political blackmail known as 'senatorial
courtesy'. Under this system, it is customary for the President,
when selecting men for all but the highest national appointments, to consult the Senator or Senators of his party from the
State in which a nominee is to serve or, less commonly, from
which a nominee comes before sending a nomination to the
Senate. If there is no Senator of his party from the State, the
President usually consults the State party chairman. If the
President fails to consult the proper Senators, they may ask their
colleagues to vote against confirmation. By 'senatorial courtesy'
Senators of both parties will usually comply, thus defeating the
nomination. For example, the Senate rejected President Roosevelt's nominee for a national judgeship in Virginia in 1939 by
72 votes to 9 and President Truman's nominee, a Virginian, for
a position on the Federal Trade Commission (a type of post
usually not subject to 'senatorial courtesy') in 1950 by 59 votes
to 14, in each case because the two Democratic Senators from
Virginia opposed the nomination.

In effect, the system usually makes the Senators the real
nominators, and the President the person who gives his consent.
Indeed, by custom, the Senators often consult members of the
House of Representatives who are of the same party about
appointments in their districts, so that some nominations are in
fact made by Representatives, though they are without a
shadow of constitutional authority.

The framers were more successful in implementing their
second purpose, to protect States with small populations. Not
that small States, as such, have been ranged against large in
senatorial controversies. It is possible to cite a few important
occasions when most of the Senators from small States voted

against most of those from large States: in 1896, for example, on a vote on a Free Silver Bill, 42 Senators defeated 35 Senators who represented eight million more people. But there has been no trace of a deliberate alliance among small States. Rather, the equal representation of States in the Senate has given protection to rural and sectional minorities. In this way, the intention of the framers to safeguard geographical minorities from the 'tyranny' of the popular majority has been substantially fulfilled.

Rural States are markedly overrepresented. The Bureau of the Census estimated that 64 per cent of the American population was urban in 1950. (It calls the population of communities of 2,500 or more inhabitants urban.) Eighteen States with between 27 (North Dakota) and 50 per cent urban population accounted for about 24 per cent of the population of all the States and elected about 38 per cent of the Senators; seventeen States with between 50 and 64 per cent urban population accounted for about 25 per cent of the population of all the States and elected about 35 per cent of the Senators; eight States with between 64 and 80 per cent urban population accounted for about 28 per cent of the population of all the States and elected about 17 per cent of the Senators; and five States with between 80 and 87 per cent (New Jersey) urban population accounted for about 24 per cent of the population of all the States and elected about 10 per cent of the Senators. In other words, States less urban than the country as a whole accounted for about half the population and elected nearly three-fourths of the Senators. The interests that benefit most from the misrepresentative character of the Senate are small farming and mining interests that are scattered across many States, often with small populations but always with two Senators each: beet-sugar-farming, wool-growing, and silver-mining interests, for example. Among sections the Mountain States benefit most.

The protection to minority interests is not based solely on the method of representation. The way the Senate conducts business is just as important. By tacit 'senatorial courtesy' legislation is rarely pressed that threatens seriously to impair sectional interests. Thus it is possible for the Senate to work with virtually no limits on debate, which it could not do were bills adversely affecting sectional minorities frequently introduced. Occasionally Senators from one section seek to pass legislation strongly opposed by Senators from another section, and the latter filibuster. The filibuster is almost invariably successful. Cloture has never been applied to subdue a sectional minority.

The best known effect of this kind of 'senatorial courtesy' has been the failure of the Senate to do anything for southern Negroes. Spasmodic efforts by northern Senators, mindful of Negro voters in their own States, to pass anti-poll-tax, anti-lynching, and Fair Employment Practices Commission bills have always been blocked by southern Senators, representing the white South. The present anti-filibustering rule, which requires the votes of 64 Senators before cloture can be applied, makes it extremely unlikely that any important civil rights legislation will be passed in the near future.

Before 1913 the third purpose of the framers, to make the Senate a conservative check on the popularly-elected House, was generally fulfilled. In the latter part of the nineteenth century, as was mentioned in Chapter 5, the Senate sometimes had the appearance of being a 'rich man's club'. But since 1913, when the Seventeenth Amendment to the Constitution made the Senate popularly elected, too, the Senate has almost lost its obvious 'plutocratic' element. In recent years it has usually been more liberal than the House of Representatives.

The usual explanation is that, despite rural overrepresentation in the Senate, all but a few Senators must take urban sentiment into account. In 1950 84 of the 96 Senators came from States with at least one city of over 50,000 inhabitants and 70 of the 96 Senators from States with at least one city of over 100,000 inhabitants. On the other hand, it has been unofficially estimated that 265 of the 435 Representatives come from districts in which rural and small-town (less than 10,000 inhabitants) voters predominate. Rural gerrymandering makes it possible for about one-half of the electorate to elect about three-fifths of the Representatives. A majority of Representatives can almost ignore the opinions of people living in cities. Since liberalism now finds its greatest support in cities, the majority of Senators are more likely to adopt liberal, or at least moderate, attitudes than a majority of Representatives.

Contrary to the expectations of the framers, the Senate has turned out to be more powerful than the House. There are several reasons for its superiority. The longer term and greater dignity of a Senator attract political leaders to the Senate rather than the House, and their appearance in the Senate enhances the prestige of being a Senator still more. It is through the Senate that most national patronage is siphoned to the State party machines. The Senate has more influence than the House over the conduct of foreign affairs, though now that many foreign commitments require appropriations the House is gaining influence in this field.

Above all, the way the Senate does business puts it in a better bargaining position than the House. Virtually unlimited senatorial debate usually makes it necessary for the House of Representatives, which works under almost continuous cloture, to concede more than the Senate when the two chambers really disagree. For spokesmen for the Senate know that a majority in the House which has the support of the Speaker can usually force concessions through, while they can plead that they cannot concede very much without provoking a filibuster in their own chamber. Similarly, virtually unlimited senatorial debate usually makes it necessary for the President to concede more to opinion in the Senate than to opinion in the House. The ultimate effect of 'senatorial courtesy' is to make the American Senate the most powerful second chamber in the world.

The legislative process is basically the same in the two Houses. The House of Representatives is more tightly organized than the Senate. The Speaker—that is, the leader of the majority party in the House—has a great deal of influence. The House Rules Committee, a bipartisan committee on which the majority party in the House has a majority of places, and which in practice is dominated by senior members of both parties, very largely determines the order of business. Standing committees are more influential in the House than in the Senate.

But this tighter organization fails to produce effective government by the majority of the House. One reason is that its power is largely negative. It can often prevent business from being taken up, but it cannot often force business through, unless it is a special piece of business like a bill reported from a joint conference committee of Senators and Representatives. A second reason, which largely accounts for the first, is that the organization often does not represent the will of the majority of the House. The nearly pervasive seniority system usually puts 'Old Guard' Republicans and southern Democrats in the Speaker's chair, on the Rules Committee, and into the chairmanships of the standing committees. These men are often more conservative than the House as a whole.

The seniority system is a substitute for a real party system of appointing men to key congressional posts. It is a sign, in both Houses of Congress, that the partisan majority is unable to direct affairs.

The major work of the legislative process is performed by the standing committees of the two chambers. About 10,000 to 15,000 bills are introduced in the House or Senate every two years, that is, during the period for which Representatives are elected. With extremely rare exceptions, every bill is referred to a standing committee for study and recommendation. The standing committees promptly bury most of the bills and eventually report back on perhaps a fifth or a third of them. About 1,500 to 2,000 acts are finally passed by both Houses, perhaps about one-half public and one-half private acts, the proportions varying a good deal from year to year. On the floor of the Houses, many of the acts pass by unanimous consent, and usually only from 120 to 160 Senate bills and from 200 to 250 House bills are debated for over a half-hour during the two-year period. Most of the discussion about legislation takes place in the committees.

Since the Legislative Reorganization Act of 1946 went into effect in 1947, there have been fifteen standing committees in the Senate and nineteen in the House. In the Eighty-third Congress there were also ten or more joint committees with members from both chambers and a varying but always small number of special and select committees, including the majority and minority party policy committees of the Senate. Each standing committee is named in accordance with the type of bills referred to it. In the Senate, for example, the Appropriations, Armed Services, Finance, Foreign Relations, and Labor and Public Welfare committees are among the fifteen. In the House of Representatives the Appropriations, Armed Services, Ways and Means, Foreign Affairs, Education and Labor, Rules, and Un-American Activities committees are among the nineteen. Overlapping of jurisdiction is inevitable, however; and part of the parliamentary tactics of the supporters of a bill is to guide the presiding officer or, in case of appeal, the chamber so that the bill is referred to the friendliest of the committees which might receive it.

The standing committees are bipartisan with their party composition usually roughly proportional to that of the whole House. With a few exceptions, each Senator serves on two standing committees and each Representative on one. Congressmen tend to find places on committees dealing with legislation of particular interest to their constituents. Committees dealing with water-resources development legislation, for example, are usually composed almost entirely of members from States or districts in which water-resources development policy is important. Committees dealing with agricultural legislation have a disproportionate number of members from agricultural areas. Committees are not, therefore, truly representative samples of the Houses as wholes.

The chairman of a standing committee is nearly always the senior member of the majority party on the committee, unless the senior member is chairman of another committee, in which case the second senior member of the majority party serves. Seniority is reckoned on the basis of continuous service. This method of selection ensures that most key committee chairmanships are held by Senators and Representatives from safe seats, that is, by 'Old Guard' Republicans and southern Democrats. The chairman has a great deal of influence over the conduct of committee business.

Committees may hold hearings, open or secret, on a bill or group of bills, at which outside persons may be heard and questioned. Minutes are kept of the hearings; and, after private discussion among committee members, reports are written for bills reported, favourably or unfavourably, to the whole House. On major bills there are usually majority and minority reports, often prepared without regard to party lines. Usually major bills are reported with substantial amendments to which a committee minority may again take exception. 'Administration measures' receive no official priority. Indeed, officially they do not exist, for all bills are introduced by members of Congress acting as individuals. In practice, 'administration spokesmen' often introduce major bills from the executive branch which are given unofficial priority.

The part standing committees play in the passage of a bill is illustrated by the legislative history of the Employment Act of 1946. At the end of 1944 a 'Full Employment' bill was drafted under the leadership of Senator James Murray, Democrat, of Montana, chairman of the War Contracts subcommittee of the Senate committee on Military Affairs, and printed in the year-end report of the subcommittee to the full committee. (Before 1947 the numbers and titles of the standing committees in the two Houses were different from what they are now.) In January 1945 Senator Murray introduced a revised version on the floor of the Senate. The sponsors of the bill had it referred to the Banking and Currency committee, chaired by Senator Robert Wagner, Democrat, of New York, a supporter of the bill. This meant that the public hearings, handled by a subcommittee of which Senator Wagner was also chairman, were held under friendly auspices.

The Banking and Currency subcommittee then went into executive (private) session, from which a new version of the bill was reported favourably to the full committee over the opposition of a minority led by Senator Robert Taft, Republican, of Ohio. The subcommittee version, amended slightly in executive session of the full committee, was in turn reported favourably to the Senate by thirteen members of the full committee, eleven Democrats and two Republicans. One Democrat and six Republicans issued a hostile minority report. The bill, amended further, was passed by the Senate on 28 September 1945.

Meanwhile, the 'Full Employment' bill was introduced in the House of Representatives by Representative Wright Patman, Democrat, of Texas. Here the bill was referred to the hostile House committee on Expenditures in the Executive Departments rather than the more friendly House Banking and Currency committee or House Labor committee. Under the chairmanship of Representative Carter Manasco, Democrat, of Alabama, who believed America is a 'republic' not a 'democracy', public hearings were conducted to help the opponents of full employment legislation.

Although by the time the House committee went into executive session it had three bills to deal with—the original bill as introduced in the House in February 1945, the version passed by the Senate in September 1945, and a bill introduced by Representative Charles LaFollette, Republican, of Indiana— the conservative majority on the committee set up a subcommittee to draft another measure. This measure, entitled an 'Employment and Production' act, was reported to the whole House in December 1945. A bipartisan majority of the full committee supported this version over the opposition of two committee minorities, an extremely conservative one of one Democrat and three Republicans, and a liberal one of three Democrats and one Republican. The measure endorsed by the majority was passed by the House. This meant that the Senate and House bills were different, but a compromise bill passed both chambers and was signed by President Truman in February 1946.[1]

The compromise bill was drafted in a joint conference committee. The joint conference committee is one of the most important pieces of American constitutional machinery, though unknown to the written Constitution. A joint conference committee is appointed for about one in ten bills that pass both chambers, and is usually required for a major bill. As its name suggests, it serves as the means for effecting a compromise between the Senate and House versions of a bill when neither

[1] For a full account of the passage of the Employment Act, see Stephen K. Bailey, *Congress Makes A Law* (New York: Columbia University Press, 1950).

chamber is willing to accept the version of the other, and is made up of members of the two Houses. In practice, the members are usually senior members of both parties from the standing committees that have dealt with the bill. Thus again congressmen from safe seats are unduly represented at a key point in the legislative process.

Both Houses have had great difficulty in restraining conference committees, which are supposed to change bills only at points where the two chambers disagree. Some of the most flagrant violations of this rule have occurred in connection with tariff legislation. Conference committees have compromised conflicting rates of duty by setting higher rates than either House, and have extended protection to commodities after both chambers have denied protection. The Legislative Reorganization Act of 1946 reaffirmed the old rule, but on one occasion in 1948 Senator J. William Fulbright satirically congratulated conferees for once again 'forthrightly disregarding the wishes of common lay Members of the Senate and the House'. The conferees are able to take liberties, particularly near the end of a session, because their reports often virtually have to be accepted.

Among the important committees of Congress are, finally, the special investigating committees. Congress, or one of its Houses, may authorize a special investigating committee, one of the regular standing committees, a joint executive-congressional commission, an executive agency, or a partly-governmental, partly-private group to conduct an investigation in its behalf. The way the purely congressional committees, special and standing, investigate reveals a good deal about Congress.

The first congressional investigation was held in 1792 into a disaster that befell a general sent to shoot Indians. From then until 1925 there were about 300 formal congressional investigations. In the last thirty years the number has expanded greatly: there were 165 investigations in the first four years of the Roosevelt administration, for example. Investigations now constitute one of the most famous, or infamous, aspects of congressional activity.

The methods of the congressional committees vary enormously, not only because the subjects investigated require different treatment, but also because what the committees attempt to do and who serves on them vary so much. Sometimes congressmen seek information directly useful to them in legislating. Sometimes they are after information, about corruption in an executive department for example, with no direct legislative purpose in mind. Often they are really seeking to give publicity to information as a means of arousing public opinion. And sometimes they are really serving the private purpose of one congressman. Thus in 1942 Representative Eugene Cox of Georgia had himself made chairman of a committee to investigate the Federal Communications Commission after the Commission had reported his illegal pressure tactics in connection with its work to the Department of Justice. He was induced to resign from the committee some time after the F.C.C. sent the facts of his illegal acceptance of a $2,500 cheque to the Speaker, but was still able to help persuade the House to cut the annual recommended appropriation for the Commission by 25 per cent.

That Representative Cox was originally made chairman of the investigating committee despite his proved direct personal interest is not typical. But it is typical that the congressmen most interested politically in the investigation serve on the investigating committee. This means that, though they are drawn from both parties, the members of the committee may not be at all representative of Congress as a whole. The Un-American Activities committee attracts the extreme right-wing, just as the investigation of lobbying by private power interests in 1935 attracted liberal Senator, now Justice, Hugo Black. In this, as in almost everything else, Congress is fragmented and each small group of congressmen goes its own way. One may speak of an overall 'congressional courtesy', a sort of legislative *laissez-faire*.

The most objectionable forms of congressional investigating tactics could be prevented by strengthening party government in Congress, so that the majority party could control, and take responsibility for, the choice of committee chairmen and their methods. Stronger party control would strike at 'congressional courtesy' of all kinds. One unfortunate result would be that desirable investigations of executive activities would be curtailed. Even the small measure of organized party control in the House of Representatives has been enough to make it a less effective investigator than the Senate of an administration that is of the same party as the majority of the chamber. On the other hand, effective party government and responsibility might reduce the need for investigations.

Bills pour out of the legislative standing committees on to the floors of the two Houses. There cliques and 'blocs' of congressmen push and resist the bills as they move and stall through the maze of procedural rules regulating the conduct of business. No one group controls the major flow of laws. In each chamber there are party committees and caucuses, party leaders, and party campaign committees; but, except when electing congressional officers and making a few patronage appointments among the staff of Congress, the parties rarely act as units. Significantly, there are not even nominal congressional party organizations embracing members in both Houses. In the absence of party control laws are passed by 'log-rolling', that is, by temporary alliances among small groups of congressmen. The majority that passes one law may not be the majority that passes the next.

What does it mean to a congressman to be virtually free from the party whip? It does not mean that he carefully studies each bill and votes on its merits. A conscientious congressman is far too busy. He is busy with committee work: attending hearings, conferring about bills, and writing reports. He is busy with constituency mail: in 1948 the average Representative received 90 letters a day and the average Senator 325. A congressman is busy with constituents: in 1948 the average Representative had ten visitors a day and the average Senator fourteen.

A congressman is busy for constituents: he presses thousands of constituents' claims on administrative agencies. This interference with the details of administration goes much further than in Great Britain, where claims taken up by M.P.'s are put to the ministers and their secretaries; for congressmen may go directly to the civil servants handling the cases they are interested in and, as a consequence of the detailed control Congress has over appropriations for the executive departments, they are able to put on a great deal of pressure. In this respect, the separation of powers between the legislative and executive branches is far less rigid in America than in Great Britain. Although widely deprecated as a corrupting influence on administration, the American practice forestalls or remedies many of the petty abuses of bureaucratic power.

Congressmen, especially Senators, receive substantial allowances for staff help. The Legislative Reorganization Act of 1946 and subsequent legislation have improved the general staffing of Congress a great deal. But for most members the congressional work-load is still staggering: in 1948, according to the *New York Times*, the average congressman arrived at his office at 8.48 a.m., left at 6.31 p.m., and with his 'homework' averaged an eleven-hour working day. Very little of his time is spent studying bills that are not referred to his committee.

On most bills a congressman must vote as someone else tells him. A congressman specializes in a few subjects and otherwise follows the lead of friends who specialize in other subjects. Informal, personal cliques are formed, as well as the more obvious 'blocs' of 'silver' Senators and 'corn' and 'cotton' congressmen. A few congressmen, by force of intelligence or appearance of intelligence, become leaders across a wide range of public policies and help create some order out of the legislative chaos. That their influence is more personal than partisan is illustrated by the career of the most important congressman of recent years, Senator Robert Taft. Because of his personal competence he became the leading Republican Senator before he was elected to a nominally important party post; and throughout President Truman's second term, despite the fact that the Democrats had a majority in the Senate, he was the most influential member of his chamber. The rare chance for developing an effective partisan legislative programme within Congress during President Eisenhower's administration, when Senator Taft's unique position in the Congress of 1953 was joined with (at least the appearance of) his co-operation with the new Republican President, ended with the Senator's death.

Fundamentally, a congressman takes his voting cues from pressure groups. He chooses whom to follow in the chamber primarily by deciding who are the most effective spokesmen for those interests which he favours or wants to placate. Naturally, the pressure groups that exert the greatest pressure on him are those important in his district. One of these 'pressure groups' may sometimes be the supporters of the national administration: when the President is very popular with the voters, many congressmen follow the lead of 'administration spokesmen' in Congress. But generally local voters seem to look to the President and congressmen for different things. It has been said that the President is now elected by consumer interests but Congress by producer interests. Presidential elections are now fought primarily on great national and international issues but congressional elections are still fought largely on issues affecting local crops and industries. 'If a legislator is sent here from a "bean" section', explained one congressman to his colleagues in 1942, 'he will—and seemingly must—protect beans. His constituents demand it to be his first interest.'

In the complexity and confusion of congressional activity, however, the unorganized local electorate loses track of its congressman. He falls primarily under the influence of the strongest groups—business, labour, large-farming, ex-serviceman, and religious groups, for example—which maintain lobbies in Washington and the State capitals and organizations in many, if not all, the constituencies. (The law requiring the registration of organizations attempting to influence national legislation and the report of their expenditures is so ineffective that it would be pointless to cite the amounts reported by the few hundred organizations that have registered.) To the extent that the national political parties have become identified with different social classes, some of the groups have tended to align themselves with the parties. Business and large-farming groups are now overwhelmingly Republican and they exercise a unifying control over Republicans, and many southern Democrats, in Congress that the formal congressional party machinery has rarely exercised; business power was the social basis of Senator Taft's influence over his colleagues. Labour groups have often been almost as effective among northern Democrats. Thus, because the majority of members within each of the major partisan groups in Congress—Republicans, southern Democrats, and northern Democrats—usually come from roughly the same kind of districts and are subject to the same kind of pressure-group influence, there is at least a moderate partisan character to most major congressional roll calls.

But other special interests still extract special favours from the government by cutting across party lines. Party leaders find it impossible to hold their lines in Congress, for example, when the American Legion, the chief ex-servicemen's organization, makes a raid on the Treasury. The most effective resistance to such a pressure group has come from the House Rules Committee, which can often block consideration of measures the majority of congressmen dislike but dare not openly oppose, and the President, who can veto legislation. Even so, the American Legion forced Congress to pass bonus bills over the vetoes of Presidents Harding, Coolidge, Hoover, and Roosevelt. (Congress overrides a veto by two-thirds majorities of those voting in each House on roll-call votes.) The story is the same, then, regardless of which party is in office.

The strong influence pressure groups have on congressmen means that congressional debate usually has no more direct effect on congressional voting than parliamentary debate on parliamentary voting. Alben Barkley, when Democratic majority leader in the Senate, once criticized his fellow members as follows:

'. . . I do not know what has happened to the Senate of the United States. I regret to say what I am going to say, but it seems to me that it has reached an all-time peak in irresponsibility of attendance on the floor of the Senate. We can get but few Senators to come here while there is under consideration one of the most important matters that will be before the Senate in weeks, involving billions of dollars worth of property; and when the debate has been concluded Senators will come trooping in, asking somebody at the door what the Senate is voting on and how they should vote. It does not present a very encouraging picture of deliberation in the Senate of the United States.'

This is, *mutatis mutandis*, the kind of criticism made of the 'party drudges' of the House of Commons. It shows how misdirected most of the criticism is.

That the choice for modern legislators is largely between voting according to party and voting according to conscience is a myth. It is largely between voting according to party and voting according to pressure group. The British M.P. votes according to party, the American congressman according to pressure group. In both cases it is usually possible to salve the conscience. Indeed, congressmen are usually willing servants of the organized interests they support. As parochial upper-middle class Americans, many congressman are attached by sympathy as well as expediency to local interests and the great organized interests which, with the exception of the labour groups, are upper middle class in outlook too. In short, congressmen are usually themselves the 'lobbyists'.

The chief advantage of legislation passed without strong pressure from party whips is said to be that it is based on the 'consensus' of members representing the diverse regional and other special interests of the nation regardless of party and that such legislation is more likely to reflect the broad yet complex, steady yet ever-changing, currents of opinion in the country than legislation passed by disciplined, transient partisan majorities. Government by 'consensus' is an ideal firmly rooted in the American constitutional tradition. Its emphasis on moderation befits a middle class society. It would be unjust to fail to recognize the efforts of many congressmen to make the ideal a reality. But it would be a mistake not to keep in mind that unless 'consensus' is guided by the President it is merely 'log-rolling'.

The shortcomings of legislation passed under pressure from special interests are that it is largely irresponsible (pressure groups do not submit their claims directly to the whole electorate), often incoherent (different combinations of 'lobbyists' pass conflicting laws), and always neglectful of great common interests (those of consumers, for example) that can be effectively represented only by responsible national parties. These are, in other words, the shortcomings of 'congressional courtesy', which in the absence of responsible party government allows little groups of congressmen to dominate segments of public policy, chiefly by entrenching themselves in the relevant legislative standing committees. In politics the whole is more than the sum of its parts, but the American Congress is made up only of the parts. No congressional organ represents the nation as a whole.

Chapter 8

The National Administration

It is convenient to begin an account of the American national administration by describing its co-ordinating organs. Of these, the prime one is the presidency, for the President is constitutionally the chief executive. However, the President needs help in supervising the conduct of administration: in January 1953 at least fifty departments and other agencies reported directly to him. His effectiveness in exercising his authority, and therefore the adequacy of the co-ordination of American national administration, largely depends on the form the help takes.

Below the presidency, the cabinet has formally been the most important co-ordinating organ. It now consists of the heads of ten departments: the Department of State, Department of the Treasury, Department of Defense, Department of Justice, Post Office Department, Department of the Interior, Department of Agriculture, Department of Commerce, Department of Labor, and Department of Health, Education, and Welfare. In June 1953 these departments employed about 85 per cent of the civilian employees of the national government. But, though the cabinet meets often and maintains its prestige as the highest advisory body to the President, it has usually failed in practice.

'White House advisers' rather than the cabinet have usually performed the task of helping the President co-ordinate the machinery of administration. Some of the advisers may have been cabinet members, but they have served as co-ordinators because of their individual personal relations with the President, not because they have been in the cabinet. Many of the advisers have not been in it. President Andrew Jackson had his 'kitchen cabinet'. President Woodrow Wilson had, among others, Colonel Edward House. President Franklin Roosevelt had his 'brains trust'. During the Second World War he had, among others, Harry Hopkins, who became the second most influential man in American government after he had left the cabinet and, indeed, while he held no official post at all.

At first President Eisenhower seemed to follow the usual practice, though perhaps he paid more homage than usual to cabinet prestige. Martin Durkin, first Secretary of Labor in the Eisenhower cabinet, when explaining his resignation from it in September 1953 to the convention of the American Federation of Labor, referred several times to efforts of the White House staff to work out proposed amendments to existing labour legislation that would satisfy him and others whose views had to be considered. He made no mention of the cabinet as a co-ordinating agency. In November 1954, however, the President created a secretariat to organize the work of the cabinet and record its decisions. His action should make cabinet meetings more useful than they have been in the past.

The failure of the cabinet to co-ordinate has been recognized in legislation that permitted the establishment of the Executive Office of the President in 1939 and has subsequently enhanced its importance. The Executive Office of the President now includes as its permanent parts the White House Office, the Council of Economic Advisers, the Office of Defense Mobilization, the Bureau of the Budget, and the National Security Council.[1]

The White House Office is composed of the Assistant to the President, other assistants, secretaries, military aides, special advisers, and their staffs. Its most important members handle presidential relations with the administrative departments and agencies, Congress, and the press. The Council of Economic Advisers, the institutional expression of Keynesian economics as filtered through the American political process, is composed

[1] Many of the references in this chapter to the details of administrative organization are based on information in the official *United States Government Organization Manual 1954–55* (Washington: Government Printing Office, 1954), which is 'revised as of July 1, 1954'. The present tense is usually used here to describe the arrangements of that date.

of three economists whose appointments are confirmed by the Senate and a small staff. Its chairman reports to the President. The Office of Defense Mobilization is responsible for working out mobilization and stockpiling plans for both current and possible future defence needs. Its head is a member of the National Security Council.

The Bureau of the Budget and the National Security Council are major co-ordinating organs. The Bureau of the Budget was created in 1921 and remained technically part of the Treasury Department until 1939, when it was transferred to the Executive Office. Its Director is appointed by the President without senatorial confirmation and is responsible to the President alone. The Bureau has become the most important instrument of presidential supervision of administrative management. It is authorized to control the relations of administrative agencies with Congress: it is the clearing house for their requests for money and proposals for legislation, though leading members of the White House Office censor the main legislative recommendations. The Bureau is charged with making studies directed towards improving administrative procedures, and with taking action to reduce duplication of efforts in the collection of statistical information by agencies.

The National Security Council was created in 1947, and put in the Executive Office in 1949, to 'advise the President with respect to the integration of domestic, foreign, and military policies relating to national security'. By law the President is chairman and the Vice-President, secretaries of State and Defense, and heads of the Foreign Operations Administration and the Office of Defense Mobilization are members. With the consent of the Senate the President may invite other secretaries and under-secretaries of the cabinet and military departments to become members. The Council receives reports from the Central Intelligence Agency, which is subordinate to it, and, for example, from the Atomic Energy Commission, which is not. It has as staff a special assistant to the President, an executive secretary, and a secretariat and since 1953 has been assisted by an Operations Co-ordinating Board, composed of the Under Secretary of State, Deputy Secretary of Defense, Director of the

Foreign Operations Administration, Director of the Central Intelligence Agency, and a representative of the President, and created to 'co-ordinate the development by departments and agencies of detailed operational plans to carry out national security policies'. In the first few years of its existence the National Security Council became by far the most important collegiate body for co-ordinating policy in the American national administration.

In December 1954 President Eisenhower created by executive order a Council on Foreign Economic Policy, with a special assistant to the President as its head and the secretaries of State, the Treasury, Commerce, and Agriculture and the Director of the Foreign Operations Administration, or their principal deputies, as its 'initial basic membership', to co-ordinate activities in the field indicated by its title. The President instructed the chairman to 'establish appropriate working relations with the National Security Council and the National Advisory Council on International Monetary and Financial Problems'. The new Council may become a permanent part of the Executive Office of the President.

The development of the Executive Office of the President since 1939 and particularly the rapid growth in the importance of the National Security Council since 1947 indicate how badly the co-ordinating machinery was needed. They raise the questions why the cabinet failed to meet the need and whether the organs that have been developed are an adequate substitute for cabinet control of administration.

An American version of cabinet government in administration failed to develop for several reasons. The first is that the American political parties do not groom a cabinet any more than they groom a President. There is no American equivalent of the British 'shadow cabinet'.

This means that most members of a new cabinet have not been accustomed, individually, to giving serious consideration to the implementation of a wide range of public policies. The Postmaster General is normally a professional politician who is chiefly concerned with distributing patronage. He is rarely interested in co-ordinating policy and administration. Other cabinet members are often men with little experience in government administration, though usually with a good deal of experience in either government or administration as, for example, ex-congressmen or ex-business men. The absence of a 'shadow cabinet' means, too, that the members of the cabinet have not been accustomed, collectively, to working together as a team. Indeed, some of them sometimes meet other members for the first time at their first cabinet meeting. The cabinet members fall naturally into the habit of dealing with the President individually.

It is nearly the root of the matter that the President has permitted, often even encouraged, them to deal with him individually. The fact that the President can override the collective opinion of the cabinet is frequently stressed in explanations of the failure of the cabinet, usually by citing the story of President Lincoln ending a discussion of a point on which all seven members of the Civil War cabinet had opposed him by saying: 'Seven nays, one aye—the ayes have it.' Doubtless, this fact makes a cabinet member prefer putting his proposals to the President in private to putting them in a cabinet meeting, where other members may persuade the President to reject them; for it is the President alone who makes the final decision in either case. But what is important is that the President has usually allowed the cabinet member to indulge his preference. The President has failed to use the cabinet as an instrument for clearing the proposals of one member with the others.

The cabinet is, in fact, not simply the creature of the President. Its membership is defined by law. The President cannot make the head of an agency a cabinet member without the consent of Congress. President Truman sought, for example, to turn the Federal Security Agency, a large national administrative unit, into a cabinet department, but Congress refused to allow him to raise the status of an agency whose head was one of the most outspoken advocates of national health insurance. After President Eisenhower took office, Congress agreed to turn the Federal Security Agency into the cabinet Department of Health, Education, and Welfare.

The President can invite others besides the formal members

to cabinet meetings. The Vice-President, the Assistant to the President, the Director of the Bureau of the Budget, and the head of the Foreign Operations Administration, for example, have attended meetings of the Eisenhower cabinet. The legal restriction on cabinet membership could be only of symbolic importance. But it does seem to have exercised some restraint on the inclusion of unofficial members and the part they have played at meetings.

Moreover, the President is not entirely free to choose the men he wants as members. Although there are no fixed customs, it is often considered necessary for him to appoint men from various factions of the coalition that has elected him and from various regions of the country. It is sometimes thought desirable that he appoint at least one Catholic, and probably most future Presidents will follow Presidents Franklin Roosevelt and Eisenhower in appointing at least one woman. It is likely, therefore, that the President soon finds that he does not work well with all the members of the cabinet whom he felt constrained to choose when entering office. And in a cabinet that has never had more than ten posts there is little scope for meeting even a few of the special claims for places and making sure that all the key presidential advisers are included.

The President's nominees must be confirmed by the Senate. Confirmation is rarely withheld, partly because 'senatorial courtesy' does not apply to cabinet posts, partly because the Senate recognizes that the President's choice of men to work directly with him ought generally to be respected, but partly because the President sometimes avoids naming the man he wants if he believes that the nomination might not be confirmed. Senatorial power thus sometimes limits further the President's freedom of choice.

Again, while the President may in theory always dismiss a cabinet member in whom he has lost confidence, Congress sometimes limits his practical power to dismiss a cabinet member who is popular there. The confirmation proceedings of a successor may be unpleasant, and so may the next committee hearings on appropriations for the department concerned. The situation should not be exaggerated. Despite the restrictions mentioned, the American President is much freer from party and legislative pressures than the British Prime Minister in selecting and changing his cabinet. But the Prime Minister receives in return control of his party and the legislature. The President does not.

The root of the matter seems to be, indeed, that when the President tries, as most new Presidents do try, to treat the cabinet as a collective unit for co-ordinating policy and administration, he finds that it puts inconvenient restrictions on his freedom of action without any obvious compensating advantages. It is true that a strong cabinet, especially if expanded into an executive-legislative council, might to some extent bridge the division between the President and Congress, as well as improve the supervision of administration, but since the President has usually been no more willing than Congress to make immediate sacrifices in order to develop a more 'responsible' relationship between the two branches, he has usually preferred to use co-ordinating machinery that ensures his 'irresponsibility'. Although many of the other officials on whom the President relies also require senatorial confirmation, some do not; and in any case the fact that there are many of them means, first, that within certain limits the President may shift co-ordinating authority from one group of officials to another without making formal changes which enable Congress to interfere (Franklin Roosevelt was adept at this game) and, second, that the President retains fully the final power of co-ordination. The sole head of the Executive Office of the President is the President.

It follows that the organs the President uses for co-ordination are not in themselves an adequate substitute for an effective cabinet. The development of the Executive Office of the President has made it physically possible, though perhaps only barely so, for the President to carry the much greater administrative burden put upon him in recent years; but the Executive Office does not itself co-ordinate all aspects of administration. Whether presidential co-ordination is as effective in American government as cabinet co-ordination in British government depends largely on the personal administrative capacity of the President. The American political system relies somewhat more than the British on a man rather than an institution. The trouble is that a President is not often chosen primarily for his administrative ability; it is largely a matter of luck if he has it. The establishment of a cabinet secretariat in November 1954, however, may be a first step in a new development of profound importance.

There are limits, in any case, to the President's control of the national administration. The structure of administration is determined by law in America in much more detail than in Great Britain. The legal relations between administrative units and the President vary a great deal: some units are fully under his direction, others are only under his direction in some respects, and others are not under his direction at all. The practical relations vary a great deal, too, though not always in accordance with the legal relations. A brief survey of the main categories of administrative units shows how mistaken it would be to equate presidential executive authority with administrative power in the American national government.

The two broadest categories are the cabinet departments and the other agencies, but it is useful to describe three groups of units separately: the independent regulatory commissions, government corporations, and judicial and congressional administrative agencies. This section deals with the first two categories, and the next section with the special aspects of the last three.

The ten cabinet departments are the core of the administration. They form a category in general more fully under the direction of the President than the others. Functions are apportioned among them on the principle of assembling in one department activities and services with a related object: the Department of State, the conduct of foreign relations; the Department of the Treasury, the conduct of national fiscal affairs; the Department of Defense, the conduct of military affairs; the Department of Justice, the enforcement of national law; the Post Office Department, the operation of postal services; the Department of the Interior, the protection and development of natural resources; the Department of Agriculture, the conduct of national agricultural and forestal policies; the Department of Commerce, the promotion of business commerce; the Department of Labor, the conduct of national labour policies; and the Department of Health, Education, and Welfare, the conduct of national social services. There are, however, real and apparent anomalies, often accounted for by the history of administrative development. The Department of the Interior, for example, is the American Colonial Office. It has administered relations with the American Indians since its establishment in 1849; as a natural extension of activities, it took over the administration of relations with the continental Territories from the Department of State in 1873; and it has gradually taken over the administration of relations with the insular possessions from the Army and Navy. (The Secretary of the Army still supervises the administration of the Canal Zone.)

In addition, there are inevitably many borderline cases. The United States Coast Guard and the United States Secret Service are parts of the Department of the Treasury, though they perform other functions than preventing smuggling and counterfeiting. The Immigration and Naturalization Service was transferred from the Department of Labor to the Department of Justice in 1940. A perennial issue in administrative politics has been whether river control projects should be undertaken by the Bureau of Reclamation of the Department of the Interior or the Army Corps of Engineers—or *ad hoc* agencies like the Tennessee Valley Authority.

Indeed, the chief source of confusion in the allocation of activities among national administrative units has not been the claims of the different cabinet departments but the use of *ad hoc* agencies outside all of them. The number of the independent agencies varies a good deal from time to time, but even if the independent regulatory commissions, government corporations, and judicial and congressional agencies are not counted, the number in the last decade has always been larger than the number of cabinet departments. The category of the other agencies includes a few large ones like the Veterans' Administration (which had more employees in June 1953 than any department except the Department of Defense and Post Office Department) and the General Services Administration and more small ones like the Federal Mediation and Conciliation Service and the National Science Foundation. It includes agencies like the Foreign Operations Administration as much subject to presidential direction as the cabinet departments and agencies like the Civil Service Commission over which presidential authority is limited.

The only general explanation of the existence of the other agencies is that it is an American habit to create new agencies to do new jobs. The habit may be freely indulged since the lack of a 'responsible' American executive makes it unnecessary to put activities in the hands of 'responsible' ministers. It is likely to be indulged since congressional factions—and sometimes the President—find it useful to establish autonomous agencies with which they and interested pressure groups may deal without interference from department heads. The habit may be rationalized by arguing that new autonomous agencies break new ground better than old departments. The success of the Tennessee Valley Authority, an independent government corporation, is now almost invariably cited to support the argument.

There are special reasons for each case. Often Congress or the President wants to avoid putting an activity in the hands of a particular department and has no feasible alternative except establishing an *ad hoc* agency. Thus, the military departments, now under the Department of Defense, have recently been the strongest departments, probably mainly because they have had the strongest professional services of the major departments; it has not been possible to assign any important activity with a large defence element to any other department; but professional military influence in the military departments has been too great to make it wise to entrust them with any activity that has much more than a defence element. The Atomic Energy Commission was created as a separate agency in 1946, partly because the experience of the T.V.A. seemed particularly apt, and partly because control of atomic energy development would otherwise have remained in military hands. The Office of Defense Mobilization, first an emergency and then a permanent agency of the Executive Office of the President, was created to direct mobilization a few months after the Korean War broke out. The Foreign Operations Administration, the successor to other *ad hoc* agencies in the same field, was created to direct the mutual security programme in 1953. (It is scheduled for dissolution at the end of fiscal 1955.)

The conservative factions that have controlled Congress for over a decade, to which the Eisenhower administration in particular has made concessions, have shown a strong hostility to the State and Labor Departments. Independent agencies have been established in their fields not only to perform new functions but to take old functions away from the departments. In 1953, for example, the Foreign Operations Administration and the United States Information Agency absorbed not only the Mutual Security Agency and the information services of independent agencies administering foreign policy programmes but also the Technical Co-operation Administration and the United States International Information Administration of the State Department. In 1947 the independent Federal Mediation and Conciliation Service replaced the United States Conciliation Service of the Labor Department. The result of conservative hostility to the Labor Department is that there are more national government employees dealing with labour policies outside the Department than in it. It is by far the smallest of the departments.

Since the general justification for creating independent *ad hoc* agencies is, however, that they are useful in breaking new ground, it should follow that most of those that do not finish their jobs should in time be grouped, if not in old departments, in more comprehensive agencies and new departments, in order to reduce the difficulties of operating a large number of separate units. This has been the general trend, helped by several official reports on administrative reform, the most important of which were issued by the presidential Committee on Administrative Management in 1937 and by the Commission on Organization of the Executive Branch of the Government, headed by ex-President Herbert Hoover, in 1949. (In 1953 Hoover took charge of a new Commission of the same name to examine national government programmes as well as administration.)

Thus three 'quasi-departments', the Federal Works Agency, the Federal Loan Agency, and the Federal Security Agency, were created by grouping existing departmental and independent units together in 1939, though all three have disappeared in subsequent reorganizations, the last becoming a new department in 1953. The General Services Administration was created from existing units in 1949 to perform 'housekeeping' functions, such as the maintenance of buildings and the purchase of standard supplies, for the national civil government.

But the trend is not pervasive. Congress opposes carrying reorganization far enough to put all agencies under effective presidential control. The Civil Service Commission, for example, remains autonomous, though the Committee on Administrative Management recommended in 1937 that it be replaced by a personnel agency in what came to be called the Executive Office of the President. Congress still does not want all its policies subject to direct presidential influence. (It should be noted that neither the Bureau of the Budget nor the Civil Service Commission is in the Treasury Department. The American Treasury has nothing like the influence of the British Treasury in administration.) And new agencies continue to be formed. The other agencies thus have a permanent place, especially as the cutting edge, in the American national administration.

The category of independent regulatory commissions is distinguished partly by their formal independence from presidential control and partly by the nature of their activities. There are now seven or eight such collegiate commissions with from five to eleven members each: the Interstate Commerce Commission, which regulates most interstate common carriers; the Federal Trade Commission, which administers certain antitrust and fair trade practices legislation; the Board of Governors of the Federal Reserve System, which administers certain banking and credit legislation; the Federal Power Commission, which regulates the interstate electricity and natural gas industries; the Federal Communications Commission, which regulates the interstate wire and the wireless communications industries; the Security and Exchange Commission; the National

Labor Relations Board; and, possibly, the Civil Aeronautics Board. The commissions are supposed to be free from presidential interference in exercising their discretion within their statutory authority. Their independence is protected by legislation requiring the President to appoint their members with the consent of the Senate for overlapping terms, varying from commission to commission, of five to fourteen years, usually requiring him to select members so as to maintain bipartisan membership, and usually preventing him from removing members, before their terms have expired, except for causes laid down in law.

In 1926 the Supreme Court held in the case of Myers *v.* United States that Congress could not restrict the President's power to remove an executive official who had been appointed by the President with senatorial consent. The decision, and in particular some of the words of Chief Justice Taft's opinion, cast doubt on the validity of the statutes protecting members of the independent regulatory commissions. In the early days of the New Deal President Franklin Roosevelt disapproved strongly of the opinions of William E. Humphrey, a member of the Federal Trade Commission who had been appointed by President Coolidge and reappointed by President Hoover. He therefore removed Humphrey, frankly admitting that he did not do so for any of the reasons laid down in law—inefficiency, neglect of duty, or malfeasance in office—but simply because 'I do not feel that your mind and my mind go along together on either the policies or the administering of the Federal Trade Commission'. In the case of Humphrey's Executor (Rathbun) *v.* United States, decided by the Supreme Court in 1935, the independence of the members of the regulatory commissions was put directly to a constitutional test.

The Court held that the statute was valid and the removal illegal. Justice Sutherland, speaking for the Court, said that the Federal Trade Commission 'cannot in any proper sense be characterized as an arm or an eye of the executive'. He said that 'to the extent that it exercises any executive function—as distinguished from executive power in the constitutional sense —it does so in the discharge and effectuation of its quasi-legislative or quasi-judicial powers, or as an agency of the legislative or judicial departments of the government.' Consequently, he decided that 'illimitable power of removal is not possessed by the President in respect of' its members.

Justice Sutherland was at this time leading the Court down several strange constitutional paths. This one arrived at the conclusion that the independent regulatory commissions were not in any one of the three separate branches of government created by the Constitution. They were a 'fourth branch', exercising quasi-executive, quasi-legislative, and quasi-judicial functions.

The practical meaning of these functions is: First, as executive bodies, the commissions supervise and enforce the observance of statutes, rules, and judicial findings by persons and corporations subject to their jurisdiction; require reports and conduct investigations; and engage in studies with a view to making new rules of their own or recommending new legislation to Congress. Second, as legislative bodies, they make rules which, if a proper exercise of their statutory authority, have the force of law. Third, as judicial bodies, the commissions hear and decide cases involving alleged infractions of statutes and rules, rival claims to licences and other benefits, and other relevant disputes. Thus the Federal Communications Commission supervises the observance of a rule governing television transmission —execution—which it has made in pursuance of its statutory authority—legislation—and decides whether a licensee has infringed the rule—adjudication. Although the commissions are not the only administrative agencies that exercise quasi-legislative and quasi-judicial functions, and that in some cases are relatively independent of the President too, the commissions are usually distinguished from the other agencies by the exceptional complexity and importance of the economic relationships with which they deal.

The independent regulatory commissions have been subjected to two main criticisms. The first is that a commission is 'both prosecutor and judge'. Many lawyers have argued that a commission should be the prosecutor and a court the judge, or at least that separate groups of administrators should perform the two roles. They have also complained bitterly about the procedures of commission hearings, especially when the commissions have sometimes shown a preference for avoiding the use of lawyers. For a long time the regular courts reflected the hostility of the legal profession to administrative justice by subjecting it to close and usually unsympathetic judicial review.

After 1937, however, the Supreme Court generally refused to allow the regular courts to hamper administrative justice. In reaction, the American Bar Association induced Congress to pass a bill in 1940 providing for crippling changes in the procedures and judicial supervision of national administrative agencies. President Roosevelt vetoed it. A less drastic Administrative Procedure Bill was enacted in 1946 to apply to all national agencies exercising quasi-legislative or quasi-judicial functions. It requires, for example, that officials who investigate and present cases for administrative adjudication take no part in deciding them, that persons compelled to appear at hearings be permitted counsel and interested parties allowed to cross-examine witnesses, and that the right to appeal to a regular court be maintained. The Supreme Court has not allowed the last requirement to prevent it from continuing to show respect for most administrative decisions. The Act, as applied, seems to have effected a reasonable compromise between administrative justice by expert agencies with mixed powers and 'the rule of law'.

The second criticism is that the independence of the commissions hampers the efficient exercise of executive power. Many students of administration have argued that the commissions should not exercise autonomous policy-making and policy-enforcing functions. They should be administratively responsible to the President for those functions, since he is responsible to the electorate. The present situation inevitably leads to conflicts between the commissions and the other parts of the national administration.

It is true that the President cannot be indifferent to the effect the commissions have on public policy. Every President in this century has tried to influence the work of the commissions by taking advantage of the opportunities to appoint and remove members, developing close relations with the members, making recommendations about appropriations for the commissions, and using his influence in Congress and the country to determine the statutory and political environment in which the commissions work.

President Roosevelt's judicial defeat in the Humphrey case increased the demand that the independence of the commissions be formally curtailed. In 1937 the Committee on Administrative Management recommended that only judicial functions be left to autonomous commissions, while administrative and legislative functions be assigned to units of regular departments. In 1940 Congress permitted the executive activities other than investigations of the Civil Aeronautics Board to be transferred to a Civil Aeronautics Administration in the Department of Commerce; the present C.A.B. is thus different from the other independent commissions. In 1949 the Hoover Commission recommended that the similar executive functions of the other commissions be turned over to the regular departments, too, apparently hoping that a less extreme general recommendation than that of 1937 would stand a better chance in Congress; the compromise adopted for some but not all of the commissions, however, has been to put the executive activities under their chairmen, who are designated in these cases by the President. In 1950 Congress agreed to abolish the United States Maritime Commission, until then one of the independent regulatory commissions, transferring its functions to the Department of Commerce. Seven quasi-executive, quasi-legislative, and quasi-judicial independent regulatory commissions remain.

Congress is generally reluctant to change their status, for while they are largely independent of the President, they are subject to congressional pressure. They require annual appropriations from Congress. Furthermore, Congress supports some of the commissions because they tend, like Congress itself, to come under the influence of interested pressure groups. The decisions of the Interstate Commerce Commission, for example, have often favoured the great railway interests, a fact that accounts both for the particularly high prestige the commission has had among conservatives in Congress and the particularly low prestige it has had among liberals on the Supreme Court:

the justices most responsible for the sympathetic review of administrative decisions generally after 1937 were markedly harsh in their review of the decisions of the I.C.C. It has been plausibly argued that the Civil Aeronautics Board has usually been dominated by its 'certificated' carriers and that the National Labor Relations Board was for a time under the influence of the C.I.O. Congress will never fully subject the independent commissions to presidential control so long as it itself is primarily subject to special pressures.

The category of government corporations has recently varied a great deal in the number of units it comprises. From 1932 to the late 1930's and early 1940's the number grew from a few to over a hundred, and then it declined: the Hoover Commission counted seventy-five in 1948 not in the process of liquidation, and there are fewer now. Most of them are attached to a regular department: the Commodity Credit Corporation of the Department of Agriculture, for example. A few are separate agencies: the Tennessee Valley Authority, for example. Most of them are wholly publicly owned: both the Commodity Credit Corporation and the T.V.A., for example; and it is with these that this discussion is concerned. They are usually engaged in financial and proprietory activities for which a form of organization used by private business is considered appropriate.

Their most characteristic feature, compared with other governmental agencies, is, or at least has been, their great latitude in managing their own affairs: they buy, sell, loan, borrow, and make and accumulate profits and losses in pursuance of their responsibilities as businesses. When they are financially self-sustaining, they are sometimes the most independent of national administrative units; for unlike the others, including the independent regulatory commissions, they do not require annual appropriations from Congress. It is therefore appropriate to add something about recent congressional efforts to curb the independence of government corporations to what has been said about the broad categories of departmental and other agencies, to which the corporations otherwise belong.

Many congressmen have distrusted government corporations partly because many of the corporations have been associated with the liberal policies of the New Deal. The T.V.A., for example, has been called by the friends of the New Deal one of the greatest achievements of public enterprise and by its enemies a symptom of, in President Eisenhower's words, 'creeping socialism'. Indeed, President Roosevelt created some government corporations without statutory authority, a practice forbidden by an act of 1945. But congressmen have been distrustful chiefly because the financially successful corporations have sometimes been immune from congressional supervision of and pressure on their personnel and administrative policies.

In 1940 Congress authorized the President to put most national agencies, including all government corporations except the T.V.A., under the central civil service system of merit appointment. This congressional decision was one of several made about that time which were based on the belief that the spoils system of appointment often benefited the President more than congressmen. (In general it is thought that the spoils system usually benefits congressmen more than the President.) The T.V.A. was exempted because it had developed, over the bitter opposition of the patronage-seeking senior Senator from Tennessee, Kenneth McKellar, an extremely good merit system of its own, which it had advertised so well that Congress dared not try to abolish it. In April 1941 the President exercised most of the authority granted to him the previous year. Congress steadily encroached on the financial independence of government corporations, until in 1945 it required that they subject themselves to annual financial scrutiny by the presidential Bureau of the Budget and the congressional General Accounting Office. This act still left corporations more independent than many congressmen wanted; but the Hoover Commission supported the corporations as a category on this point; and the reduction in the number of corporations has had a soothing effect.

Finally, there are the administrative units in the judicial and legislative branches of the national government: the Administrative Office of the United States Courts; and the Office of the Architect of the Capitol, Library of Congress, Government Printing Office, United States Botanic Garden, and General

Accounting Office. Most of them are where they are because of the services they provide for the courts and Congress. The unit that has the greatest effect on general administration is the General Accounting Office.

The General Accounting Office prescribes accounting systems for the administrative agencies, authorizes them to draw money from the Treasury, and audits their accounts. The last two activities are often referred to as pre-auditing and post-auditing, for the General Accounting Office has asserted the right when authorizing the drawing of money to check the legality of the purpose for which it is to be (or has been) spent, and thus the accounts of the agencies are in a sense audited twice. Many administrators object strongly to this arrangement. They argue that operating agencies ought to be allowed to spend money as they think proper up to the amount permitted them by Congress. If the General Accounting Office thinks that the money is wrongly spent, it should report the matter to Congress. It should not be allowed to prevent agencies from spending money (or force them to refund it) on the basis of what may be its erroneous interpretation of congressional intent.

The head of the General Accounting Office is the Comptroller-General of the United States, appointed by the President with the consent of the Senate for a term of fifteen years and removable before the expiration of his term only by joint resolution of Congress for specific cause or by conviction on impeachment. In the 1930's a Republican-appointed Comptroller-General, serving out the last years of his term under the New Deal, clashed repeatedly with New Deal agencies in exercising his pre-auditing function. When his term expired in 1936, President Roosevelt showed his displeasure with the existing arrangement by delaying the appointment of a successor. In 1937 the Committee on Administrative Management recommended that the pre-auditing function be transferred to the Treasury Department. Congress refused to follow this recommendation. In 1949 the Hoover Commission made more cautious proposals, which were modified by Congress in an act of 1950 providing that more accounting was to be done by the executive agencies themselves but that general supervision was to remain with the General Accounting Office. In this, as in much else, Congress perpetuates unsatisfactory administrative arrangements in order to avoid strengthening presidential authority.

The internal organization of the administrative units naturally varies a great deal, but it is possible briefly to give some idea what it is like, particularly in the cabinet departments, and to say something about how civil servants are appointed.

The general structure of a department is as follows: At the top is a single department head: the Secretary, the Attorney General, or the Postmaster General. Below him are usually a deputy head and a number of assistants, some of whom supervise groups of operational units. The most striking deviation from the usual arrangement is that the Department of Defense has, besides the Secretary of Defense and his subordinates in the central Department, three 'secretaries' as heads of the 'departments' of the Army, Navy, and Air Force, though the autonomy of the three branches implied by their titles has been steadily reduced since the creation of the comprehensive national defence establishment in 1947. The top officials at the departmental level are appointed by the President with the consent of the Senate. Some of the others are appointed by the heads of the departments, often subject to the approval of the President.

The highest operational unit of a department is usually referred to as a bureau, though it may be entitled, for example, a 'service', an 'office', or an 'administration'. A bureau may be organized on the basis of function, work process, clientèle, territory, or a combination of two or more of the simple bases. Functional bureaus are most common: the Bureau of the Census in the Department of Commerce and the Forest Service in the Department of Agriculture, for example. Work process bureaus are organized to bring together highly specialized personnel or types of equipment: the Office of Business Economics in the Department of Commerce, for example. Examples of clientèle bureaus are the Bureau of Indian Affairs in the Department of the Interior and the Women's Bureau in the Department of Labor. Examples of territorial bureaus are the Bureau of Far Eastern Affairs in the Department of State and the Southwestern Power Administration in the Department of the Interior, though the latter is functional too. Bureau chiefs are appointed by the President with the consent of the Senate, the President alone, or the heads of the departments.

The subdivisions of bureaus may also be organized on any of the bases mentioned, though not necessarily on the same bases as the bureaus they are in. The degree of subdivision and sub-subdivision depends on the size and work of the bureau. At some point, however, most bureaus have field services about the country. About nine out of ten national civil servants work outside Washington. The pattern of field services is extremely confused. Departments, bureaus in the same departments, and other agencies differ greatly in the way they divide the nation into areas and delegate authority to field offices. The great majority of employees below the bureau chiefs are appointed by the departments.

Most of the large non-departmental agencies have single heads: the Veterans' Administration and the Foreign Operations Administration, for example; but some have collegiate directorates: the T.V.A. and the Atomic Energy Commission, for example; and so do most of the small non-departmental executive agencies. Collegiate directorates are perhaps useful in agencies like the independent regulatory commissions, especially when exercising their judicial functions. But they are subject to more internal dissension than is probably desirable in large operating agencies. The three heads of the T.V.A. quarrelled so bitterly in the 1930's that the President had to remove the chairman in 1938; and the five heads of the Atomic Energy Commission quarrelled in 1954 over the special position its chairman had assumed. Except for this difference at the top, most of the generalizations about departmental organization and personnel apply to the other agencies. If large enough, the agencies are divided and subdivided as the departments are, with extensive field services. In general, the methods of appointment are presidential appointment with senatorial confirmation at the top and agency appointment below.

An important aspect of an appointment, however, is the

degree and kind of partisan influence that can be brought to bear on it. On this aspect the method of appointment is not an accurate guide. Although most grades of civil appointees picked by the President with senatorial consent are partisan appointees, some are not: Foreign Service Officers, for example. Although most civil appointees picked by the departments and agencies are merit appointees, some are not: some clerks and most legal advisers in various departments and agencies, for example. The distinction between partisan and merit selection is confused further not only by the absence of consistent distinctions between posts filled in the two ways but also by the presence of different kinds of partisan and merit selection and discrepancies between the form and reality of appointments.

Thus some partisan appointees requiring senatorial confirmation are subject to 'senatorial courtesy': national district judges and postmasters, for example. Others are not: Supreme Court justices and cabinet officers, for example. The first are sometimes called party patronage appointees and the second non-patronage political appointees. More fundamentally, some partisan appointees are picked for posts which are supposed to be administered impartially: the clerks, legal advisers, district judges, and postmasters already mentioned, for example. Others are picked for posts which are recognized as 'policy-making': cabinet officers and some bureau chiefs, for example. The distinction between party patronage and non-patronage political appointees is applied more usefully in this connection.

The merit type of selection in the American civil service is defined broadly to mean non-partisan appointment and narrowly to mean appointment on the basis of demonstrated relative fitness. The narrow definition leaves room for kinds of non-partisan patronage, such as 'old school tie' patronage, which seems to play a part, for example, in promotions in the Foreign Service. On the whole, however, Americans have been determined to avoid drawing particular grades of appointees from particular classes, on the basis either of social origin or of education, to the extent the British have drawn them. The most persuasive argument against the extension of the merit system has always been that it would substitute social for partisan patronage. Those responsible for merit system recruitment have sought to avoid criticism in that respect by doing very little to encourage some of the ablest graduates of American universities to enter the permanent civil service. The resultant loss has been partly compensated for by leaving the top posts in the administration available for non-patronage political selection of able business executives and professional men to an extent not possible, at least in peacetime, in the British civil service.

It is commonly held in America that non-patronage political selection is proper if confined—as the better definition of the term requires—to 'policy-making' posts; that merit selection is proper for 'administrative' posts; and that patronage selection is never proper. Consequently, politicians try to conceal improper appointments behind proper forms. It has been the practice for some time, for example, to appoint postmasters who are subject to senatorial confirmation from merit system examination lists and to give them permanent appointments. But it is understood that only acceptable members of the party in power get on the lists. On 25 June 1953 President Eisenhower, for another example, withdrew about 66,000 posts in the United States from the merit system protection previous Presidents had given them so that those found to be of 'a confidential or policy-determining character' could be made subject to political rotation. ('Confidential' posts like those of chauffeur and stenographer to an important official are at the other end of the scale from 'policy-determining' posts.) The excuse for the action gave a semblance of respectability to the promise of more patronage for the Republicans.

Obviously it is very difficult to estimate the extent to which the spoils system still exists in American national administration. In October 1952 the *New York Times* reported that the extension of the merit system in recent years had gone so far that probably only about 30,000 posts were subject to easy political manipulation in a total of about 2,380,000 national civil service posts in the United States. In January 1953 it reported that the Civil Service Commission had been asked to prepare a list of about 170,000 posts in the United States which could be filled by political appointment, at least when they fell vacant; and the list did not include the postmasterships referred to above, which fall vacant at the rate of about 4,000 a year. In June 1953 President Eisenhower made it possible to add about another 66,000 posts to the list.

Opportunities for political manipulation are not always taken, however: for example, about four-fifths of the lawyers in the Justice Department not under the merit system stayed on when Democratic President Roosevelt replaced Republican President Hoover. It is likely that only a small fraction of the posts affected by President Eisenhower's action will in fact be classified as subject to political rotation. Rotation in office is made difficult, moreover, by 'veterans' preference' in obtaining and keeping government jobs. It is still too early to say exactly what the first partisan turnover in administration in twenty years will really mean for a service that has undergone enormous changes in size, activities, and methods of recruitment in the meantime. But at the end of the first eighteen months of the new administration the reductions in force resulting from the curtailment of government expenditure and services had affected many more employees than the spoils system.

In any event the effects of the spoils system on the present civil service are much less important than the effects of the methods of congressional committees and the heads of the administration in examining the loyalty of civil servants to the United States. Perhaps the present situation was unavoidable: the American permanent civil service had not gained sufficient professional prestige to be left to 'purge' itself discreetly, largely free from partisan attempts to make political capital out of disclosures or alleged disclosures of disloyalty; and once the loyalty issue became a major political one, it lent itself naturally to the stunts of Senator Joseph McCarthy and Attorney General Herbert Brownell. 'McCarthyism' has done most damage in America to the civil service and its impact on recruitment will affect American national administration for a generation.

Chapter 9

The Presidency

John Locke described three kinds of power: legislative, that is, power to make laws; executive, that is, power to carry out laws; and federative, that is, power to conduct foreign relations and to make war and peace. Under this classification the executive function is the simple enforcement of legislation by administrators and judges and the federative function is distinguished from it by a degree of discretion required in dealing with foreign states. Although the framers of the American Constitution referred to legislative, executive, and judicial power, Locke's distinction between executive and federative power has found a place in the interpretation of the powers of the American presidency, and it is convenient to consider presidential activities in Locke's terms. The President is the chief legislator, the chief executive, and the chief conductor of foreign policy in the American political system.

In each role his connection with Congress is of prime importance. The first three sections of this chapter describe the particular constitutional and extra-constitutional character of the connection in the conduct of legislative, executive, and federative activities. The last section discusses the general problem of presidential-congressional relations, which is now the most important problem of the structure of American government.

First, the President as the chief legislator. The Constitution puts the President at the beginning and end of the legislative process. It provides that he 'shall from time to time give to the Congress information of the state of the Union, and recommend to their consideration such measures as he shall judge necessary and expedient'; and it provides that every bill 'which shall have passed the House of Representatives and the Senate, shall, before it become a law, be presented' to him. He may use one of two vetoes. The first may be used while Congress is in session: within ten days, except Sundays, after a measure has been delivered to him, the President may return it to the House of Congress in which it originated together with his objections to it. (Otherwise it becomes law whether he signs it or not.) This veto may be overridden by two-thirds majorities of both Houses. The second veto may be used if Congress adjourns before the constitutional ten days have passed: the President may then exercise a 'pocket veto' simply by not signing a measure. This veto is absolute.

The custom is that the President prepares regular State of the Union messages, dealing with the general conduct of affairs, for the annual convenings of Congress and such special messages, dealing with particular subjects, as he may wish to submit from time to time. The messages were rarely important in the nineteenth century; but in the Progressive Era President Theodore Roosevelt made some use of his regular messages and President Taft of his special measages to present presidential views on legislation to Congress and the country; and President Wilson restored the early practice, which President Jefferson had dropped, of delivering messages in person. The regular State of the Union address is now usually delivered that way, broadcast and telecast while the President delivers it, and frequently used as a thinly-veiled appeal to the public to put pressure on Congress in the President's behalf.

The history of the State of the Union address reflects the history of presidential recommendation of legislation. Alexander Hamilton put a number of important legislative proposals to Congress as the spokesman for President Washington in the first years under the Constitution, but President Jefferson preferred to use his influence behind the scenes, and most subsequent presidents made little use of their right to make formal suggestions. The reputation of the strongest presidents of the nineteenth century—Jackson, Lincoln, and Cleveland—rests on their use of executive power, often to resist congressional encroachments, rather than on the guidance they gave congressional legislation. Theodore Roosevelt and, even more, Woodrow Wilson took firm personal leads in proposing measures again. The practice is now well established. The presidential programme is the prime basis of congressional legislative activity; and though congressmen like to criticize the President for wanting to 'dot the i's and cross the t's' of legislation, they expect him to tell them fairly clearly what he wants.

President Jackson was the first President to make use of the veto power as a major instrument of presidential policy, though he vetoed only twelve measures in eight years. Over a half-century later President Cleveland vetoed 584 measures, many of them private veterans' pension bills, in eight years. His vetoes accounted for more than half of all presidential vetoes before Franklin Roosevelt took office in 1933. Roosevelt vetoed 371 measures, including for the first time a general revenue bill, by regular veto and 260 measures by pocket veto. The fact that he vetoed 631 measures in twelve years, though his party was nominally in control of Congress all the time, indicates the extent to which the President and Congress may represent different conceptions of the public interest.

The Constitution does not provide the President with power to influence directly the middle stages of the legislative process. The framers of the Constitution may have anticipated that once the President made his proposals, he would wait until he saw what measures were passed before interfering in the legislative process again. But the rise of political parties with presidential candidates as their standard-bearers inevitably meant that the President became interested in legislation at every stage. The popularity of a partisan administration depends partly on what Congress does. The President's problem is to turn his interest into influence. Presidents have used several means, but they have been only intermittently successful.

The President may threaten to use the veto as a means of influencing the content of legislation before it reaches him. Theodore Roosevelt was the first President to use the threat extensively, and Harry Truman has been the President to make the most frequent and open, though often unsuccessful, use of it.

The technique partly compensates for the lack of an item veto, that is, the right to veto part of a bill while approving the rest. The President may also threaten to withhold patronage from congressmen who refuse to support his proposals. The threat has often been effective at the beginning of an administration, especially when the President's party has just returned to office. This is the practical basis of the romantic notion that presidential-congressional relations begin as a 'honeymoon'—and the less romantic notion that they often end in separation or divorce. President Eisenhower was criticized for postponing the fight for his major legislative recommendations until after the traditional 'honeymoon' period was over, but he also stretched out the distribution of patronage by ordering a review of 'policy-determining' posts that might be made subject to political rotation.

The President's position as head of the bureaucracy is an important source of influence. Administrative agencies may obtain information, publicize points of view (though congressmen watch public relations activities closely), and draft bills for him. As the task of legislating becomes increasingly difficult, congressmen often have to turn to the administrative experts for some guidance. Congressmen often have to delegate legislative power to the administrative agencies too, though the doctrine of the separation of powers makes so frank a description of their action constitutionally improper. In several important areas of public policy, such as tariff-rate policy, Congress now exercises general supervision over administrative policy-making instead of legislating in detail.

The President's positions as the elected representative of the national electorate and as party leader (though the distinction between these two positions may not be clear, it means a great deal, for example, to President Eisenhower) are other sources of influence. Direct appeals to the people to let their congressmen know how they feel about the President's programme are sometimes effective. Appeals to the party loyalty of congressmen sometimes work too, particularly when an election is near and the President seems popular among the voters. Finally, the personal relations the President and members of his official and unofficial groups of advisers have with congressmen of both parties are extremely important. The administration takes part in bipartisan 'log-rolling'. By an adroit use of presidential popularity, partisan pressure, and 'log-rolling', for example, the Eisenhower administration scored several legislative victories in the last months of the Eighty-third Congress, particularly in forcing part of its agricultural programme through despite the opposition of the 'farm bloc'. In sum, the President is now, from the beginning to the end of the legislative process, the chief legislator.

Presidential influence over legislation is limited, however, by the caution with which congressmen view presidential-congressional co-operation. They think that it entails a degree of presidential leadership they do not want. And they have the means to reduce the effectiveness of every constitutional power and extra-constitutional source of influence the President has.

The President may propose measures to Congress, and 'administration spokesmen' may introduce bills drafted in the executive branch, but congressmen often rewrite the bills in standing committees and sometimes ignore or reject the President's proposals altogether. The congressional power to dispose of legislative recommendations is more important than the President's power to make them.

The President may veto legislation, but Congress may override the regular veto. It has been estimated that through 1936 about one in six regular vetoes of public bills and about one in eighty regular vetoes of private bills were overridden. All told, of 1,190 regular vetoes delivered by the presidents before President Eisenhower, 71 were overridden, just over half of them during the terms of three presidents: fifteen of the twenty-one regular vetoes of President Johnson, whom the House of Representatives impeached and the Senate failed to convict by only one vote short of the required two-thirds majority, were overridden; nine of the 371 regular vetoes of President Franklin Roosevelt were overridden (including the veto of the Revenue Act of 1944); and twelve of the 180 regular vetoes of President Truman, who faced a Republican majority in Congress during 1947-8, were overridden (including the vetoes of the Taft-

Hartley Labor-Management Relations Act of 1947 and the Revenue Act of 1948). Roosevelt's success in exercising the veto power, however, was well above average.

Congress reduces the effectiveness of the veto power by putting 'riders' on bills the President may feel unable to veto. Thus Congress put a 'rider' on an appropriation bill in 1943 specifying that no money was to be paid to three government employees whom certain congressmen disliked. President Roosevelt denounced the 'rider' but felt constrained to sign the bill. In 1946 in the case of United States v. Lovett the Supreme Court held that the 'rider' was an unconstitutional bill of attainder, thereby providing an unusual ending to an oft-told tale.

The President's threat to withhold patronage from uncooperative congressmen of his own party is often overcome by 'senatorial courtesy'. The influence the President derives from his position as the head of the bureaucracy is reduced by his inability to control it completely. Some administrative agencies work more closely with congressional committees than with the President. The influence he derives from his positions as the head of the nation and the head of the party is limited by the strength of local pressures in congressional districts and the lack of strong party discipline in Congress. What the administration gains by engaging in congressional 'log-rolling' must be paid for: the Eisenhower administration postponed its efforts to secure tariff reforms as part of the price paid for its successes in the Eighty-third Congress. In sum, Congress very often does not do what the President wants.

The President's reaction to the limits on his legislative influence has sometimes been to assert the doctrine that he can legislate on his own. Presidents Lincoln and Johnson claimed the right to determine the southern 'reconstruction' policy of the national government. During the Second World War President Roosevelt was angered by the success with which the 'farm bloc' obstructed price control legislation in Congress. He announced: 'In the event that the Congress should fail to act, and act adequately, I shall accept the responsibility, and I will act. . . .' The threat was effective.

President Truman's order putting the private steel industry

under government control during a labour dispute in 1952 was an application of the doctrine of independent legislative power. The President had refused to follow the procedure laid down in the Taft-Hartley Labor-Management Relations Act and, after having failed to settle the dispute his own way, ordered the seizure on his own authority. In the case of Youngstown Sheet & Tube Co. *v.* Sawyer the Supreme Court ruled that the order was invalid. Justice Black held in the Opinion of the Court (in which four other justices concurred) that

'the President's power to see that the laws are faithfully executed refutes the idea he is to be a lawmaker. The Constitution limits his functions in the lawmaking process to the recommending of laws he thinks wise and the vetoing of laws he thinks bad. . . .

'The Founders of this Nation entrusted the lawmaking power to the Congress alone in both good and bad times. . . .'

The doctrine of independent legislative power is indeed dangerous, but the frequent conflict between the President and Congress leads to dangerous situations. A fair deduction from the various opinions in the Youngstown case—there were one Opinion of the Court, five concurring opinions, and one dissenting opinion; the justices divided six to three on the merits of the case—is that a President with a regard for the niceties of constitutional language may in fact do a great deal on his own without interference from the Court. The history of the American presidency leaves no doubt that it has been an office of expanding power. Only by more effective presidential-congressional co-operation can the growth of independent presidential power be prevented.

Second, the President as the chief executive. The Constitution provides that the President shall be commander-in-chief of the national armed forces; that he shall nominate and with the advice and consent of the Senate appoint the officers of the United States, though Congress may vest the appointment of inferior officers in the President alone, the courts of law, or the heads of departments; and that 'he may require the opinion, in writing, of the principal officer in each of the executive departments, upon any subject relating to the duties of their respective offices'. It gives him the power, which Locke held to be properly vested in the executive, 'to grant reprieves and pardons for offences against the United States, except in cases of impeachment'. There are also two broad constitutional provisions that the President 'shall take care that the laws be faithfully executed' and that 'the executive power shall be vested in a President of the United States of America'. Upon these several clauses rests the President's position as the chief executive of the United States.

His powers are broad enough that an able and tenacious President who knows how to appeal to public opinion can turn the ways the laws are enforced into a major instrument of presidential policy. The vigorous administration of President Theodore Roosevelt, for example, strengthened the civil service merit system, created a national conservation policy, and expanded governmental supervision of the activities of large corporations with the aid of relatively little new legislation. The administration of President Franklin Roosevelt kept the tone of American government liberal after 1937 largely by the use of executive power; for Congress became increasingly conservative during the last half of Roosevelt's tenure of office.

The President's control of the executive branch is restricted, however, by Congress, which shapes the structure of the administrative hierarchy and virtually names many of the executive appointees. Some administrative units, like the independent regulatory commissions, are formally independent of presidential direction and others nominally in the cabinet departments and other agencies responsible to the President are practically independent. Bureau chiefs whose relations with Congress are particularly good can often work virtually free from the supervision of their administrative superiors: J. Edgar Hoover of the Federal Bureau of Investigation of the Department of Justice is a well-known example. As was pointed out in Chapter 8, Congress has not permitted a full reform of the national administration that would strengthen presidential influence and weaken its own influence over certain agencies.

Traditionally, legislative control of administration has rested primarily on the power of the purse. The American Congress has retained much more of the substance of the power than the British Parliament. Congressional power of the purse remains the foundation of congressional influence in American administration. The key to comprehending the balance of power between the President and Congress with respect to the national administration is an understanding of American national government budgeting procedures.

A brief outline of the process of budget-making is as follows: The fiscal year of the national government begins on July 1. The Bureau of the Budget starts preparation of the annual budget about fourteen months before it goes into effect, spending the time from May to December of the preceding year in shaping the budget as it will be delivered by the President to Congress. Although the budget is not officially delivered until Congress convenes in January, subcommittees of the Committee on Appropriations of the House of Representatives sometimes receive parts of the budget for study as early as October. Then, after the subcommittees have made detailed studies and changes, the full Appropriations committee considers the budget recommendations and drafts several budget bills, which it presents to the whole House. Thereafter, the budget measures follow essentially the same procedure through the House and Senate as other bills, though they receive special treatment that assures them of the necessary priority. Consideration of the budget is a slow process, however, and the bills are frequently not ready for the President's signature when the fiscal year begins.

General congressional supervision of administrative finance has to be by 'rule of thumb'. Congressmen are usually well aware of the direct effects of budget changes on their constituents. When they cut President Truman's original budget proposals for fiscal 1952 by a record net amount—according to one estimate by about $6,000,000,000 in an original budget of about $85,000,000,000, though some of the 'cuts' were merely postponements of appropriations—they reduced appropriations for national defence and foreign aid but increased appropriations for the agricultural price support programme and veterans' services and pensions. They also give vent to their distrust of and faith in certain programmes. For fiscal 1952 they reduced the recommended appropriations for education and research and increased those for atomic energy development. But they struggle against 'bureaucratic waste' with blunt instruments. They make flat reductions in appropriations and provisions for staff, for example, without regard for the varying effects the reductions have on the administrative units concerned.

Indeed, congressional supervision of administration must be similar to congressional legislative activity. There is no effective organization in Congress to exercise general control. Therefore, each little clique of congressmen acquires inordinate influence over the section of public administration in which it is particularly interested. Congressmen work themselves on the subcommittees on appropriations that deal with the agencies most directly affecting their special interests. Through the increases and reductions they make in the President's budget, through the statements they make to the administrators during hearings, and through the reports they write, members of the subcommittees and committees exercise detailed as well as general oversight of the several parts of the national administration. The congressional subcommittees and their staffs act as a second budget bureau.

The authority of the executive Bureau of the Budget within the national administration has been supported by legislation that prevents agencies from asking Congress for more money than the Bureau requests for them. But congressmen encourage agency heads to break the law, in spirit if not in letter, on the ground that otherwise the Bureau would deprive Congress of useful information. (It is certainly true that the growth of the Bureau as the best-informed body on administrative finance and management has partly accounted for an increased guidance from the executive in budgetary matters.) Congressmen are particularly anxious that the Bureau does not restrict the agencies that provide 'pork'. The Army Corps of Engineers works closely with congressmen in arranging civil engineering projects in their districts, though even it fails to satisfy them completely. In 1951 the Director of the Bureau of the Budget said that between September and December 1949, while the budget for fiscal 1950 was being prepared for submission to Congress, 200 congressmen asked the Bureau to put estimates for particular projects in its recommended budget for the Corps.

And as congressmen help friends (and themselves), they punish enemies. Each agency head knows that he must not do certain things if he wants favourable treatment of the recommended appropriations for his agency. The taboos are sometimes explicit. It was pointed out in 1943, for example, that a congressman from a fruit-growing district had regularly imposed a ban on the expenditure of money by the Department of Agriculture to test the effects of fruit sprays on the consumers of fruit. More often the taboos are simply understood. Other congressmen will usually support an aggrieved member against an executive department. This is one more facet of 'congressional courtesy'. Often the President's only recourse is to appeal to public opinion, but while the President may be able to protect the main outlines of his budget, he usually cannot expect to arouse public opinion over the details.

The pressure groups that benefit from 'congressional courtesy' in legislation benefit from 'congressional courtesy' in legislative oversight of administration. They are able to exact special favours from administrative agencies, indirectly through friendly congressmen and directly through their own pressures on the agencies. It is worth stressing that Congress has created and maintains an administrative structure that is subject to the same disjunctive special pressures to which it itself is subject. 'Log-rolling' in the American Congress supports 'log-rolling' in the national administration.

Throughout the history of presidential-congressional relations in administrative affairs, the President has resisted congressional encroachments by claiming that a large measure of executive authority may be exercised free from legislative interference. Congress and President Jackson, for example, fought over the President's assertion that he could control the policy of the Treasury Department despite legislation that appeared to make the Department primarily an instrument for carrying out the financial powers of Congress. The Senate and President Cleveland fought over the President's refusal to allow the Senate to see papers relating to the suspension of government employees. In May 1954 Senator McCarthy put in an extreme form a congressional demand that employees of the national government should not be restrained by the President from giving information about executive decisions and personnel to Congress:

'. . . I would like to notify those 2 million Federal employees that I feel it is their duty to give us any information which they have about graft, corruption, communism, treason, and that there is no loyalty to a superior officer which can tower above and beyond their loyalty to their country.'

In reply President Eisenhower had his Attorney General put the executive position in temperate but firm words:

'. . . The Executive Branch of the government has the sole and fundamental responsibility under the Constitution for the enforcement of our laws and presidential orders.

'They include those to protect the security of our nation which were carefully drawn for this purpose. That responsibility cannot be usurped by any individual who may seek to set himself above the laws of our land or to override the orders of the President of the United States to federal employees of the executive branch of the government.'

The Senate select committee of 1954 which proposed that the Senate censure Senator McCarthy for some of his words and actions recognized that Congress should show respect for 'reasonable' executive regulations dealing with the disclosure of confidential or 'classified' information and pointed out that federal employees who disregarded them ran the risk of incurring penalties. But the committee agreed with Senator McCarthy that Congress had the right to obtain 'any information, even though classified, if it discloses corruption or subversion in the executive branch', and decided that the form of his appeal, though 'improper', was 'motivated by a sense of official duty'. It did not recommend censure on this point. It suggested that senatorial leaders should confer with executive officers about the procedures for giving confidential data to Congress.

Although the exact constitutional rights of the two branches have rarely been clearly determined by the Supreme Court, the presidential case for autonomous administrative power clearly rests on much firmer grounds than the case for autonomous legislative power. The President needs to have a good deal of freedom of action in executing the laws. Chief Justice Taft pointed that out most forcefully, perhaps too forcefully, in the Myers case when the Court upheld the right of the President to dismiss an executive official who had been appointed with senatorial consent without consulting the Senate about his dismissal. (But the sweeping generalizations of the Myers opinion were modified in the Humphrey case when the Court held invalid the President's dismissal of a Federal Trade Commissioner.) It is worth noting, too, that in 1890 in the case of *In Re* Neagle the Supreme Court held that the President can order an officer to enforce not only the acts of Congress but also 'the rights, duties, and obligations growing out of the Constitution itself, our international relations, and all the protection implied by the nature of the government under the Constitution'. (The majority of the Court rendered a strong opinion in this case; the executive order in question, which had been issued without statutory authority, had been given to a deputy United States marshal, Neagle, in order to protect a Supreme Court justice whose life had been threatened; the case arose because Neagle shot the man who had made the threat as the man attacked the justice.) Independent executive power as defined in the Neagle and other cases—though the decisions dealing with the constitutional rights of the executive contain many inconsistencies—would seem to embrace a good deal of what Locke called the prerogative, if not independent legislative power. The use of independent executive authority has indeed gone very far in time of war. The decision of the Youngstown steel seizure case of 1952 gives Congress only an illusory protection from the President's attempts to make policy on his own.

Third, the President as the chief conductor of foreign policy. The framers of the Constitution divided the federative power between the President and Congress. From the clause 'he shall receive ambassadors and other public ministers' is derived the President's power to recognize and withhold recognition from a foreign government, but this is apparently his only unrestricted power—and Congress has sometimes sought to interfere with it. The Constitution provides that the President 'shall have power, by and with the advice and consent of the Senate, to make treaties, provided two-thirds of the Senators present concur; and he shall nominate, and by and with the advice and consent of the Senate, shall appoint ambassadors, other public ministers and consuls'. It provides that the President shall be commander-in-chief of the armed services but empowers Congress to make rules for their governance and to declare war. These constitutional arrangements of 1787 subjected the executive conduct of foreign affairs to more legislative control in the United States than anywhere else.

In practice the President has more autonomous power in this field than in any other. He has avoided some of the difficulties involved in treaty-making under the Constitution by entering into executive agreements with other countries, which either require no congressional action or only a simple majority vote in both Houses. Important executive agreements during the Second World War, for example, were the destroyers-naval bases agreement with Great Britain in 1940, which required no congressional action, and the lend-lease agreements with Great Britain and other United Nations, which required simple acts of Congress. Executive agreements are as legally binding as treaties, and more executive agreements than treaties have been made. No distinction can be made between their subjects; indeed, agreements have sometimes replaced treaties the Senate has failed to ratify: an agreement pursuant to an act of Congress admitted Texas in 1845 after the Senate defeated a treaty of admission in 1844; and President Theodore Roosevelt made an agreement with Santo Domingo in 1905 extending United States control over that country after the Senate failed to ratify a treaty. But there are obvious reasons why an undertaking like the North Atlantic Treaty of 1949, with its long-term commitment of vital importance to Western European security, should be given a form that makes the strength of the commitment manifest.

The President reduces the effect of senatorial influence over diplomatic appointments by using agents who do not need senatorial confirmation. In 1791 President Washington informed the Senate that he had 'employed Mr. Gouverneur Morris, who was on the spot' to confer with the British Government about the further enforcement of the treaty of peace between the two countries. President Franklin Roosevelt's use of Harry Hopkins in keeping in touch with Prime Minister Churchill during the Second World War is well known. The President circumvents congressional power to declare war by waging war without a declaration. Presidents have sent naval units to fight the Barbary States, Marines to occupy Caribbean countries, and armed forces to repel aggression in Korea without declarations of war. Furthermore, though Congress occasionally tries to put restrictions on the movement of the armed forces, the President has maintained his authority to deploy them as he sees fit; when congressmen asserted that they would not provide the funds to send the American battleship fleet on a world cruise, President Theodore Roosevelt sent it on its way and challenged Congress not to appropriate the money to bring it back. And the President can provoke a declaration of war by his action: when President James Polk sent troops into a disputed area with Mexico in 1846, he helped produce a border incident that led to a declaration of war.

The Supreme Court has rationalized the role the President plays in the conduct of American foreign policy. In 1936 in the case of United States *v.* Curtiss-Wright Export Corporation Justice Sutherland was again responsible for a strange interpretation of the American Constitution. He explained, first:

'As a result of the separation from Great Britain by the colonies, acting as a unit, the powers of external sovereignty passed from the Crown not to the colonies severally, but to the colonies in their collective and corporate capacity as the United States of America. . . .

'It results that the investment of the federal government with the powers of external sovereignty did not depend upon the affirmative grants of the Constitution. The powers to declare and wage war, to conclude peace, to make treaties, to maintain diplomatic relations with other sovereignties, if they had never been mentioned in the Constitution, would have vested in the federal government as necessary concomitants of nationality. . . . As a member of the family of nations, the right and power of the United States in that field are equal to the right and power of the other members of the international family. Otherwise, the United States is not completely sovereign.'

In short, in international affairs the powers of the national government are not defined by the constitutional delegation of powers from the States but by international law. In international affairs the States do not exist.

Justice Sutherland explained, next:

'Not only, as we have shown, is the federal power over external affairs in origin and essential character different from that over internal affairs, but participation in the exercise of the power is significantly limited. In this vast external realm, with its important, complicated, delicate and manifold problems, the President alone has the power to speak or listen as a representative of the nation. . . . As Marshall said in his great argument of March 7, 1800, in the House of Representatives, "The President is the sole organ of the nation in its external relations, and its sole representative with foreign nations." '

And then, in effect, the argument moves from John Marshall to John Locke:

'It is important to bear in mind that we are here dealing not alone with an authority vested in the President by an exertion of legislative power, but with such authority plus the very delicate, plenary and exclusive power of the President as the sole organ of the federal government in the field of international relations—a power which does not require as a basis for its exercise an act of Congress, but which, of course, like every other governmental power, must be exercised in subordination to the applicable provisions of the Constitution. It is quite apparent that . . . congressional legislation which is to be made effective through negotiation and inquiry within the international field must often accord to the President a degree of discretion and freedom from statutory restriction which would not be admissible were domestic affairs alone involved.'

Here, unmistakably, is the federative power.

Most major presidential policies, however, ultimately require congressional support. Just as a list of examples may be given to show how the President evades congressional restraints, so may a list be given to show how Congress asserts itself. When congressional legislation is needed to implement an international compact, the Senate may insist on a treaty form or lay down the conditions of an executive agreement. The UNRRA agreement of 1943, for example, had to be implemented by congressional appropriations. The Senate required that the draft text be submitted to the Committee on Foreign Relations and that the agreement itself be incorporated in a joint resolution of Congress as the price for evading the two-thirds rule. The great majority of treaties submitted to the Senate have in fact been ratified without change, but some of the rejections and ratifications-with-amendments that amount to rejections have been important: the defeat of the Treaty of Versailles is the most famous example. Technically, only the President may terminate an international undertaking, but Congress may do so in effect even with the President's disapproval: the Japanese exclusion provisions of an immigration act of 1924 ended the friendly Gentleman's Agreement of 1908 which had virtually excluded the Japanese.

Congress provided most of the impulse within the national government leading to the War of 1812 and the Spanish-American War. It has sometimes sought to guide the President in according or withholding recognition of foreign governments: it urged the recognition of the American states that revolted against Spain before President James Monroe accorded them formal recognition in 1822; and it has expressed its strong opposition to the recognition of Communist China in recent years. It has sometimes forced the pace in other ways: in 1948–50 it appropriated money for military aid to the Chinese Nationalists and Franco Spain before President Truman asked for it; and though the President resisted direct dictation of his policy, he had to make concessions on those points in order to hold support for his general foreign aid programme.

Indeed, the President often seeks to assure the success of his main policies by co-operating with Congress. The efforts to develop and maintain presidential-congressional and bipartisan co-operation in foreign policy have received a good deal of attention in recent years, but many of the techniques have not been new: for example, Democratic-Republican President Madison included a Federalist Senator and the Speaker of the House of Representatives (who resigned from Congress to accept their commissions) in the delegation to negotiate the treaty ending the War of 1812; Whig President Zachary Taylor's Secretary of State, John Clayton, worked closely with Senators of both parties, particularly Democratic Senator W. R. King, Chairman of the Foreign Relations Committee, in negotiating and obtaining approval of the Clayton-Bulwer Treaty with Great Britain in 1850; and Republican President William McKinley named three Senators (who did not resign from the Senate), including the Chairman of the Foreign Relations Committee and one Democrat, in the delegation to negotiate the treaty ending the Spanish-American War. The defeat of the Treaty of Versailles was partly the result of President Wilson's refusal to take elementary precautions: he took no Senator and a Republican with no real standing in his party with him to Europe. The Republican presidents who followed him named key Senators of both parties as delegates to important conferences: the Washington Arms Conference of 1921 and the London Naval Conference of 1930, for example.

During the Second World War President Roosevelt was anxious to avoid a repetition of Wilson's blunders in the formal negotiations for a post-war settlement, though he kept the informal negotiations, from the 'Atlantic Charter' meeting with Churchill in 1941 to the Yalta meeting with Churchill and Stalin in 1945, in his own hands. The Democratic Secretaries of State under Roosevelt and Truman worked closely with congressmen of both parties and used members of both parties as key advisers in their efforts to create and maintain presidential-congressional co-operation and bipartisanship in foreign policy. (The practice of using members of the other party as major advisers was not followed by Eisenhower's Republican Secretary of State, John Foster Dulles, in his first two years in office.) A feature of the presidential-congressional co-operation has been the unusual deference paid to opinion in the House of Representatives; for appropriations have become extremely important in the conduct of American foreign policy. A feature of the bipartisanship was the unusual agreement between Secretary of State Cordell Hull representing President Roosevelt and John Foster Dulles representing Governor Dewey that discussions of the post-war United Nations organization during the 1944 presidential election would not be partisan.

The most significant aspects of the recent developments, however, have been the range and duration of co-operation. Co-operation has shaped the American part in creating UNRRA in 1943, the United Nations organization in 1945, the Rio Inter-American Treaty of 1947, the Marshall Plan in 1947, the North Atlantic Treaty of 1949, the Mutual Defense programme in 1949, the Japanese Peace and ANZUS treaties of 1951, and the South-East Asia Collective Defense Treaty of 1954. The achievements seem even more impressive when it is recalled that the Democrats held the presidency and the Republicans controlled Congress during 1947-8. Of necessity, the initiative has usually come from the President, though it has often been concealed by arranging for Congress to pass resolutions before the President takes formal action. But the support of congressmen of both parties has been essential. The late Senator Arthur Vandenberg, Republican, of Michigan, deserves more than anyone else to be known as the 'architect' of the most effective presidential-congressional co-operation in foreign policy in the history of the Republic.

Each branch dislikes the price it must pay, however. Presidential guidance has led to a reaction against it in Congress. In 1953-4 Senator John Bricker, Republican, of Ohio, led an attempt to amend the Constitution in order to restrict the treaty power and to subject executive agreements to more congressional control. On 26 February 1954 a mild version of the

'Bricker Amendment' sponsored by Senator Walter George, Democrat, of Georgia, failed to pass the Senate by one vote short of the necessary two-thirds majority. It is likely that further attempts will be made.

The Eisenhower administration opposed the 'Bricker Amendment', including the George version. The George version proposed only two changes of substance:

'A provision of a treaty or other international agreement which conflicts with this Constitution shall not be of any force or effect.

'An international agreement other than a treaty shall become effective as internal law in the United States only by an act of the Congress.'

The first proposal makes explicit what most constitutional lawyers are sure is already implicit: that a treaty, though made 'under the authority of the United States', is no more valid when it conflicts with the Constitution than an act of Congress, supposedly 'made in pursuance' of the Constitution. Only the fact that the Supreme Court has never held a treaty invalid on constitutional grounds makes the point debatable. The second proposal seems reasonable, especially since it would appear to allow Congress to continue to pass general acts like the Reciprocal Trade Agreements acts, which authorize the negotiation of a number of executive agreements. It would not be necessary to pass an act after each agreement is made. (It has been estimated that over four-fifths of the executive agreements made under the present arrangements are based on or receive statutory support.)

Administration spokesmen proclaimed their faith in constitutional provisions that had stood the test of over a century and a half. Their objections were obviously based, however, on the use they expected Congress to make of the second proposal. The price the President must pay for congressional support in foreign as in domestic affairs is deference to congressional 'logrolling' pressures, and the George version would permit Congress to force the President to pay a higher price. It is worth emphasizing that congressional support for the Marshall Plan was partly bought by administration concessions to the 'China lobby' in Congress. The limits of presidential influence in Congress force the President to become a 'log-roller' too. In all his roles—as the chief legislator, the chief executive, and the chief conductor of foreign policy—the President finds presidential-congressional co-operation inadequate. As a result, he seeks to preserve and extend his independent powers.

Finally, the general problem of presidential-congressional relations. The difficulties of presidential-congressional relations have had a long history, which began in President Washington's first term and had its most dramatic moment in the impeachment trial of President Andrew Johnson in 1868. The framers of the Constitution made presidential-congressional relations 'irresponsible' by making the President and Congress largely independent of each other. They made it difficult for the same faction to control the presidency and both Houses of Congress at the same time by making the modes of election and the terms of office different. Although the President's party has nominally controlled both Houses of Congress for his full term during ten of the fifteen terms since 1897—the record before 1897 was much worse—the hope of the framers has continued to be essentially fulfilled. The political parties have consisted of many loosely organized factional interests. They have only intermittently had sufficient coherence and discipline to ensure effective co-operation between the President and 'his majorities' in Congress. The breakdown point in presidential-congressional relations was reached only in Johnson's administration, following a civil war; it has usually been possible for the President and Congress, whatever its partisan composition, to agree on more than a minimal programme; but it has usually been impossible for them to agree on anything like a full one.

The increased importance of American national government in this century has enhanced the authority of the President, who is at the head of the expanded and expert bureaucracy. The growth of presidential leadership in the early years of the century was marked by the change in emphasis in Woodrow Wilson's essays on American government: he wrote a penetrating account of 'congressional government' in 1885 and a stirring description of the opportunities for presidential leadership in 1908 in which he came to the frequently quoted conclusion that the President's 'office is anything he has the sagacity and force to make it'. He made a good deal of it in his own tenure of the office. The growth of presidential leadership was accelerated after President Franklin Roosevelt took office in 1933, and it is now almost inconceivable that the long-term trend will be reversed. President Eisenhower sought for a time to make a virtue of lack of leadership, but he has pressed recommendations on Congress, put his views on a wide range of subjects in news conferences that are reported and now televised throughout the nation, and explained his policies in speeches to the people on a scale not approached by President Hoover a quarter of a century ago.

Yet the President often fails to carry Congress with him. President Wilson's foreign policy was wrecked in the Senate. President Roosevelt was able to lead Congress in his first years in office, under the pressure of the great depression, but not in the years immediately before the American entry into the Second World War. His war leadership was largely independent of Congress. Despite the achievements of presidential-congressional co-operation in foreign policy since the War, President Truman's relations with Congress often degenerated into mutual name-calling.

A perennial source of presidential-congressional disagreement is that the President represents the whole of America and Congress its parts. Perhaps more important at present is that the President depends primarily on the support of urban voters and most congressmen, especially senior congressmen, depend on the support of rural and small-town voters. In other words, the President and Congress represent respectively the post-1933 and pre-1933 aspects of American politics. The difference is greater when the President is a Democrat because a Democratic President is even more dependent on urban support than a Republican one. But the division between presidential and congressional politics exists in both parties.

In this situation the President and Congress have strengthened the institutions of conflict. It was pointed out in the preceding chapter that the use of the Executive Office of the President instead of the cabinet to co-ordinate administration has protected the President's 'irresponsibility'. It was pointed out several times in this chapter that the President has sought to develop his independent powers as well as his influence in Congress. For its part, Congress reformed itself in the Legislative Reorganization Act of 1946 that cut back the growth of standing committees and expanded the staffs of the committees, the Legislative Reference Service of the Library of the Congress (which collects information, chiefly from published sources, for committees and members), and the Offices of the Legislative Counsels of the two Houses (which assist committees and members in drafting legislation). Congressmen hope to make their own organization efficient and expert, and thus reduce their dependence on executive guidance. They, too, seek to develop their independence.

In sum, American congressmen accept a large measure of presidential leadership only when they feel strongly that something must be done. Then they are willing to face the fact that on the whole the President, as head of the national administration, is better able to give the lead than they. They accept presidential guidance in grave, sharply defined crises like those produced by the great depression of the early 1930's and the Russian threat of the late 1940's, though they quite properly insist that the President justify his proposals. (The fact that a few of the first proposals of President Roosevelt were rushed through Congress in 1933 virtually without consideration has given plausibility to the charge that the New Deal Congresses were 'rubber stamps', but the great majority of the New Deal measures were examined closely and amended in important respects.) However, when a sense of crisis is lacking, or when the crisis is not clearly defined, congressmen are less willing to give their support. It is easier to win congressional approval, for example, of remedial than of preventive measures: of a Marshall Plan than of Point Four.

As a result, the President often tries to win approval of his proposals by imparting a sense of immediate need—and, sometimes unintentionally, an expectation of quick results. He thus makes it appear that American policy is determined in a succession of panics. The attempt of the Eisenhower administration to create a sense of crisis in Congress and the country about the Indo-Chinese situation in the spring of 1954 is a case in point. The truth is that American presidential-congressional co-operation works best in crises, real or artificial, with the result that the current long continuous international tension tends to be treated as a series of short discrete crises to which the American political system responds.

What is required, then, is a more satisfactory continuous relationship between the President and Congress so that the President may exercise a steady guidance in congressional 'consensus'. Formal amendments to the Constitution are extremely unlikely to be adopted. But an increase in the President's political influence in Congress is likely to develop from the slow growth of urban post-1933 influences in congressional politics. Students of American politics argue a great deal about the extent to which the structure of the national parties in and outside Congress can be—or ought to be—reformed to encourage the change. It seems certain, however, that when political conditions become propitious, presidential-congressional relations will be improved, whether sufficiently or not, within the framework of the Constitution of 1787.

Chapter 10

State and Local Government

Each of the forty-eight States has a written Constitution, which, like that of the nation, is superior to and more difficult to amend than ordinary law. A State Constitution, however, is usually less 'constitutional' than the national one: it contains more clauses dealing with other matters than the organization of the government and the definition of civil liberties and rights. It also describes the governmental system in more detail.

As a result, few State Constitutions are brief. The length of the Constitution of the United States, including its amendments, is usually put at from 6,000 to 7,500 words. A few State Constitutions are about the same length; but the great majority are at least twice as long; and a few are at least six to ten times as long. State Constitutions have, on the whole, grown in length through the years, whether by the addition of amendments to old Constitutions or by the substitution of new Constitutions for old. The California legislature estimated in 1947 that its State Constitution of 1879, originally about 16,000 words long, had grown to over 72,000 words by the addition of 256 amendments.

Framers of the most recent Constitutions have sought to avoid excessive length. Although the framers of the Missouri Constitution of 1945, the first completely revised State Constitution adopted after 1921, produced a text said to be about 30,000 words long, it is estimated that they thus reduced the length of the State Constitution by about 11,000 words. Although the framers of the New Jersey Constitution of 1947 produced a text longer than that replaced, the new Constitution, including the long article giving the schedule by which it took effect, is not more than twice the length of the national Constitution. Even its comparatively brief provisions, however, reflect the common practice of putting or retaining what amount to definitions of public policy, normally the province of ordinary law, in the constitutional text. The reason for the practice is that it is harder, at least in form, to change policies given constitutional protection.

Thus the New Jersey Constitution declares that the State legislature 'shall provide for the maintenance and support of a thorough and efficient system of free public schools for the instruction of all the children in the State between the ages of five and eighteen years'. It protects the existing tax exemption of 'real and personal property used exclusively for religious, educational, charitable and cemetery purposes'. It provides for the tax exemption of 'real and personal property to an aggregate assessed valuation not exceeding five hundred dollars' possessed by any 'citizen and resident of this State now or hereafter honorably discharged or released under honorable circumstances from active service in time of war in any branch of the armed forces of the United States' or by the 'widow of any citizen and resident of this State who has met or shall meet his death on active duty in time of war in any such service', during her widowhood. Concessions to educational, religious, and ex-servicemen's pressure groups are very common in the State Constitutions.

Almost all State Constitutions contain more definitions of policy than the New Jersey Constitution. The shortened Missouri Constitution, while no longer retaining a prohibition of duelling, provides, for example, that the State legislature shall not have the power 'to authorize lotteries or gift enterprises for any purpose, and shall enact laws to prohibit the sale of lottery or gift enterprise tickets, or tickets in any scheme in the nature of a lottery'. It declares that the State legislature

'shall provide an annual tax of not less than one-half of one cent nor more than three cents on the one hundred dollars valuation of all taxable property to be levied and collected as other taxes, for the purpose of providing a fund to be appropriated and used for the pensioning of the deserving blind as provided by law.'

Among the provisions of other State Constitutions, according to a list compiled in the 1940's, are a ban on removing timber from State forests and a limit on the duration of prize-fight rounds to not more than three minutes each.

The details of the financial clauses of State Constitutions are often written to protect or help special groups. Maximum tax rate provisions protect property owners in general: the Missouri Constitution provides that the tax rate on intangible personal property shall not exceed 8 per cent of its yield. Exemptions, like those quoted from the New Jersey Constitution, protect certain classes of owners. Part of the revenue is allocated to particular purposes, as in the provision of the Missouri Constitution relating to the deserving blind. The Missouri Constitution also declares that:

'. . . All appropriations of money by successive general assemblies shall be made in the following order:
    First: For payment of sinking fund and interest on outstanding obligations of the State.
    Second: For the purpose of public education.
    Third: For the payment of the cost of assessing and collecting the revenue.
    Fourth: For the payment of the civil lists.
    Fifth: For the support of eleemosynary and other institutions.
    Sixth: For public health and public welfare.
    Seventh: For all other State purposes.
    Eighth: For the expense of the general assembly.'

Other financial restrictions in State Constitutions include requirements of uniform tax rates for all kinds of property, prohibitions of certain taxes, and severe curtailment of the borrowing power. Both the Missouri and New Jersey Constitutions, for example, contain provisions for submitting to popular referenda proposals entailing the assumption of debts above certain strict limits.

Local government finance especially is often put in a constitutional strait-jacket. On the one hand, rate limits and exemptions restrict the yield of the prime source of local tax revenue, the general property tax. On the other hand, allocations of revenue take a share of what yield there is. Restrictions on borrowing sometimes hamper the development of capital improvements. In a few States the restrictions have also been a source of minor constitutional amendments raising the debt limits of particular local communities. It should be pointed out that while provisions of the Missouri and New Jersey Constitutions have been cited to illustrate recent impositions or reaffirmations of constitutional financial restrictions, the Missouri Constitution of 1945 made, for example, the limits on local tax rates somewhat more flexible than in the past and the New Jersey Constitution contains no absolute rate restrictions at all.

Constitutionally, State governments are not governments of enumerated powers. They possess all powers other than: those delegated to the national government by the national Constitution; those, if any, delegated to the local governments by the State Constitutions; and those reserved to the people by the national and State Constitutions, as in their Bills of Rights. Yet some of the State powers are defined in the State Constitutions as parts of the concessions to special interests illustrated above and, since it is not clear precisely what powers the State governments have retained, in order to reverse or forestall the invalidation of State legislation by the State courts. Thus, after the highest court of New York State held a workman's compensation law invalid in 1911, a constitutional amendment was adopted granting the power to enact such a law. The New Jersey Constitution of 1947 declares that 'the clearance, replanning, development or redevelopment of blighted areas shall be a public purpose and public use, for which private property may be taken or acquired', provided just compensation is paid. In effect many State governments have become governments of enumerated powers.

Many of the details of the State Constitutions relating to State powers are designed to eliminate abuses by the political branches. The States charter business corporations in the

United States. Bribing State legislators to pass special charters was for a long time a notorious corrupt practice in American politics, which reformers sought to curb even before the Civil War. It is common, therefore, for State Constitutions to ban special charters. Many Constitutions also contain provisions setting certain standards for general incorporation acts.

Most State Constitutions prohibit or severely restrict the enactment of private, special, or local legislation generally. The Missouri and New Jersey Constitutions forbid the passage, for example, of such legislation: changing the law of descent; affecting the estates of minors or persons under disability; vacating any road, street, alley, or town plot; changing the venue in civil or criminal cases; summoning or empanelling grand or petit juries; regulating the management of public schools; granting any corporation, association, or individual the right to lay down a railway track; or granting any corporation, association, or individual any exclusive right, privilege, or immunity. The last provisions reinforce the ban on special charters.

Most State Constitutions extend the prohibitions to include local acts affecting the internal affairs of counties and municipalities. The passage of local acts has often been used in the American States to penalize political opponents of the dominant factions in the legislatures. The fact that the dominant factions have almost always consisted mainly of rural representatives has meant that the brunt of the penalties has fallen on the cities. The attempt to remove the abuse by constitutional prohibition, however, may not prevent it taking another form. General legislation, particularly financial legislation, may in effect discriminate against city governments too. Efforts to improve the structure of State government by detailed constitutional descriptions of the separation of powers, which will be referred to in the next section, have also been only partly successful.

Constitutions are likely to reflect the political ideals of their communities. American State Constitutions have often reflected the political good intentions of State citizens in their detailed provisions, moreover, because constitutional conventions, by far the most common bodies for drafting constitutional revisions, have often attracted people who do not deign to engage in

STATE AND LOCAL GOVERNMENT

ordinary politics but seek to hedge in by constitutional restrictions the 'rascals' who do. Fortunately, the distinction between 'reformers' and 'politicians' now seems to be diminishing. The prospects are promising that members of most constitutional conventions will henceforth think somewhat less about how to make bad government impossible and somewhat more about how to make good government possible. On the whole, the members of the New Jersey convention of 1947 set an unusually fine example.

Since the conventions are elected by the people, they are usually responsible to them and not to the ordinary organs of the government. In some States the legislature can restrict the subjects with which a convention may deal. Thus the New Jersey convention of 1947 was not allowed to alter representation in the State legislature, which as in almost every State favours rural voters. In other States the legislature cannot interfere with the work of the convention at all. In these States the rural interest often obstructs a movement for a convention, but may permit the establishment of a constitutional commission to submit proposals to the legislature.

In any case a plan for major constitutional revision is usually submitted to a popular referendum. Likewise, amendments to a State Constitution, initiated either by the legislature (in almost all States) or by petition of the voters (in about one-fourth of the States), are submitted to the people in almost all the States. In nearly one-fourth of the States a special majority of some kind is required for adoption: a majority of all votes cast in the election in which an amendment appears on the general ballot, for example. The proponents of an amendment must, therefore, arouse sufficient interest in it to overcome the voter fatigue induced by the long ballot. Some idea of the variations in ease and frequency of amendment is given by pointing out that the Tennessee Constitution of 1870 was not amended until 1953, by which time the Louisiana Constitution of 1921 had had over 300 amendments (and had become over 180,000 words long). The ease and frequency with which new Constitutions are adopted varies, too, though the fact that some States have carried out major revisions without making formal substitutions makes comparisons misleading: the Massachusetts Constitution of 1780, for example, was 'rearranged' by a convention in 1919. The great majority of the present State Constitutions, however, are basically late-nineteenth- and early-twentieth-century documents. No State Constitution—no written Constitution anywhere—has withstood the passage of time so well as the Constitution of the United States.

Indeed, paradoxically, though the provisions of State Constitutions are generally much newer than those of the national Constitution, they are often more out of date. They have often defined too precisely the state of political thought and the balance of political forces at a given time; and while amendments are frequently added in many States, they do not adjust old clauses to new circumstances quickly. The clauses and laws perpetuating rural overrepresentation have perhaps the worst effect, since rural overrepresentation perpetuates in turn other clauses ill adapted to an increasingly urban society. The national Constitution also preserves rural overrepresentation, but without producing a comparable secondary effect. Its provisions permit a wide measure of adaptation by law, interpretation, and usage. The framers of 1787 wrote a Constitution which is reasonably brief and obscure. But in constitution-making, as in much else, good writing has been more admired than emulated.

Although the refrain of any discussion of the detail of State and local government must be that it varies from State to State, it is possible to generalize about the basic structure of American State government as defined by the State Constitutions. Like the national Constitution, each State Constitution has a Bill of Rights, generally containing the sort of seventeenth- and eighteenth-century definitions of rights found in the national document, though the New Jersey Constitution of 1947, for example, adds to the usual list a declaration that persons 'in private employment shall have the right to organize and bargain collectively'. It would be a mistake to say that the States have copied the nation; for the thirteen original States had Constitutions before the nation, and the national Bill of Rights contains provisions found in some of them. New States received the common American heritage.

Like the national Constitution, too, each State Constitution provides for the separation of powers among three branches: an executive branch headed by a single elective chief executive, the Governor; a legislative branch consisting of two roughly equal chambers, except in Nebraska, which has had a uni-cameral legislature since 1937; and a judicial branch. Provisions for the separation of powers were also present in American government before the Constitution of 1787 was written: a large measure of separation of powers had been present in colonial governments; and the doctrine was explicitly pro-claimed as fundamental to its constitutional system in the Mas-sachusetts Constitution of 1780, for example. But the national Constitution had a profound impact on subsequent State con-stitution-making, even in the original States. At the time it was written there was a good deal of variety among the institutions of the several States, though most States had weak executive and strong legislative branches, measured by either the old colonial or new national standard. Traces of the influence of varying early governmental systems may still be detected among the original States; New York has a stronger Governor than North Carolina, for example, as under their first Constitutions. The general effect of the national model, however, has been to induce a more uniform pattern of executive-legislative rela-tions in the United States than would otherwise have been the case.

The main difference between national and State constitu-tional arrangements is the greater measure of direct democracy in the latter. Most States have several directly elected officers besides the Governor, most often the Lieutenant-Governor (though some States do not have this office at all), Secretary of State, Treasurer, Auditor or Comptroller, Attorney General, and the head of the educational services. In most States also the voters elect most or all of the judges. About one-fourth of the States permit the electors to petition and then vote for the recall of executive officers, and perhaps judges, before their terms have expired. About a score of States permit the voters to initiate or challenge the enactment of bills by petition; initiated bills may be ratified in some States only by popular referendum and in others also by the State legislature; challenged bills are submitted to the voters. Constitutional provisions that require the submission of bills entailing the creation of debts to popular referendum were mentioned in the last section; and similar provisions sometimes apply to intoxicating beverage or gambling bills, for example.

The working of State government may be briefly described by considering the State Governor as a legislator as well as an executive officer. Like the President of the United States, the State Governor is formally placed at the beginning and end of the legislative process. He may send messages to the legislature, and in many States he may convene special sessions that must consider proposals he sends them and nothing else. The power to convene special sessions, which the President and every Governor have, is more important in State than national government anyway, since regular sessions are usually more infrequent—in over three-fourths of the States they are biennial—and often constitutionally restricted in duration—to about sixty days, for example. The Governor of every State except North Carolina has the power to veto legislation. The veto may be overridden by majorities ranging from a simple majority of those voting in each chamber of the legislature to a two-thirds majority of the full membership in each. In half the States the latter rule applies.

The Constitution of the State of Washington permits the Governor to veto any section of any bill while approving the rest. The New Jersey Constitution, for example, contains the following provisions:

'To avoid improper influences which may result from intermixing in one and the same act such things as have no proper relation to each other, every law shall embrace but one object, and that shall be expressed in the title. This paragraph shall not invalidate any law adopting or enacting a compilation, consolidation, revision, or rearrangement of all or parts of the statutory law. . . .

'No general law shall embrace any provision of a private, special, or local character.'

If enforced, the prohibitions make the normal veto power somewhat more effective. The following provision, also found in the New Jersey Constitution, makes it more flexible:

'. . . The Governor, in returning with his objections a bill for reconsideration at any general or special session of the Legislature, may recommend that an amendment or amendments specified by him be made in the bill, and in such case the legislature may amend and re-enact the bill. If a bill be so amended and re-enacted, it shall be presented again to the Governor, but shall become a law only if he shall sign it within ten days after presentation; and no bill shall be returned by the Governor a second time.'

On the other hand, the New Jersey Constitution curtails the opportunities for exercising a pocket veto by requiring a recall of the legislature in special session forty-five days, Sundays excepted, after it has adjourned *sine die* for the sole purpose of receiving veto messages, unless the forty-fifth day falls on or after the last day of the legislative year, in which case the Governor has a pocket veto. This provision strikes at the gubernatorial veto power at what is usually its strongest point. For most bills passed in the short State legislative sessions often do not reach the governors, the great majority of whom have an absolute power of pocket veto, until the legislatures are about to adjourn.

In the intermediate stages of legislation, the Governor, like the President, relies on patronage, party, personal contacts, and public opinion.

Legislative machinery in the States is generally even less integrated than in the nation. In almost all States each House has a set of committees; in the others the two Houses have a joint set. There are more legislative standing committees, on the average, in a State legislature than in Congress. Although nearly all State legislatures are organized along party lines, party influence is usually weaker in State than national policy-

making, particularly in virtually one-party States. The extreme
congestion of business in the last days of State legislative sessions,
when many bills from the committees are passed by almost completely irresponsible 'log-rolling', is due to the weakness of
general supervision of legislative activity as well as to the short-
ness of the sessions. A few State Constitutions have sought to
prevent congestion by requiring split sessions: in general, bills
are to be introduced in the first part and passed or rejected in
the second; but the device has not worked well. The Massachusetts legislature, one of the very few with a full set of joint
committees, has rules which pace the passage of legislation
effectively. Technical improvements in procedure, however,
strike at effects instead of causes.

In an effort to give the content of legislation more coherence,
legislative councils have been set up in most States since 1933,
usually consisting of members from both parties in each House
and in a few cases also the Governor or his appointees. The
councils try to prepare the ground for the legislative work of the
sessions, and in at least a few States they have succeeded in improving legislative integration. Since the Governors do not
usually work with them, however, they have not usually fos-
tered executive-legislative co-operation. Like the growth of the
administrative staff of Congress, the development of the legislative councils seems to have been primarily the result of the
desire of legislators not to become dependent on the expert
advice of the executive bureaucracy. In a few States administrative agencies seem to have strong influence in the legislature:
in New York, for example. But in most the executive branch
probably has less influence than in the nation.

The Governor is a weaker chief executive than the President.
His power to appoint the members of the central State administration is limited by the popular and, much less commonly,
legislative election of several of the most important executive
officers of the State as well as by the requirement that most of
his appointees must receive the approval of the upper House of
the State legislature in the great majority of States and of an
executive council in most of the others. Moreover, he is often
required to appoint members of a comparatively large number

of regulatory and supervisory boards for long and overlapping terms, perhaps on a bipartisan basis, and perhaps with regard for technical qualifications prescribed by law. His power to remove is limited by the status of most elective officers, who can be removed only by conviction on impeachment (and perhaps recall), and by the status of some elective and appointive officers, who may be protected from removal, for example, at least to the extent that the upper House or executive council must concur in the Governor's decision. His power to direct is limited, partly by the Constitution, partly by law, much more than the President's.

In this century the trend has been to enhance the Governor's administrative authority. The framers of the New Jersey Constitution of 1947 made the most radical changes, though the State legislature has not integrated the administrative system as much as the Constitution permits. Under the new as under the old Constitution of the State, only the Governor is elected by the people; and under the new Constitution, only the State Auditor is elected by the legislature. The new Constitution provides that all administrative agencies, except temporary commissions, shall be allocated 'among and within not more than twenty principal departments, in such manner as to group the same according to major purposes so far as practicable'. It declares that each 'principal department shall be under the supervision of the Governor'. It provides that the 'head of each principal department shall be a single executive unless otherwise provided by law'. Such single executives are appointed by the Governor with the consent of the State Senate and serve at his pleasure, except that the Secretary of State and Attorney General serve full terms with the Governor. If a board or commission is made head of a department, the Governor appoints the members with the consent of the Senate but may remove them only 'in the manner provided by law'. Such boards or commissions may, when authorized by law, appoint principal executive officers for their departments, who must be approved by the Governor and may be removed by him 'upon notice and an opportunity to be heard'.

At the beginning of 1953 five of the fourteen principal departments were headed by a board or commission: Agriculture, Civil Service, Education, Institutions and Agencies, and Public Utilities. The other principal departments were: State, Banking and Insurance, Conservation and Economic Development, Defense (dealing with State 'National Guard' and civil defence activities), Health, Labor and Industry, Law and Public Safety, the Treasury, and State Highway Department.

Another trend in State administration has been the slow growth of the merit system of appointment. All States have a partial system now, though in perhaps only about half of them is it fairly extensive and effective. This trend helps the Governor, too, since patronage appointments are usually dispensed under a State form of 'senatorial courtesy' but the Governor is usually blamed by the public for corruption and incompetence in administration.

As in the national government, the balance of power between the chief executive and the legislature in administrative affairs is partially reflected in budgetary procedures. In Arkansas the legislative council makes the budget recommendations, assisted in part by the budget division of the Department of Finance and Administration. In a few States a budgetary board or commission, usually consisting of the Governor as chairman and either a few other executive officers or two other executive officers and two legislators as members, prepares the executive budget. In most States the Governor supervises the work, though the direct responsibility is usually in the hands of another executive officer. At the preparatory stage, then, the Governor's influence is sometimes nominally and often actually less than the President's.

At the legislative stage it can be greater. A few State legislatures, for example, cannot in general increase the amounts or insert new items of expenditure in the budgets. In three-fourths of the States the Governor has the right to veto items of an appropriation bill. In some States he also has the right to reduce items of expenditure in a bill as part of his veto power; but, unaccompanied in these States by any check on legislative increases of budget estimates, this right makes it convenient for legislators to please their constituents by raising amounts which they believe the Governor will feel constrained to cut back despite the unpopularity he incurs. In sum, the Governor is usually able, if he wills, to check the worst abuses arising from legislative 'log-rolling'.

It may seem that in some respects presidential leadership and gubernatorial leadership are taking different courses. During the last two periods of strong presidential leadership, the Progressive Era and the New Deal period, there was much stronger gubernatorial leadership on the broad questions of public policy that received most popular attention in the first than in the second. In the Progressive Era the fight for fundamental constitutional reform and government supervision of business practices was waged as vigorously, and sometimes as effectively, by State governors like Robert LaFollette of Wisconsin, Woodrow Wilson of New Jersey, and Hiram Johnson of California, as by presidents like Theodore Roosevelt and Woodrow Wilson. In the New Deal period the fight for economic recovery was waged primarily by President Franklin Roosevelt. Leading governors of the last decade, like Thomas Dewey of New York, Earl Warren of California, and Adlai Stevenson of Illinois, have usually won their reputations as governors chiefly as effective administrators and advocates of 'clean government'. Constitutional trends strengthening the gubernatorial veto, administrative, and budgetary powers support the growth of this kind of strong governor.

The obvious explanation is that the traditional functions of the national government, foreign policy and defence for example, have become much more important politically and many economic and social functions seem to have been shifted from the State governments to the national government. Consequently, presidential leadership in the nation overshadows gubernatorial leadership in the States. Yet within its field gubernatorial leadership in matters of policy usually serves, as does presidential leadership, as the guiding force, if any, of legislative 'consensus' and the protecting force, if any, of the general interest.

State legislatures are badly organized. They are misrepresentative. St. Louis, Missouri, had about 860,000 inhabitants in 1950; it is probably the only city of comparable size or larger in the United States that has representation proportionate to its population in even one House of the State legislature. The Missouri Constitution of 1945 contains a provision that seeks to ensure that apportionment in the State Senate will always be adjusted to changes in the distribution of population; for failure to reapportion is the chief cause of rural overrepresentation in the Houses of State legislatures that are supposed to be based on population. The United States Conference of Mayors estimated in 1949 that the urban three-fifths of the population elected only one-quarter of the State legislators.

The Governor of a State is fairly elected. (However, the Democratic party of Georgia, which elects all its governors, uses an electoral vote system based on county units that greatly favours rural counties.) The legislature is often unfairly dominated by rural and small-town voters. If it is true that the President and Congress tend to represent 'two nations', it is even more true that the State Governor and legislature often tend to represent 'two States'. Gubernatorial influence in the legislature is sometimes virtually the only influence in it reflecting the interests of the State as a whole. Unfortunately, like presidential influence in Congress, it often has inadequate effect.

The structure of American local government varies not only from State to State but also within the States. The Constitution or laws of a State often allow some of the local communities, usually cities, a measure of 'home rule' in defining the organs and powers of their governments. In 1950 New Jersey, for example, authorized the voters of cities to choose among no fewer than fourteen forms of governmental organization; and Illinois permits the voters of a county to decide whether to vest the powers of local government in the county government or to divide them between it and smaller governmental units. On the other hand, the State sometimes restricts the authority of particular cities in particular fields. In Massachusetts, for example, the Governor of the State appoints the head of the police of Boston but of no other city. This variety of American local government should be kept in mind in reading any general statements about it.

In the late eighteenth century the important units of local government in the thirteen original States were: the county, present in all the States and predominant in the South; the town, mixed with the county in the Middle States and predominant in New England; and the chartered municipality, a few of which were scattered among the States outside New England. This beginning helps account for the general pattern of American local government to-day. County government exists almost everywhere. Strong county government is important throughout the South and in most of the West. Strong town government is important in New England. A mixture of county and township government, the township being a type of town appropriate to less compact communities, is important in the Middle Atlantic States and most of the Midwest. Incorporated municipalities are important throughout the country. In addition, myriads of single-purpose (or at least almost single-purpose) authorities, most of them school districts, have been created, though many of the school districts are now being consolidated or abolished. They have been associated especially with the region comprising the States of Iowa, Kansas, Minnesota, Missouri, Nebraska, and North and South Dakota. The numbers of the different kinds of local government units in the United States in 1952 were given in Chapter 4.

Counties, towns, and municipalities usually and townships and special districts always are part of a two- or multi-tier system of local government. Cities in Virginia and a few in other States, for example, are the equivalents of English county boroughs, but they are exceptions to the general rule.

A county is partly governed by a board in every State but Rhode Island, whose counties are not governmental units. The board is almost always elective. More than two-thirds of the county boards have fewer than six members. A very few have over fifty members. The county board exercises at least part, if not all, of the rule-making powers and some of the administrative powers of the county government. There are separately elected (occasionally appointed) officers, such as the sheriff, prosecuting attorney, coroner, and clerk, who exercise other administrative powers largely independently. County judges are also separately elected or appointed.

A town, which is now usually rural, because urban towns have become incorporated municipalities, is governed by an annual town meeting, though in the larger towns a partial system of representation may be used. The town meeting elects a board of selectmen or town council to serve as its executive committee and other officers and committees, such as the town clerk and school board, to carry out specific functions. A township is governed by either an elective board or a single elective officer with an elective advisory board, but at least a vestige of a town meeting is present in some States. A municipality is governed by an elective mayor and council, commission, or council. A special district is usually governed by an elected or, less often, State or county appointed board.

The most important type of incorporated municipality, and the local government with the most intensively developed range of local functions, is the city. Lesser municipalities may be called villages or boroughs, though the nomenclature is by no means uniformly used. In some States all municipalities are called cities, divided into classes. The city has been the focus of American experiments with forms of government in this century.

The once standard form is the mayor and council city government. It is still found in many small and medium-sized cities and in the very large ones. The mayor is a directly elected officer, whose relations with the council are similar to those of a Governor with a State legislature. At one time city councils, on the analogy of Congress and State legislatures, were usually bicameral, but they are rarely so now. They are usually small bodies of about ten to thirty members, elected by wards or at large or both. The New York City Council has twenty-six members and the Chicago City Council fifty. In the cities where the mayor is weak—with only limited power of appointment, control over other officials, and veto, if any, on council activity—the council is thus usually small enough to be able to control the city government in some detail. For over half a century, however, the trend has been to strengthen the mayor.

Since 1900 many cities have adopted the commission form of government. The commission usually consists of five members, all of whom are elected by the voters of the whole city. Municipal administrative units are grouped in a corresponding number of departments, each commissioner heading a department. One of the commissioners serves formally as the mayor, designated as such either by the voters or, less frequently, his colleagues; but he usually has no authority in that capacity. The commission itself is the co-ordinating administrative authority as well as the rule-making authority of the city.

Since 1914 many cities have adopted the council-manager or commission-manager form of government. As in the commission form, there is a small council or commission headed by a titular mayor, and the council is the rule-making authority of the city. But it hires a professional administrator, the city manager, as the head of administration. The commission and council manager forms of government are among the reforms sponsored by the Progressives in local government. Another was that local government elections should be non-partisan; and local government elections in the majority of cities that have adopted the commission or council-manager forms of government (and in many of those that have not) are at least nominally so.

The new forms of government eliminate some of the wasteful and irresponsible obstruction that is associated with mayor and council government, but they have drawbacks. The commission form lacks adequate provision for the administrative co-ordination required in all but the smallest cities. The council-manager form is rationalized by a distinction between policy and administration that is hard to make manifest, especially in very large cities. The commission form has lost ground fairly rapidly, largely to the commission-manager or council-manager form, after its early gains. The manager form continues generally to gain ground, even in counties, a few of which now have county managers, but was abandoned in Cleveland, the largest city (about 910,000 inhabitants in 1950) that adopted it. The strengthening of the mayor in the mayor and council form has been the most successful reform in the metropoli. (The mayor and council form is not incompatible, of course, with the use of

238

professional administrators under the mayor.) Similarly, non-partisan politics has proved more practicable in small communities than large. Perhaps what is most needed, especially in large cities, is better partisan politics.

Municipal administration usually deals with police and fire protection, health and sanitation, planning and zoning, roads and other public works, public utilities, and public welfare. In 1950, moreover, about one-third of the cities with more than 25,000 inhabitants administered educational services; otherwise, overlapping units of local governments administered them. Other overlapping units often deal with some aspects of the activities already mentioned, but they do not add others to the list. Rural local administration, though less developed than urban, has about the same general range of activities. None of the categories is dealt with exclusively by local administration, however: the State administers directly some aspects of all of them.

The pattern of local and State administration is confused further by the fact that local government units are both local governments and administrative units of the State. It is impossible to draw a precise line between local activities carried on in pursuance of local powers and those carried on in administering State powers, though it may be said that the municipalities have more activities of the first kind than the other local governments. In any case the strength of local governments in the United States has rested on both governmental powers and administrative autonomy. The devolution of the administration of many State functions on local authorities has meant that the functions have been executed by officials who are usually locally elected or appointed and subject to little central administrative supervision. State officials usually lack the power to veto their selection and often lack the power to veto or alter their decisions. Since the State duties of local officials are legally defined by the State legislatures, the State courts exercise some control over them; but judicial oversight is not a substitute for administrative direction.

Moreover, the political environment favours local units of government. The political parties are highly decentralized. So, in some respects, is the press. The absence of national newspapers like those in England does not mean that accounts of national politics usually have a strong regional flavour. The national press services and syndicated columnists (and, in another medium, the national radio and television networks and commentators) have largely killed that. But it does mean that the papers most Americans read cover local politics more thoroughly than the papers most Englishmen read. These facts probably partly explain why American reactions to national politics are tending to become more uniform throughout the country without, for example, forcing local elections to be fought largely on national issues.

Local government and administration is becoming relatively less important in the American States, however. The State governments have taken over parts of functions once almost entirely delegated to or devolved on local authorities. They have established State police forces, for example, which often act only as highway patrols, but more often perform other duties as well; and more and more they administer educational services, legally a State function in every State, directly.

The States have increased the degree of administrative supervision of local officials when the officials administer State functions. State supervision of educational services still administered locally, for example, is ever more exacting. The States have also increased the degree of administrative supervision of local officials when the officials administer local functions. Supervision of local government financial procedures, for example, is ever more exacting, too. Supervision of local personnel policies, however, has developed much more slowly, except in education. This is one reason why the merit system is very weak in local administration, except in education.

One cause of the decline in the relative importance of local government is that its general structure is grossly inefficient, consisting of many small and overlapping units, which are often too small in size and power to administer activities effectively as single units and usually unwilling or unable to administer them effectively in co-operation. On the whole, resistance to State centralization is much more easily overcome than resistance to local government reform; consequently, State-local administration is improved much more by centralization than by local consolidation. Another cause is fiscal. As the nation is a more effective tax collector than the States, so the States are more effective tax collectors than the local units. Probably no amount of local government reform can eliminate the difference.

American general property taxes are the fiscal equivalent of English 'rates', though on capital rather than annual value. In theory they are usually levied on almost all forms of property, but in practice they are collected primarily on real estate. In 1915 the States raised about half their tax revenue from property taxes and local governments about nine-tenths of theirs. In 1951 the States raised about 28 per cent of their tax revenue from motor fuel taxes and vehicle licences; about 22 per cent from general sales, gross receipts, and use taxes; about 17 per cent from individual and corporation net income taxes; about 6 per cent from alcoholic beverage taxes and licences; about 5 per cent from tobacco taxes; about 13 per cent from other sales taxes and licences; about 2 per cent from severance taxes on the extraction of natural resources; about 2 per cent from death and gift duties; and about 4 per cent from property taxes. In 1951 local governments raised about 88 per cent of their tax revenue from property taxes—and most of the rest from sales taxes and licences.

The practical limits of State tax yields are set partly by State competition, because large differentials in State tax rates may drive taxable activities from heavily taxing to lightly taxing States. The practical limits are set partly, too, by national tax policy; for example, the existence of the national income tax as well as State competition holds down State income taxes. (Some States do not levy them at all.) But State governments have been able to shift from property to other taxes. On the other hand, local tax competition severely restricts local use of non-property taxes. Local tax competition and constitutional, legal, and political barriers restrict the use of property taxes too. Unable to exploit sufficiently either new or old sources of tax revenue, local governments surrender some functions to the States and receive increased amounts of State grants-in-aid in order to maintain, and develop, others. The grants are often accompanied by administrative controls, which could usually be imposed by the State legislatures anyway, but which are more easily accepted when attached to grants.

Local political forces resist the centralizing trend in the States as in the nation. The State legislatures often provide that the revenue of certain State-imposed taxes be turned over, in whole or part, to the localities roughly on the basis of the collections in them. This is a way of supplying money without strings. Furthermore, the rural-small-town group that controls most State legislatures often arranges that to the extent grants-in-aid help local governments most in need of money, they are more likely to help rural rather than metropolitan areas. One effect of this policy is to sustain local units of rural government that would otherwise have to lose either more of their functions or their separate identities.

The prospects for rural local government reform are therefore bad. The prospects for metropolitan local government reform are perhaps worse. The problem of metropolitan government is not merely State and local. It is interstate. Many of the metropolitan areas extend across State lines: for example, greater New York City is in New York and New Jersey; greater Chicago is in Illinois and Indiana; greater Philadelphia is in Pennsylvania and New Jersey; and greater St. Louis is in Missouri and Illinois. It has been politically impossible for several decades for great cities to extend their boundaries and functions even within their States in order to cover their whole metropolitan areas and absorb the functions of other governmental units. Although increasing use is made of interstate metropolitan administrative agencies—the Port of New York Authority created by a compact between New York and New Jersey in 1921 is their model—interstate city governments are utopian.

Perhaps the extension of great cities is not the way to change the present situation in which, for example, the suburbs have markedly lower tax rates than the central cities though suburban residents use central city services. But the State legislatures refuse to adopt fiscal policies that would change the situation at least within their States. The present condition of metropolitan government is not encouraging for those who really want effective State and local government in America—as distinct from those who defend States' and local rights because they do not want effective government at all. For the failure to deal with the problem of metropolitan government weakens State as well as local government. The centralizing pressures in the United States are now strong enough that, if the lesser units of government fail for long to provide at least the minimum standard people expect of a service, the national government will be induced to intervene.

Chapter 11

The Judiciary

The national Constitution of 1787 and its amendments are detailed in their description of the national judicial power and the procedures the national courts must follow. Article III, Section 2, of the Constitution provides that the national judicial power shall extend

'to all cases, in law and equity, arising under this Constitution, the laws of the United States, and treaties made, or which shall be made, under their authority;—to all cases affecting ambassadors, other public ministers and consuls;—to all cases of admiralty and maritime jurisdiction;—to controversies to which the United States shall be a party;—to controversies between two or more States;—between a State and citizens of another State;—between citizens of different States;—between citizens of the same State claiming lands under grants of different States, and between a State, or the citizens thereof, and foreign states, citizens, or subjects.'

The Eleventh Amendment declares that the national judicial power shall not be construed, however, to extend to any suit brought against one of the States of the Union by citizens of another State or by citizens or subjects of any foreign state.

Article I, Section 9, of the Constitution prohibits the suspension of the writ of habeas corpus except in cases of rebellion or invasion and the enactment of bills of attainder and ex post facto laws. Article III, Section 2, requires that a criminal trial shall be by jury in the State where the crime shall have been committed. The Bill of Rights prohibits, in the Fourth Amendment, unreasonable searches and seizures and the issuance of general warrants. It declares, in the Fifth Amendment, that no person shall be tried for a capital or otherwise infamous crime unless on an indictment of a grand jury, put twice in jeopardy for the same offence, compelled in any criminal case to be a witness against himself, or deprived of life, liberty, or property without due process of law. It requires, in the Sixth Amendment, that an accused person shall have the right to a speedy and public trial by an impartial jury of the State and district in which the crime shall have been committed, to be informed of the nature and cause of the accusation, to be confronted with the witnesses against him, to have compulsory process for obtaining witnesses in his favour, and to have the assistance of counsel. It provides, in the Seventh Amendment, for trial by jury in suits at common law, where the value in controversy shall exceed twenty dollars, and for the finality of a jury's determination of fact. And it prohibits, in the Eighth Amendment, excessive bail, excessive fines, and cruel and unusual punishments.

Since the adoption of the Fourteenth Amendment, which prohibits a State from depriving any person of life, liberty, or property without due process of law, some of the procedural restrictions of the national Bill of Rights have eventually been applied to State judicial action too. In addition, State Constitutions have their own Bills of Rights, which apply to State courts.

The national Constitution gives few details, however, about the structure of the national judicial system. It establishes one Supreme Court and grants it original jurisdiction in all cases affecting ambassadors, other public ministers, and consuls and in which a State shall be party. It provides that the President shall nominate and with the advice and consent of the Senate appoint the judges of the Supreme Court and of such inferior courts as Congress may establish. It declares that the judges of both the Supreme and inferior courts shall hold office during good behaviour and receive a compensation which shall not be diminished during their continuance in office. But the definition of the appellate jurisdiction of the Supreme Court within the national judicial power, the number of judges on the Supreme Court, and the organization of the inferior courts—indeed, whether there shall be any inferior courts at all—are matters left entirely to the discretion of Congress.

At a time when many Americans feared a strong national judiciary, the framers did not specify a detailed structure. During the struggle over ratification of the Constitution, its proponents could point out that the Constitution permitted the new national government to rely almost exclusively on the State courts if it wished. Congress need not provide for any national court except the Supreme Court. The first Congress, however, established a complete national judiciary, though Congress has always allowed the State courts some share of cases arising under the national judicial power. The American judiciary consists, then, of a full set of national courts and forty-eight sets of State courts, the latter differing in details from State to State.

Moreover, though the organization of the national judiciary is based on congressional rather than constitutional provisions, its fundamental structure is rarely changed. At present, except for, first, special 'legislative courts' like the Court of Customs and Patent Appeals and most courts in the possessions and, second, the Court of Claims (against the national government), which was formerly a 'legislative court' but is now designated a 'constitutional court' by Congress, there are three kinds of national courts. At the bottom are eighty-four district courts in the States, two district courts in the possessions, and one district court in the District of Columbia. Above them are ten circuit Courts of Appeals in the States and one circuit Court of Appeals in the District of Columbia. At the top is one Supreme Court of nine justices.

There is also a small administrative machine. In 1922 the Chief Justice of the Supreme Court was given the power to convene an annual conference of national senior circuit court judges at which the state of national judicial business is considered and plans made accordingly. The Chief Justice may temporarily shift district judges—in June 1954 there were 229 district judgeships in the States—to districts with congested dockets. In 1939 Congress established the Administrative Office of the United States Courts under a director appointed by the Supreme Court and supervised by the national judicial conference. The Office helps the lower courts in the management of their routine affairs and provides information and makes recommendations about the handling of judicial business. These administrative arrangements help keep the national judicial system fairly efficient, though it is overburdened with business at the present time.

State Constitutions prescribe the structure of State judicial systems in some detail. Like the national judiciary, a State judiciary is always hierarchial, comprising several levels of trial and appellate courts. The levels are commonly as follows: at the bottom are the justices of the peace and other courts of petty jurisdiction; above them are courts of general trial jurisdiction; and at the top is the supreme court of the State. In some States there are intermediate courts of first instance between the justices of the peace and the general trial courts. In some States there are intermediate appellate courts between the general trial courts and the supreme court. (The titles of the courts are sometimes confusing: in New York State, for example, the 'Supreme Court' is a general trial and intermediate appellate court and the 'Court of Appeals' is the supreme court.)

A few States retain the once fairly common division between equity and common law courts. The States have special courts to deal with special problems like juvenile delinquency. In general, State law involves a wider range of subjects that bring heavy dockets than national law. Almost inevitably, then, a State judicial system is more complex than the national system.

A State system is also usually less efficient. Many States have formal provisions for administrative arrangements, directed by either the highest court, a judicial conference, or an administrative agency, but few have an administrative machine that works well. The State judicial process is generally often needlessly slow and expensive. Reform is difficult, partly because the details of the State judicial system are often defined in the State Constitution, and chiefly because the legal profession is strongly entrenched in American politics. Lawyers are usually reluctant to change the systems to which they are accustomed. The United States is the place to study English judicial archaisms in operation.

247

The growth of administrative justice, however, which is often quicker and cheaper than judicial justice, has impelled the bench and bar to try to improve the judicial process. The New Jersey Constitution of 1947, for example, created a highly integrated judicial system, modelled in several respects on the present English system. The following clause gives some idea of the nature of the system it reformed: 'There shall be a County Court in each county, which shall have all the jurisdiction heretofore exercised by the Court of Common Pleas, Orphans' Court, Court of Oyer and Terminer, Court of Quarter Sessions, Court of Special Sessions and such other jurisdiction consistent with this Constitution as may be conferred by law.' The Constitution grants the Chief Justice of the State Supreme Court extensive administrative powers, in order to make the system flexible enough to meet changes in the flow of judicial business with the minimal delay.

The Supreme Court of the United States is not only at the apex of the national judicial hierarchy but also in effect the highest court of each State system for what are known as 'federal questions'. 'Federal questions' involve some right or immunity claimed under the national Constitution, laws, or treaties. The great majority of cases in America do not raise 'federal questions', but the some that do, perhaps in the course of proceedings, allow the national courts to help shape the framework of State justice. The broad clause of the Fourteenth Amendment that prohibits a State from depriving any person of life, liberty, or property without due process of law gives the national Supreme Court a good deal of influence over State judicial procedures.

The work of the Supreme Court may be illustrated by that of a single annual term. In the 1952–3 term the Court ruled on the merits of 198 cases in 110 full opinions and 61 memorandum orders. (A full opinion records and explains the grounds for a decision or decisions; a memorandum order records a decision or decisions and perhaps gives a very brief clarifying statement or citation to a controlling precedent.) It refused to rule on several times that number of cases. Petitions for the writ of *certiorari*, which appellants may apply for but not demand, enable the Court to examine most of the claims put to it and to sift out those it hears. The writ is granted on the affirmative vote of four of the nine justices, though after argument it can be dismissed by a majority of the Court as improvidently granted. In 1952-3, of the 198 cases heard, 88 came before the Court by right of appeal (though even in such cases the Court has a good deal of discretion in practice in accepting them), and 110 by writ of *certiorari*. Forty-nine cases came directly from national district courts, 86 from circuit Courts of Appeals, four from other national courts, and 59 from State courts. No case came before the Supreme Court under its original jurisdiction.

The decision of the Court is that of a majority of justices hearing the case. For a case disposed of in a full opinion a member of the majority usually writes what is known as the Opinion of the Court. Other justices of the majority may write concurring opinions. The justices of the minority usually write collective or individual dissenting opinions. In 1952-3 the decision of the Court was unanimous in 24 of the 110 instances when full opinions were rendered and 41 of the 61 instances when memorandum orders were rendered. Besides 104 signed and six per curiam Opinions of the Court, 32 concurring and 89 dissenting opinions were written.

The figures show that the Supreme Court handles few cases. Its original jurisdiction is infrequently invoked. Diplomatic personnel are almost invariably exempted from its jurisdiction by international law, and cases involving consular personnel without diplomatic immunity and in which a State is party, unless in the latter circumstance the other party is another State of the Union, may be tried by other courts, which have concurrent jurisdiction. On the other hand, cases on appeal once overburdened the Court. When former President William Howard Taft took office as Chief Justice in 1921 the Court was more than a year behind in its work. Taft initiated a number of reforms, including the establishment of the national judicial conference mentioned earlier, of which the most important was a drastic change in the statutory definition of the appellate jurisdiction of the Supreme Court. He turned the Court into an effective pressure group that lobbied what was known as the 'judge's bill' through Congress in 1925, sharply curtailing the right of appellants to demand a review of their cases.

Under the 1925 Act and subsequent amendments, the right of appeal is limited to only a few circumstances. Most of them may be described briefly, if it is kept in mind that in cases coming to the Supreme Court of the United States national laws and treaties may be declared invalid only on the ground that they conflict with the Constitution of the United States and State laws (including constitutional provisions) only on the ground that they conflict with the Constitution, laws, and treaties of the United States. (In other cases State courts may declare State laws invalid on the ground that they conflict with the State Constitutions.) The Supreme Court of the United States takes a case on appeal: when any national court declares a national law invalid in a civil action involving the United States or its officers; when a national district court, for example, declares a national or State law invalid in a civil action or restrains the enforcement of an order of the Interstate Commerce Commission in a civil action brought by or against the United States; when a national circuit Court of Appeals declares a State law invalid; and when a State court of last resort rejects a claim that a State law is invalid or declares that a national law or treaty is invalid. (It may seem strange that a State court has the power to declare that a national law or treaty conflicts with the national Constitution, but since the Constitution specifically requires that State judges shall be bound by it, the right of a State court to determine the constitutionality of national legislation is as well-grounded as that of a national court.) The Supreme Court of the United States also answers questions of law arising in cases before and certified by national circuit Courts of Appeals or the national Court of Claims. (Three of the 88 cases which came to the Supreme Court in 1952–3 by right of appeal were on certificate from Courts of Appeals.) The Supreme Court has discretion to take a case on writ of *certiorari* in a great many circumstances. With extremely few exceptions, Congress has granted it a discretionary right of review in cases that somehow fall within the national judicial power as defined in the national Constitution (and that are presented for consideration at the proper stage of litigation.) By accepting only a limited number of cases the Court keeps abreast of its docket.

One effect of giving the Supreme Court such a wide measure of discretion over the cases it hears has been that the share of difficult cases has increased since 1925. The Court has laid down principles for assessing the claims raised in requests for writs of *certiorari*, in order to reject the routine ones and to accept those 'where there are special and important reasons' for taking them. It will, for example, usually take a case involving an issue upon which two circuit Courts of Appeals have disagreed or a case raising an important question of national law upon which the Supreme Court has never ruled. The relative increase in difficult cases before the Court is one reason why the ratio of non-unanimous to unanimous decisions has risen markedly in recent decades.

It is important in considering the work of the highest court in the land to remember that the great majority of cases are decided in the lowest courts. More than nine in ten cases tried by American courts are finally decided by the first courts that hear them. Furthermore, in most of the cases that are appealed, the higher courts accept the findings of fact of the trial courts. Appellate courts are usually concerned with general rules of law and deal directly with only a relatively few cases. As the highest appellate court, the national Supreme Court is furthest removed from the everyday work of the judicial system. It is much more concerned with general rules, which guide not only the work of the lower courts but also to some extent the work of the other branches of the government, than with trying cases. Indeed, the scope of its rule-making authority makes it a political institution of prime importance in the American governmental system.

Congress has varied the number of members on the Supreme Court. In 1789 it provided for a court of six justices, in 1801 five, in 1807 seven, in 1837 nine, and in 1863 ten. In 1866 it provided that as members died or retired from the Court the membership should drop to seven justices. In 1869 it again provided for a court of nine justices. The membership has remained constant since, though had President Franklin Roosevelt's Court Plan of 1937 been enacted, the number on the Court would have varied between nine and fifteen.

Presidential nominations to the Supreme Court are not subject to 'senatorial courtesy'. Although some of the nominees have been rejected by the Senate, there has been only one rejection since 1897: in 1930 President Hoover's nomination of John Parker, a North Carolina Republican, was defeated because of Parker's alleged anti-trade-union bias in one of his decisions as a member of an inferior national court and his anti-Negro statements in his campaign, ten years earlier, for the governorship of his State. Presidents have some regard for the sectional and religious composition of the Court in making nominations, but there are no fixed customs. They also consider the views of the men they appoint. Thus President Theodore Roosevelt wrote to Senator Henry Cabot Lodge when considering the nomination of the Chief Justice of Massachusetts for the Supreme Court of the United States: 'I should like to know that Judge Holmes was in entire sympathy with our views . . . before I would feel justified in appointing him.'[1] The President decided that the judge's opinions were satisfactory, and nominated the man who became the most famous associate justice in the history of the Court.

Presidents usually appoint men of their own party, and though most presidents have required a fair standard of fitness in their appointees, appointments are often rewards for political service. Many appointees have had some judicial experience. But since almost all lesser judicial appointments, national and State, are partisan appointments and most State judges are elected as partisan candidates, earlier judicial experience does not imply a judicial career so much as a step on the political ladder. Some Supreme Court justices come directly from other benches or law schools, but most of them come directly from political or administrative office, whatever their earlier back-

---

[1] Henry Cabot Lodge, ed., *Selections from the Correspondence of Theodore Roosevelt and Henry Cabot Lodge: 1884–1918* (London: Charles Scribner's Sons, 1925), I, 519. Quoted with permission of the publishers.

ground. Thus presidents have often appointed high officials of the Department of Justice to the Court, with the result that in some cases involving the national government as many as four justices have excused themselves on the ground that they have been connected with the cases at an earlier stage.

Technical legal competence is not the prime requisite of an able Supreme Court member anyway. Many of Justice Benjamin Cardozo's admirers felt that one of the greatest legal craftsmen in the country proved less effective on the national Supreme Court, on which he served from 1932 to 1938, than as chief judge of the New York State Court of Appeals, from which he was elevated. Supreme Court justices are perforce politicians, for the Supreme Court is a political institution. If the justices are good politicians, they can receive most of the legal competence they need from the bright young secretaries who come to them from the law schools.

All national judges, except members of some of the 'legislative courts' who serve fixed terms, may be removed only on conviction by the Senate on an impeachment by the House of Representatives. Only one Supreme Court justice has been impeached: Samuel Chase in 1804–5. The Jeffersonians sought to use impeachment proceedings to break the Federalist hold on the Supreme Court. But Chase was not convicted, and the attempt was abandoned. Although a few judges of inferior national courts have been removed by impeachment, the process has proved too cumbersome even to use it as often as it should be used. Security of tenure has abuses.

State experience has shown, however, that lack of security of tenure has greater abuses. State judges are usually elected or appointed for fixed terms, though their chances of re-election or re-appointment, and therefore their sense of security of tenure, are sometimes very good. In a few States, moreover, judges are subject to recall by petition and vote of the electorate, though the procedure is rarely invoked. Justices of the national Supreme Court have had occasion to comment on the electioneering atmosphere that may accompany the dispensing of justice in State courts.

Opinions about the general quality of the decisions of the

courts often depend on the extent to which the critics accept the beliefs on which the judges have based their decisions. But it is probably fair to say that of the 90 men who have served on the Supreme Court of the United States, a few have been exceptionally able justices, many have shown adequate ability, and a few have been of poor calibre. Other national judges have, on the whole, been less able, though there have been noteworthy exceptions like Judge Learned Hand, who recently retired from the Court of Appeals for the second judicial circuit. State judges have been of poorer calibre than national judges, though again there have been noteworthy exceptions.

Whatever their real merits, most judges work in an institutional environment that gives them the appearance of dignity and integrity. In a country where political controversy often degenerates into personal vituperation, judges, especially United States Supreme Court justices, have been comparatively immune from the worst forms of personal attacks. The exceptional denunciation is thus all the more shocking, particularly when one Supreme Court justice publicly impugns the work of another, as Justice Robert Jackson unjustifiably impugned the work of Justice Hugo Black in 1946. The Supreme Court of the United States and to a lesser extent the other American courts, benefit from what Walter Bagehot called the deferential element in government. Courts in almost every society do, but there is a special reason in the United States. In America the Constitution takes the place of the Crown as the symbol of unity above party. The courts, particularly the Supreme Court, by establishing themselves as the guardians of the Constitution, share the respect with which that document is held.

The American courts have successfully asserted what is known as 'the American doctrine of judicial supremacy'. The doctrine is that the courts, ultimately the Supreme Court of the United States on 'federal questions', have the right to review the activities of all agencies of government in order to determine whether they are legally and constitutionally valid.

Chief Justice Marshall enunciated the doctrine in the case of Marbury v. Madison in 1803. William Marbury sought to obtain his commission as justice of the peace in the District of Columbia from Secretary of State James Madison. Under a provision of the Judiciary Act of 1789 he invoked the original jurisdiction of the Supreme Court to request the issuance of a writ of mandamus. The Court held, with Marshall writing the Opinion of the Court, that an act of Congress which extends the original jurisdiction of the Supreme Court to subjects not listed in the relevant constitutional clause—'cases affecting ambassadors, other public ministers and consuls, and those in which a State shall be party'—conflicts with the Constitution.

What then should the Court do? The Constitution does not give an explicit answer. But Marshall said that it was the duty of the Court to declare what law governs the case before it. When two laws conflict, it must obey the higher. Since the Constitution is the highest law, the Court must obey it when it conflicts with any other. Therefore in Marbury v. Madison the Court must declare that the Constitution and not the act of Congress governs the case. The Court did not grant Marbury his request on the ground that it lacked jurisdiction to do so.

Conflict with higher law means in appropriate cases an excess of authority under higher law. Since the national government is a government of delegated powers, for example, its actions must not conflict with the Constitution by exceeding those powers. Since most American administrative agencies derive their powers from legislation, for example, their actions must not conflict with the legislation by exceeding the powers granted thereunder. They must not, in other words, be *ultra vires*.

Judicial review works upwards by stages. If an administrative order of a national agency is challenged, the Court will first determine whether it conflicts with congressional legislation. If it determines that it does, the Court will refuse to recognize the validity of the order. If it determines that it does not, the Court will next determine whether the congressional legislation authorizing the order conflicts with the Constitution. If it determines that it does, the Court will refuse to recognize the validity of the order and the legislation. If it determines that it does not, the Court will apply the order to the case. The example is given on the assumption that the challenger attacked the validity of both the order and the legislation. For as a general rule a court will work upwards only so far as the brief of the challenger demands.

Controversy about American judicial activity has distinguished three main aspects of judicial review: review of administrative action, of State action under the national Constitution, and of national congressional and presidential action and State legislative and executive action under the national and State Constitutions respectively.

It has always been generally accepted that the courts ought to exercise some control over administrative action. They ought to make sure that administrators do not exceed the powers granted to them by the legislatures. The chief dispute over judicial oversight of administration, particularly administrative rule-making and administrative justice, arose from the fact that until recently the courts, led by the national Supreme Court, often subjected administrative action to more judicial control than the legislatures intended. The courts sometimes insisted, for example, on their right to determine *de novo* the facts upon which administrative rules and decisions were based. Since 1937, however, the Supreme Court has led the trend to show administrative judgments great respect. Consequently, as was pointed out in Chapter 8, Congress passed the Administrative Procedure Act of 1946 in order partially to reinforce 'the rule of law' in the national government. Whatever the merits of this act, it can no longer be said that in general judicial review of American national administration hampers administrative action contrary to the wishes of a democratically elected legislature.

The most controversial aspect of judicial review in the early years of the Republic was the right of the national Supreme Court to declare State action to be contrary to the national Constitution. Chief Justice Marshall's decisions on this point ran against the strong States' rights sentiment in the country. But it has been generally recognized since that the absence of either a national executive or a national legislative veto on State action in the American federal system makes a national judicial veto indispensable. A State must not be allowed to interfere unduly with national concerns. 'I do not think', said Justice Oliver Wendell Holmes, 'the United States would come to an end if we lost our power to declare an Act of Congress void. I do think the Union would be imperilled if we could not make that declaration as to the laws of the several States. For one in my place sees how often a local policy prevails with those who are not trained to national views. . . .'[1] Justice Holmes himself was an eloquent critic, while he was on the Supreme Court from 1902 to 1932, of decisions of the Court declaring State social legislation unconstitutional on the ground that it infringed liberty or took property without due process of law; but his criticism was directed at the policy not the power of the Court; and since 1937, again, the Court has changed its policy.

Since judicial review of State action under the national Constitution, though exercised by State as well as national courts, is ultimately directed by the national Supreme Court, it may be justified on the ground that it is the exercise of national authority over a subordinate government. It may thus be differentiated from judicial review of congressional and presidential action under the national Constitution, also ultimately directed by the national Supreme Court, and of State legislative and executive action under the State Constitutions, ultimately directed by the highest courts of the States. The review of the activities of the co-ordinate branches of government has been the most controversial aspect of judicial review since the Civil War.

Marshall's defence of judicial supremacy in Marbury v. Madison rests on the assumption that the Court is able to judge whether an act conflicts with the Constitution better than Congress and the President. If this assumption is accepted, Marshall's case is sound; for if an act does conflict with the Constitution, the Court must obviously obey the latter, since the Constitution is the highest law of the land. But should the assumption be accepted? The provision of the Judiciary Act of 1789 declared to be contrary to the Constitution in Marbury v. Madison, for example, was passed by a Congress in which

---

[1] *Collected Legal Papers* (London: Constable and Company, Ltd., 1920), pp. 295–6. Quoted with permission of the publishers.

several framers of the Constitution were members and James Madison, the 'Father of the Constitution', was a floor leader. The Act was signed by President Washington, who had been the presiding officer at the constitutional convention. Both Congress and the President apparently believed that the constitutional clause granting the Supreme Court original jurisdiction in some cases did not preclude Congress from granting it original jurisdiction in others. Yet in 1803 the Supreme Court, only one of whose members had been at the constitutional convention, declared that this was a misinterpretation of the Constitution.

The real issue in the controversy over judicial review is not what should the Court do when it finds that an act conflicts with the Constitution but should the Court find that an act conflicts with the Constitution when most of the members of the other branches of government believe that it does not. Marshall's opponents argued that the principle of co-ordinate branches of government implied that each branch had the right to interpret the meaning of the Constitution for itself. Ex-President Thomas Jefferson wrote in 1819 that 'each department is truly independent of the others, and has an equal right to decide for itself what is the meaning of the Constitution in the cases submitted to its action; and especially where it is to act ultimately and without appeal.' President Andrew Jackson wrote in 1832:

'The Congress, the Executive, and the Court must each for itself be guided by its own opinion of the Constitution. . . . The opinion of the judges has no more authority over Congress than the opinion of Congress has over the judges, and on that point the President is independent of both. The authority of the Supreme Court must not, therefore, be permitted to control the Congress or the Executive when acting in their legislative capacities, but to have only such influence as the force of their reasoning may deserve.'

While these arguments attacked the premises of judicial supremacy, however, they did not directly challenge the right of the Court to declare a measure to be unconstitutional.

Chiefly because judicial review of the co-ordinate branches received comparatively little attention before the Civil War, the Court's claim to make the final determination was allowed to stand almost by default. When this aspect of judicial review received a great deal of attention after the Civil War, the Court had acquired a prescriptive right. The controversy over national judicial decisions affecting congressional and presidential powers, like that over decisions affecting State action, has focused on policy rather than power, with the year 1937 once more marking a decisive shift in policy.

But the Court has recognized that in some circumstances it is wisest to apply Jefferson's theory. It treats some subjects as 'political questions', concerning which the decisions of the political branches of government are accepted as final. Thus, Congress may decide conclusively whether a State has a 'republican form of government' as required by the Constitution; Congress may decide conclusively whether an amendment to the Constitution has been duly ratified; and the President may decide conclusively who is the *de jure* or *de facto* ruler of a territory. Indeed, the President's exercise of his independent powers, especially in foreign affairs, consists largely of 'political questions', so that the argument about national judicial power as it affects the co-ordinate branches has focused on review of congressional action. The Court decides, however, what subjects are 'political questions'. Its definition has varied: for example, the procedure for ratifying amendments has been examined by the Court in the past. The doctrine of 'political questions' does not, therefore, infringe the basic doctrine of judicial supremacy.

State judicial supremacy under State Constitutions is similar to national judicial supremacy under the national Constitution, but there are differences in a few States. The national Supreme Court has refused to give advisory opinions on the constitutionality of proposed legislation because it conceives its function to be merely to declare what law applies to a case before it, when it will if necessary hold that a law is unconstitutional. But the highest courts of ten States do give advisory opinions, though the opinions do not bind the courts in subsequent cases. The use of advisory opinions might have become more common had it not been for the widespread adoption after 1915 of a better device, the declaratory judgment. The great majority of States and the national Congress have enacted laws permitting courts to declare what the law is in a genuine controversy between two parties after an act has been passed but before action under it has taken place. (The national Supreme Court has upheld the validity of declaratory judgment legislation on the analogy of injunctive procedure.) Unlike an advisory opinion, a declaratory judgment is a legal precedent.

Three State Constitutions require an unusual majority before a court may declare an act of the legislature void. Despite the criticism of judicial decisions in the late nineteenth and early twentieth centuries, however, State constitution makers have not sought to impair the legal supremacy of the courts. In the States, as in the nation, a judicial interpretation of a constitutional provision may be overruled only by a subsequent decision —for the American supreme courts are not bound by the principle of *stare decisis*—or by a constitutional amendment. American constitutional provisions mean what the judges say they mean.

The legal fiction is that the courts interpret instead of make law. In fact their legal supremacy inevitably makes them policy-determining organs, and as such subject to political pressures. The following account of the practical relations between the Supreme Court and the elective branches of the national government illustrates the point.

The Supreme Court has not often set aside the judgment of Congress. It has invalidated the provisions of national law in about eighty cases. In most of these cases only part of a statute, often a minor part, has been declared void. Only eight or ten statutes have been held unconstitutional in their entirety. Since 1789 Congress has passed over 70,000 acts, of which over 30,000 have been public acts. Statistically, the incidence of judicial review on congressional legislation has been extremely slight.

But to strike down a national law is to drop a pebble in the legislative pool, creating a disturbance that ripples out from the point of contact across a considerable surface of potential legislation. When the Supreme Court declared in the 1870's and 1880's that national executive action and legislation protecting the rights of Negroes from the private acts of white Southerners exceeded the constitutional powers of the nation, it helped doom the newly-freed slaves to a subjugation not much better than they had suffered before. When the Supreme Court declared a national income tax law void in 1895, it prevented the use for nearly two decades of what has proved to be the most important fiscal instrument of the national government. When the Court ruled in several cases that Congress could not regulate the production of commodities that flow in interstate commerce, it crippled national efforts to strike at child labour and other widely condemned labour practices until, after 1937, the decisions were overruled. The Court not only held the particular acts void but also discouraged Congress from passing others.

After the Civil War the Court exercised its power to invalidate legislation much more than before. In the mid-1930's it pushed its power to the breaking point. In seventeen months it held void all or part of eleven major national acts dealing with the problems of the depression. The whole course of the New Deal was threatened by decisions that put new restrictions on national powers just when the national government was exercising power as never before. President Franklin Roosevelt thought that two reasons for the fact that the decisions of the Court reminded him of 'the horse-and-buggy age' were that by 1937 six of the nine justices on the Court were over 70 years old and he had not had a chance to appoint anyone to the Court in his first term in the White House. The average age of the 'nine old men' was over 71; those over 70 had served on the Supreme Court at least ten years. In February 1937 the President submitted to Congress a plan for increasing the membership of the Supreme Court by one additional justice for every justice of the original nine over 70 years of age who had served ten years on the Court and who refused to retire (the total number of additional justices was never to exceed six); thus, in any event, Roosevelt would be able to appoint six new justices of New Deal persuasion to the Court.

After a bitter struggle the plan was defeated. During the

struggle the Court threw its weight against the plan by revealing a new attitude towards New Deal legislation; or, more strictly, the justice who held the balance of power between the more conservative and the more liberal members of the Court revealed a new attitude: 'A switch in time saved nine.' (It is now known that the relignment took place on one important case before the President announced his proposals, but the decision was not rendered until after the announcement.) Social and regulatory legislation was sustained. In addition, one of the conservative justices announced that he intended to retire at the end of the current term. The President lost the battle but won the war. By the end of 1941 seven justices were Roosevelt's appointees; and in 1943, after the last of Roosevelt's appointees had replaced an earlier one, the average age of the nine justices on the Court was about 56. Only three minor provisions of national acts have been held void since 1937.

In November 1954 President Eisenhower nominated John Harlan of New York to fill a vacancy on the Court. He was 55. Of the eight justices on the Court, four had been appointed by Roosevelt, three by Truman, and one—Chief Justice Earl Warren—by Eisenhower. The average age of the eight was about 64.

One lesson to be drawn from the events of 1937 is that a direct challenge to the independence of the Supreme Court is politically dangerous. A more subtle lesson is that it is part of the art of judicial statesmanship not to obstruct the elected branches of the government too much. When the Supreme Court struck down liberal social legislation in the late nineteenth and early twentieth centuries, it did so at a time when the country was sharply divided on its merits and many members of the political branches were glad to be able to support liberal measures in principle while pointing out that 'the Constitution' did not permit them. But when the Court struck down liberal legislation in the 1930's, it did so at a time when the electorate had endorsed the New Deal by large majorities and most members of the other branches of the government believed firmly in the necessity for at least some of the legislation. In this context the Court had in fact much less scope in reviewing legislation.

Mr. Dooley observed that the Supreme Court follows the

election returns. The justices may follow the returns at some distance and make modifications in the course of government policy on the way, but they must follow the general direction of government action. The Court of the mid-1930's was not the first to tilt against windmills. The Court of 1857 tried to control national slavery policy, with disastrous results for its prestige in the North. The truth is that the prime function of the interpretation of the Constitution by the Supreme Court is to rationalize the exercise of governmental power under a Constitution which is, in general, hard to amend readily. The Supreme Court is, in effect, a continuous constitutional convention. So long as the Court performs its function moderately well it enjoys great prestige and a fair measure of power; when it refuses to do its job, its prestige falls and the elective branches begin to put pressure on it.

There are several ways in which judicial decisions may be made responsive to public opinion. Constitutional amendments may alter the course of judicial interpretation. But the amending process is too cumbersome to use often. More common is presidential screening of nominees to the Supreme Court according to their views on major public policies. A President fortunate enough to have several vacancies occur while he is in office can help mould the attitude of the Court, perhaps for a generation. This is an intermittent method of keeping judicial opinion consonant with the main flow of public opinion, but it is the second best there is.

The best is to develop a tradition of judicial self-restraint. The Court should on the whole accept the spirit of Jefferson's and Jackson's argument. Justice Holmes preached judicial self-restraint in his famous dissenting opinions. A liberal minority iterated his sermon through the mid-1930's. 'Courts are not the only agency of government that must be assumed to have capacity to govern,' wrote Justice Stone in the case of United States v. Butler in 1936, in perhaps the most biting dissent from 'interpretation of our great charter of government which proceeds on any assumption that the responsibility for the preservation of our institutions is the exclusive concern of any one of the three branches. . . .'

Roosevelt's appointments gave the liberals a majority (and raised Stone to the chief justiceship). Except when dealing with civil liberty and civil rights cases, most of the justices have appeared to accept the need for self-restraint in judging the constitutionality of legislation. They have decided that they must be active in keeping the political process free, but once they have done their best to protect civil liberties, the democratic suffrage, and racial equality, they must accept almost anything that comes out of the process. The justices have not always lived up to their standards, and it is too early to assess the permanent impact of their efforts on the traditions of the Court, but the Court has faced the political implications of its work more frankly than ever before. The exercise of American judicial supremacy is, in consequence, very different to-day from what it was a generation ago.

Chapter 12

Private Rights

Both the framers of the Constitution of 1787 and those who insisted that a Bill of Rights be added to it sought to provide constitutional safeguards for private rights. So did the authors of the amendments to the Constitution associated with 'reconstruction' after the Civil War. State Constitutions contain similar clauses. Thus, since the courts have been the final interpreters of constitutional provisions, judicial protection of private rights has been an important aspect of the American system of government. It is convenient to put the rights in three categories: economic rights; civil liberties; and civil rights. This chapter deals with the protection that the decisions of the Supreme Court have given to each category and the limits of judicial protection of freedom.

First, the protection of economic rights. Under Chief Justice Marshall the Supreme Court held that State laws rescinding land grants, altering the charter of a private corporation, and infringing creditor rights impaired the obligation of contracts in violation of Article I, Section 10, of the Constitution. Under Chief Justice Taney the Court allowed the States more scope in contract cases but held in the Dred Scott case that congressional legislation prohibiting slavery in part of the national domain was an unconstitutional deprivation of property without due process of law. The important period of judicial protection of economic rights from government action, however, was the half-century from 1886 to 1936. The chief beneficiaries were the wealthy and business classes.

In terms of constitutional doctrine the protection was often

265

indirect. The Court held the national income tax law void in 1895, for example, not on the ground that it infringed private rights, but primarily on the ground that parts of it constituted a direct tax within the meaning of Article I, Section 9, of the Constitution and therefore should have raised revenue in proportion to the distribution of population among the States. In order to overrule this decision the Sixteenth Amendment of 1913 granted Congress the power to tax incomes 'from whatever source derived' without regard to the distribution of population. Despite the words of the Amendment the Court declared in subsequent cases that the national government still did not have the power to tax income derived from the lease of State oil-lands, for example, on the ground that the oil-lands were State instrumentalities immune from national government taxation. The practical effect for private persons of intergovernmental tax immunity, which applied to national as well as State instrumentalities, was, in the example cited, partly to relieve business men who held oil-lands leases of the burden of taxation. Similarly, the practical effect of the constitutional doctrine that national regulation of production for commerce invaded States' rights was, as was pointed out in Chapter 2, often to free business men from effective regulation by any government.

Direct constitutional protection of economic rights was based primarily on the clauses of the Fifth and Fourteenth Amendments, relating to national and State action respectively, that forbid the governments to deprive 'any person' of 'life, liberty, or property, without due process of law'. (The Court frequently referred to the equal protection of the laws clause of the Fourteenth Amendment as well, but it rarely gave it more meaning than the due process clause in cases simply involving economic rights.) In the 1880's and 1890's the Supreme Court read three meanings into the due process clauses which had not, on the whole, been there before. It held, first, that a corporation was a person. The effect was to extend protection directly to the most important form of business organization.

The Court held, second, with the Dred Scott case the only precedent, that the substance of government action could violate due process. The Court had previously explained that the words 'due process of law' were intended to convey the same meaning as 'by the law of the land' in Magna Carta: 'settled usages and modes of proceeding'. Due process was fair procedure: a proper trial, for example, by an impartial judge and jury. In other words, the constitutional clauses applied to the way things were done. The Court now explained that due process was also fair substance: in 1898, for example, it invalidated a State law setting railway rates, not because the governmental process the State used was improper, but because the economic criteria used in determining the rates did not guarantee a 'fair return'. In other words, the constitutional clauses also applied to what was done.

The Court held, third, in the case of Allgeyer *v.* Louisiana in 1897, that the liberty mentioned in the due process clauses

'means, not only the right of the citizen to be free from the mere physical restraint of his person, as by incarceration, but the term is deemed to embrace the right of the citizen to be free in the enjoyment of all his faculties; to be free to use them in all lawful ways; to live and work where he will; to earn his livelihood by any lawful calling; to pursue any livelihood or avocation, and for that purpose to enter into all contracts which may be proper, necessary and essential to his carrying out to a successful conclusion the purposes above mentioned.'

The effect of this doctrine of the liberty of contract was to raise business activities to the status of economic rights which the Court protected from 'unreasonable' government action. In an extreme form this doctrine prevented the national and State governments from regulating in any way the prices and terms of service of businesses not 'affected with a public interest'. The Court invalidated State laws regulating the resale price of theatre tickets and licensing the sale of ice, for example, because ticket agencies and ice companies were not businesses 'affected with a public interest'.

Among the most important liberty of contract cases were those concerned with labour relations and conditions. The Court claimed that its doctrines protected the rights of workers as well as business men, but the protection was often in a form working men did not appreciate. Thus the Court invalidated national and State laws banning the 'yellow dog' contract, which required as a condition of employment that a worker undertake not to join a trade union, because they abridged both the worker's and employer's liberty of contract. The most notorious cases were those involving maximum hour and minimum wage legislation, especially Lochner *v.* New York in 1905, in which the Court held invalid a New York State law limiting the number of hours a baker might contract to work to sixty hours a week and ten hours a day. The following passages from the Opinion of the Court illustrate how the Court applied the due process clause to the substance of legislation, invoked the doctrine of the liberty of contract, and wrote its prejudices into the law of the land:

'. . . The general right to make a contract in relation of his business is part of the liberty of the individual protected by the Fourteenth Amendment of the federal Constitution. . . . Under that provision no State can deprive any person of life, liberty, or property without due process of law. The right to purchase or to sell labor is part of the liberty protected by this Amendment, unless there are circumstances which exclude the right. . . .

'. . . In every case that comes before this Court, therefore, where legislation of this character is concerned, and where the protection of the federal Constitution is sought, the question necessarily arises: Is this a fair, reasonable, and appropriate exercise of the police power of the State, or is it an unreasonable, unnecessary, and arbitrary interference with the right of the individual to his personal liberty, or to enter into those contracts in relation to labor which may seem to him appropriate or necessary for the support of himself and his family? Of course the liberty of contract relating to labor includes both parties to it. The one has as much right to purchase as the other to sell labor. . . .

'The question whether this Act is valid as a labor law, pure and simple, may be dismissed in a few words. There is no reasonable ground for interfering with the liberty of person or the right of free contract, by determining the hours of labor, in the occupation of a baker. . . .

'. . . We do not believe in the soundness of the views which uphold this law. . . . Statutes of the nature of that under review, limiting the hours in which grown and intelligent men may labor to earn their living, are mere meddlesome interferences with the rights of the individual. . . .

'. . . It seems to us that the real object and purpose were simply to regulate the hours of labor between the master and his employees . . . in a private business, not dangerous in any degree to morals, or in any real and substantial degree to the health of the employees. Under such circumstances the freedom of master and employee to contract with each other in relation to their employment, and in defining the same, cannot be prohibited or interfered with, without violating the federal Constitution.'

It should be noted that for legislation regulating the hours of bakers no process could be due process.

Justice Holmes, dissenting, wrote:

'This case is decided upon an economic theory which a large part of the country does not entertain. If it were a question whether I agreed with that theory, I should desire to study it further and long before making up my mind. But I do not conceive that to be my duty, because I strongly believe that my agreement or disagreement has nothing to do with the right of a majority to embody their opinions in law. It is settled by various decisions of this Court that State constitutions and State laws may regulate life in many ways which we as legislators might think as injudicious or if you like as tyrannical as this, and which equally with this interfere with the liberty to contract. Sunday laws and usury laws are ancient examples. A more modern one is the prohibition of lotteries. The liberty of the citizen to do as he likes so long as he does not interfere with the liberty of others to do the same, which has been a shibboleth for some well-known writers, is interfered with by school laws, by the post office, by every State or municipal institution which takes his money for purposes thought desirable, whether he likes it or not.

'The Fourteenth Amendment does not enact Mr. Herbert Spencer's Social Statics . . . . a constitution is not intended to embody a particular economic theory, whether of paternalism and the organic relation of the citizen to the state or of *laissez-faire*. It is made for people of fundamentally differing views, and the accident if our finding certain opinions natural and familiar or novel and even shocking ought not to conclude our judgment upon the question whether statutes embodying them conflict with the Constitution of the United States.

'. . . I think that the word "liberty" in the Fourteenth Amendment is perverted when it is held to prevent the natural outcome of a dominant opinion, unless it can be said that a rational and fair man necessarily would admit that the statute proposed would infringe fundamental principles as they have been understood by the traditions of our people and our law. It does not need research to show that no such sweeping condemnation can be passed upon the statute before us. . . .'

In some instances the majority of the Court accepted legislation that workers wanted, but on the whole during the half-century from 1886 to 1936 the Court showed a pronounced anti-labour bias. It was harsh in its decisions dealing with strikes and picketing and with legislation designed to protect strikes and picketing. It extended the application of the Sherman Anti-Trust Act to trade union practices. It was in general unsympathetic in its review of social legislation.

In recent years the class bias has disappeared, and with it most of the canons of constitutional interpretation which protected economic rights. The Supreme Court began to curtail intergovernmental tax immunity and abandoned the use of the doctrine that some businesses were not 'affected with a public interest' before 1937. Since 1937 it has curtailed intergovernmental tax immunity much further, allowed Congress to regulate production for commerce, largely abandoned the doctrine that the due process clause applies to the substance of legislation affecting economic rights, and repudiated the doctrine of the liberty of contract. In 1941 the Court declared in the case of United States *v.* Darby: '. . . it is no longer open to question that the fixing of a minimum wage is within the legislative power and that the bare fact of its exercise is not a denial of due process. . . . Nor is it any longer open to question that it is within the legislative power to fix maximum hours . . .'; and it announced in the case of Phelps Dodge Corporation *v.* National Labor Relations Board that later decisions had 'comptetely sapped' the decisions against the validity of laws prohibiting the 'yellow dog' contract 'of their authority'.

For a time, indeed, the Court was zealous in its protection of trade union activities. It not only upheld the rights to strike and picket peaceably but also exempted trade unions almost entirely from anti-trust legislation. As a result, it permitted some flagrant instances of trade union abuse of power which it might have curbed. The question arose whether, if a conservative Congress and conservative State legislatures passed anti-trade union regulatory legislation, the Court might invalidate it on due process grounds. By the time cases testing such legislation reached the Court, however, President Truman's appointees had leavened the 'Roosevelt Court' with sufficient conservatism to prevent invalidation, even of some acts which might have been held to curb the civil liberties of trade unionists. And in the case of Lincoln Federal Labor Union *v.* Northwestern Iron & Metal Co. in 1949 a unanimous Court upheld the right of State legislators and constitution-makers to ban the closed shop. The Court pointed out to trade union leaders that they 'now ask us to return, at least in part, to the due process philosophy that has been deliberately discarded. . . . Just as we have held that the due process clause erects no obstacle to block legislative protection of union members, we now hold that legislative protection can be afforded non-union members.'

The present attitude of the Court is not based on a reluctance to use its power to protect freedom. Rather it is based on a doubt whether the invalidation of legislation because it interferes with economic rights does, in its total effect, protect freedom. Legislation interfering with the economic rights of one person may protect or expand the economic rights of others. Thus for the Supreme Court to invalidate it in order to protect the economic rights of one person may be to restrict the economic rights of others. To strike down a law that forbids a man from working more than ten hours a day may protect the liberty of the man who wants to work more hours, but it may also remove a barrier to the economic coercion of other men.

In short, most legislation affecting economic rights strikes a balance between conflicting interests. It is one of the functions of a representative government to strike the balance. For the Supreme Court to set aside the judgment of the political branches is not, in general, to protect freedom as a whole but to readjust the balance. That is why the critics of earlier decisions have convinced the present Court that it should use its power to review economic and social legislation very sparingly. The Court now believes that it may use its power more appropriately to protect civil liberties and civil rights; for protection of one man's liberty to speak, to publish, to vote, and to send his children to school on an equal footing does not, in general, restrict another man's liberty to do the same. The Court has read this distinction into Justice Holmes's dissenting opinions, and Justice Holmes is the spiritual father of the present generation of Supreme Court justices.

Second, the protection of civil liberties. Again it is necessary to distinguish between substance and procedure, in this instance between substantive freedoms and procedural rights, in order to explain the decisions of the Court. Substantive freedoms are freedoms of religious exercise, speech, the press, assembly, and petition, referred to in the First Amendment of the Bill of Rights. Procedural rights are rights connected with a fair trial: rights to the writ of habeas corpus, an impartial hearing, and the assistance of counsel, for example. (A summary of those specified in the national Constitution was given in the second paragraph of Chapter 11.) In the American federal system the States are normally more likely to infringe both kinds of civil liberties than the nation; for the States are primarily responsible for protecting the health, welfare, morals, and safety of their citizens, that is, for exercising what is known in American constitutional law as the police power; and the State courts try something like nine-tenths of the cases tried by American

courts. National infringement of civil liberties, especially substantive freedoms, has been largely confined to a few brief
periods.

The Supreme Court dealt with a very few civil liberty cases
before the Civil War. It ruled, undoubtedly correctly, that the
Bill of Rights applied only to national government action. The
only national action seriously abridging civil liberties before the
Civil War was the passage and enforcement of the Sedition Act
of 1798. No cases under it reached the Supreme Court. The
Jeffersonians allowed the Act to expire when they took office in
1801, and the President pardoned those convicted by the lower
courts.

During the Civil War President Lincoln seriously interfered
with civil liberties in suppressing pro-Confederate activity in
States that remained in the Union, especially by authorizing
military authorities to suspend the privilege of the writ of
habeas corpus in their districts. Chief Justice Taney, as circuit
judge in Maryland (Supreme Court justices rode circuit until
1891), attempted in vain to assert his authority over the action
of military commanders carrying out the President's orders.
After the War was over, the Supreme Court roundly denounced
the use of military commissions instead of the civil courts. But
Lincoln had certainly had cause to argue that a civil war
creates a situation in which it may be necessary to set aside
some constitutional rights temporarily in order to preserve the
constitutional system which protects them at other times.

In the years immediately after the Civil War, the northern
policy of 'reconstructing' the southern States abridged the
liberties of former Confederates. In two minor cases the
Supreme Court struck down State and national laws putting
disabilities on ex-Confederates as bills of attainder and ex post
facto laws. But in general the Court avoided ruling on 'reconstruction' legislation, fearful of a Congress that nearly removed
a President from office on impeachment, until Congress itself
tired of 'reconstruction'. Then the Court intervened to strike
down laws that endeavoured to secure the civil rights of
Negroes, on the ground that Congress could not protect Negroes
from the acts of private persons.

S

From 'reconstruction' days to the First World War almost all Supreme Court cases dealing with civil liberties involved procedural rights. Congress did not abridge substantive freedoms; and though the Fourteenth Amendment, adopted in 1868, now made it possible for the Court to protect civil liberties from State action, the Court confined its protection to procedural rights only. The framers of the Amendment probably intended that the clause prohibiting States from abridging the privileges or immunities of citizens of the United States should, in effect, apply the Bill of Rights, including the guarantees of substantive freedoms in the First Amendment, to the State governments. But the Court refused to give the clause any distinct legal significance. Furthermore, it reserved the doctrine of 'substantive due process' for economic rights only. In civil liberty cases the chief question involved in the Court's application of the due process clause of the Fourteenth Amendment was what procedural rights it protected.

The Court tried to apply a logical construction of the provisions of the Constitution. It held that no phrase of the Constitution is without distinct meaning (though in fact, as was just pointed out, it failed to give the privileges or immunities clause any); the phrase 'due process of law' appears in the original Bill of Rights among several definitions of rights: the substantive freedoms of the First Amendment, immunity from unreasonable searches and seizures, immunity from trial unless on an indictment of a grand jury, immunity from self-incrimination, and the right to the assistance of counsel, for example; therefore, due process of law does not include the rights specifically mentioned. The Court held, further, that the phrase 'due process of law' means the same in the Fourteenth Amendment as in the Fifth Amendment of the Bill of Rights; therefore, the clause in the Fourteenth Amendment does not include the rights specifically mentioned in the Bill of Rights either. This construction is known as the Hurtado rule, since in the case of Hurtado v. California in 1884 the Court used this reasoning to permit California to dispense with grand jury indictments. The rule was adequate at a time when the Supreme Court was not in fact examining criminal procedures very closely.

The rule was breached, however, after the First World War. One reason was that the Court had already enunciated an analysis of civil liberty clauses that could be used instead. In the last years of the nineteenth century the United States acquired several overseas possessions—Puerto Rico and the Philippine Islands, for example—that did not have Anglo-Saxon traditions of justice. The Supreme Court held that the national government was not bound to obey all the provisions of the Constitution in governing what the Court called 'unincorporated' territories. The national government had to respect 'fundamental' but not 'formal' constitutional rights. The Court determined in each instance whether a right was 'fundamental' or 'formal'. It said that the immunity from a bill of attainder or ex post acto law and probably the substantive freedoms, for example, were 'fundamental' and held that the rights of grand jury indictment and jury trial, for example, were 'formal'. Thus the Court had found a natural law doctrine of civil liberties in 'insular' cases which it might substitute, at least in part, for its logical construction of the due process clause of the Fourteenth Amendment in State cases whenever it decided that the latter interpretation was unsatisfactory.

During the First World War Congress passed legislation restricting substantive freedoms more in some respects than the Sedition Act of 1798. It was made a crime, for example, punishable by a maximum penalty of a $10,000 fine and twenty years' imprisonment, to use 'any language intended to bring the form of government of the United States, or the Constitution of the United States, or the flag of the United States, or the uniform of the army or navy of the United States, into contempt, scorn, contumely, or disrepute'. On the whole, John Lord O'Brian, head of the War Emergency Division of the Department of Justice, exercised a restraining influence in the enforcement of such provisions. But during the War and in the subsequent Bolshevik scare the actions of the Postmaster General in censoring postal privileges, local United States attorneys in enforcing national legislation, local prosecuting attorneys in enforcing the similar legislation of several States, and private individuals of organizations like the American Protective

League in 'helping' the authorities led to a number of cases in lower courts. The growth of intolerant organizations like the revived Ku Klux Klan led to extralegal restrictions on freedom.

A few cases reached the Supreme Court after the armistice but while the Bolshevik scare was raging. In 1919 in the case of Schenck v. United States a unanimous Court, led by Justice Holmes, upheld the conviction of a man charged under national legislation with conspiring to stimulate insubordination in the armed forces. Justice Holmes laid down this criterion: 'The question in every case is whether the words are used in such circumstances and are of such a nature as to create a clear and present danger that they will bring about the substantive evils that Congress has a right to prevent.' A unanimous Court also upheld the conviction of Eugene V. Debs, the leading American Socialist, for his opposition to the War.

Near the end of 1919 Justices Holmes and Brandeis broke with the majority of the Court in the case of Abrams v. United States, in which the majority upheld the conviction of men who had published leaflets opposing Allied attacks on the Russian Bolshevik government. The case is of historic importance because of the eloquent passage in Justice Holmes' dissent, expressing a philosophy later accepted by the Court. Justice Holmes' dissenting opinions in the Lochner and Abrams cases are his most famous expressions of opinion concerning the judicial function in cases involving economic rights and civil liberties respectively. In the Abrams dissent Holmes wrote in part:

'Persecution for the expression of opinions seems to me perfectly logical. If you have no doubt of your premises or your power and want a certain result with all your heart you naturally express your wishes in law and sweep away all opposition. To allow opposition by speech seems to indicate that you think the speech impotent, as when a man says that he has squared the circle, or that you do not care wholeheartedly for the result, or that you doubt either your power or your premises. But when men have realized that time has upset many fighting faiths, they may come to believe even more than they believe the very foundations of their own conduct that the ultimate good desired is better reached by free trade in ideas,—that the best test of truth is the power of the thought to get itself accepted in the competition of the market; and that truth is the only ground upon which their wishes safely can be carried out. That, at any rate, is the theory of our Constitution. It is an experiment, as all life is an experiment. Every year, if not every day, we have to wager our salvation upon some prophecy based upon imperfect knowledge. While that experiment is part of our system I think that we should be eternally vigilant against attempts to check the expressions of opinions that we loathe and believe to be fraught with death, unless they so imminently threaten immediate interference with the lawful and pressing purposes of the law that an immediate check is required to save the country. . . . Only the emergency that makes it immediately dangerous to leave the correction of evil counsels to time warrants making any exception to the sweeping command, "Congress shall make no law abridging the freedom of speech". Of course I am speaking only of expressions of opinion and exhortations, which are all that were uttered here; but I regret that I cannot put into more impressive words my belief that in their conviction upon this indictment the defendants were deprived of their rights under the Constitution of the United States.'

During the next few years the majority of the Court continued to sustain convictions under national and State legislation over the opposition of Justice Holmes and, even more, of Justice Brandeis.

State cases kept challenging the Hurtado rule, which had the effect of preventing the Court from using the due process clause of the Fourteenth Amendment to protect both the substantive freedoms and the procedural rights specified in the Bill of Rights from State action. In 1925 in the case of Gitlow v. New York the Court, though it upheld the conviction of Gitlow under State anti-seditious legislation, gave way partly on the doctrinal point: 'For present purposes we may and do assume that freedom of speech and of the press—which are protected by the First Amendment from abridgement by Congress—are among the fundamental personal rights and "liberties" protected by the due process clause of the Fourteenth Amendment from impairment by the States.'

In the 1920's the Court was called on to deal with cases under the provisions of the Fourth Amendment concerning searches, seizures, and warrants at a time when law-enforcement authorities were using new devices like wire-tapping machinery and finding it very difficult to obtain evidence of violations of the Prohibition Amendment and legislation unless they searched swiftly-moving bootleggers without warrants. These cases made the justices think more carefully about the essentials of fair procedure. Furthermore, the Court showed more concern than in the past about the treatment of Negro defendants in southern courts; and in the case of Powell v. Alabama in 1932, arising from the trial of Negro defendants in the famous 'Scottsboro case', the Court breached the Hurtado rule—though it did not disturb the decision of the Hurtado case—on a question of procedural rights. After citing a few cases in the economic field in which the Court had held that the payment of just compensation for private property taken for public use, required by the Fifth Amendment of the Bill of Rights, was also required by the due process clause of the Fourteenth Amendment and the Gitlow case in the field of substantive freedoms, Justice Sutherland wrote:

'These later cases establish that notwithstanding the sweeping character of the language in the Hurtado Case, the rule laid down is not without exceptions. The rule is an aid to construction, and in some instances may be conclusive; but it must yield to more compelling considerations whenever such considerations exist. The fact that the right involved is of such a character that it cannot be denied without violating those "fundamental principles of liberty and justice which lie at the base of all our civil and political institutions" . . . is obviously one of those compelling considerations which must prevail in determining whether it is embraced within the due process clause of the Fourteenth Amendment, although it be specifically dealt with in another part of the federal Constitution. . . . While the question has never been categorically determined by this court, a consideration of the nature of the right and a review of the expressions of this and other courts, makes it clear that the right to the aid of counsel is of this fundamental character.'

The effect of the new construction of the due process clause of the Fourteenth Amendment was to increase enormously the opportunities for national judicial protection of civil liberties. Supreme Court justices became ever more eager to take advantage of the opportunities through the 1930's and early 1940's; and while the ardour of the Court cooled in the late 1940's and early 1950's, it still protects civil liberties to-day more carefully, at least in some respects, than at any time before 1925.

The lines of decisions since 1925 in cases involving procedural rights have been complex, but a few generalizations may be made about them. First, the generalization the Court itself makes is that among the procedural rights which are protected against national infringement by the Bill of Rights are some which are now protected against State infringement by the due process clause of the Fourteenth Amendment and some which are not: for example, the right to the assistance of counsel, which in some circumstances includes the right to the assistance of counsel whether the defendant wants it or not, and the immunity from unreasonable searches and seizures are; and the immunity from trial unless on an indictment of a grand jury, the right not to be a witness in a case against oneself, and the immunity from double jeopardy are not.

Second, the Court is in fact, though not yet clearly in the rationale of its decisions, abandoning the clear-cut distinction the two lists imply. The Court has sometimes ruled, on the one hand, that the right to be given the assistance of counsel, though now protected by the national Constitution in both national and State courts, must be respected more carefully in the former, controlled by 'the specific guarantees found in the Sixth Amendment', than in the latter, controlled by the 'less rigid and more fluid' concept of due process of law in the Fourteenth Amendment. In other words, a right 'brought over' from the Bill of Rights is not necessarily 'brought over' completely. The Court has indicated, on the other hand, that while the explicit constitutional immunity from double jeopardy does not restrict State action, the due process clause of the Fourteenth Amendment puts some limit on harassing a defendant in State courts. In other words, a right not 'brought over' from the Bill of Rights may in fact be partly 'brought over'. The truth is that the judges of the Supreme Court are not applying formulae of constitutional interpretation but their own sense of justice.

Finally, the Court has, on the whole, enforced the guarantees of procedural rights in both national and, where applicable, State cases more effectively than ever before. The most important exception is that it has weakened the content of the immunity from unreasonable searches and seizures, though it has extended its scope to State action. The Court has continued to be faced, as in the Prohibition cases, with the conflicting needs of private rights and effective law-enforcement. Although its decisions have, in consequence, been particularly erratic in this field, their net effect has been to make the immunity less protective. The Court is under pressure also to attenuate the constitutional immunity from self-incrimination, which it still applies as a barrier to national action only, especially as the immunity affects congressional investigations. (Otherwise the Court exercises very little control over congressional investigating procedures.)

In cases involving substantive freedoms, which have been protected against both levels of government since the Gitlow case, the Court has accepted the philosophy of the Abrams dissent, though it has applied it in various ways. In the early 1940's it made the phrase 'clear and present danger', which Holmes had first used in the Schenck case, a cliché of constitutional law. It gave it great force as a test of whether government action affecting civil liberties dealt with a situation that justified the action. The Court held, for example, that the validity of a statute depended on whether it dealt with a 'clear and present danger' not only in the instant case brought under it but in any conceivable case which might be brought under it. The reason for this rule was that the mere existence of the statute restricted freedom. 'Where regulations of the liberty of free discussion are concerned . . .', the Court held in the case of Thornhill v. Alabama in 1940, 'it is the statute, and not the accusation or the evidence under it, which prescribes the limits of permissible conduct and warns against transgression.'

Moreover, the Court kept setting a higher standard, at least in State cases. It finally admitted it had departed from one of the principles of the exercise of judicial review: the presumption of the constitutionality of legislation. The principle is that the burden is always supposed to be on a challenger of a statute to prove its invalidity. But in the case of Thomas *v.* Collins in 1945 the Court held: '. . . the usual presumption supporting legislation is balanced by the preferred place given in our scheme to the great, the indispensable democratic freedoms secured by the First Amendment.'

Major beneficiaries of the protection of the Court were the religious sectarians, the Jehovah's Witnesses, though the legislation they challenged was of general application. Laws requiring pedlars of religious literature to take out pedlars' permits were held to abridge their liberty. Legislation taxing religious canvassers was held invalid on the same ground. (Legislation banning the use of child labour in such activities was sustained.) The conviction of Witnesses who played anti-Catholic phonograph records in Catholic neighbourhoods on the charge of inciting a breach of the peace was reversed. (The conviction of a Witness who called a town marshal a 'God damned racketeer' and 'damned Fascist' was upheld.) Orders of Boards of Education which required school children to salute the flag were first sustained and then held invalid. In the last case, West Virginia State Board of Education *v.* Barnette in 1943, Justice Jackson said for the Court:

'The very purpose of a Bill of Rights was to withdraw certain subjects from the vicissitudes of political controversy, to place them beyond the reach of majorities and officials and to establish them as legal principles to be applied by the courts. One's right to life, liberty, and property, to free speech, a free press, freedom of worship and assembly, and other fundamental rights may not be submitted to vote; they depend on the outcome of no elections. . . .

'If there is any fixed star in our constitutional constellation,

281

it is that no official, high or petty, can prescribe what shall be orthodox in politics, nationalism, religion, or other matters of opinion or force citizens to confess by word or act their faith therein. If there are any circumstances which permit an exception, they do not now occur to us.'

The Court found its position as the guardian of freedom embarrassing when it came to review national abridgement of substantive freedoms in the Second World War. The most important abridgement was the displacement and detention of about 70,000 Nisei, American-born citizens of Japanese descent. (Japanese-born residents were ineligible for citizenship and could be detained as alien enemies.) In 1944 in Korematsu v. United States the Court, though very disturbed, sustained the action of the national government in evacuating the Nisei from the west coast. The majority salved its conscience by pretending to find 'circumstances of direst emergency and peril', though the dissenting justices showed that when the danger of Japanese invasion seemed greatest, the military authorities did not remove the Nisei to relocation centres, and when the danger ebbed but anti-Japanese feeling became intense, they did. The Court denounced attempts to restrict the movements of some of the Nisei who had been individually cleared of suspicion. After the War it denounced the substitution of military tribunals for civil courts in Hawaii during the War. But the later decisions could not make up for the failure of the Court to meet a crucial test of its doctrines in the Korematsu case.

During the Communist scare after the War the Court has openly retreated from its advanced position. The Court of the late 1940's and early 1950's has been less willing to find a civil liberty issue involved in a case than the Court of the late 1930's and early 1940's. When it has found it, it has been less willing to make the 'clear and present danger' doctrine a stringent test. In 1951, for example, in the case of Dennis v. United States the Court upheld the conviction of eleven Communist leaders for conspiring to advocate the overthrow of the government by force and violence. Chief Justice Vinson said of the 'clear and present danger' test: '. . . neither Justice Holmes nor Justice

Brandeis ever envisioned that a shorthand phrase should be crystallized into a rigid rule to be applied inflexibly without regard to the circumstances of each case. Speech is not an absolute, above and beyond control by the legislature when its judgment, subject to review here, is that certain kinds of speech are so undesirable as to warrant criminal sanction.' None the less, the Chief Justice sought to fit the decision within the formula. He argued that the existence of a group aiming at the overthrow of the government and attempting to prepare its members to 'strike when the leaders feel the circumstances permit' constitutes the requisite danger, even though the date of the uprising may seem remote and its success unlikely. Justices Black and Douglas dissented.

It is important, however, not to exaggerate the extent of the retreat. If the Supreme Court has abandoned the extreme—probably excessive—position it took a few years ago, it has not stopped insisting that there be more justification for government action in civil liberty cases than in most others.

Third, the protection of civil rights. The Fourteenth Amendment contains a clause that no State shall 'deny to any person within its jurisdiction the equal protection of the laws'. The Supreme Court has held that the due process clause of the Fifth Amendment requires the nation to grant equal protection too. The Fifteenth and Nineteenth Amendments prohibit both levels of government from abridging the right of citizens to vote on account of race, colour, or previous condition of servitude and on account of sex. These several provisions are the constitutional bases of what may be called the national civil rights of Americans.

It is useful to note the distinctions that may be made between civil liberties and civil rights. The Bill of Rights defines civil liberties in seventeenth- and eighteenth-century terms. They are liberties of the subject, of which the government may not unduly deprive him. A subject who believes that the government infringes his liberties unduly asks a Court to declare the action invalid. He presents, the Court recognizes, a justiciable issue.

Civil rights differ from ordinary civil liberties, and ordinary economic rights too, in two ways. First, they give a subject a further ground on which to challenge infringement of his liberty: the deprivation itself may be valid, but its unequal imposition or effects on different subjects may not. Second, they give the subject a ground on which to demand the privileges bestowed by governments. As a distinct constitutional basis of action the second ground has been of much greater practical importance than the first.

Modern democratic governments give as well as take away. They grant widely the privilege to vote, to send children to free schools, and to receive the benefits of social services, for example. If these privileges are often referred to as rights—and may indeed be made duties, by compulsory school attendance laws for example—it is because they are now recognized as almost fundamental in democratic societies. Constitutional law often lags behind. Under the traditional constitutional definitions of civil liberties a subject may not ask a Court to force the government to grant him the benefits it bestows. He is not able, in other words, to present a justiciable issue. The constitutional guarantee of the equal protection of the laws, for example, may enable him to present one.

In civil rights cases, especially those involving questions of privileges, the Supreme Court has frequently had to deal with the position of the Negro race. In 1880, for example, it held invalid in separate cases the provisions of a State law and the action of a State judge excluding Negroes from juries. In 1896 it sustained a State law that required railways to provide 'equal but separate' (later usually referred to as 'separate but equal') accommodations for whites and Negroes. In 1899 it permitted a southern county to provide a high school for whites without providing one for Negroes. In 1903 Justice Holmes wrote an Opinion of the Court in which he said that the Court had no practical means of protecting the suffrage rights of Negroes in the South. In 1908 the Court sustained a State law requiring a university to teach whites and Negroes separately. Since some States systematically but informally excluded Negroes from their juries in practice, the one judicial vindication of the civil rights of Negroes in these cases was of little importance.

Then the Court began to examine State action more closely. In 1914 it declared invalid a State law that permitted grossly unequal railway accommodations to be offered the segregated races. In 1915 it held invalid the so-called 'grandfather clause' of the Oklahoma Constitution, which set lower suffrage requirements for the lineal descendants of those who had voted for any form of government or who had lived abroad before the adoption of the national Fifteenth Amendment, as a patent discrimination against Negroes. In 1917 it held invalid a city zoning ordinance that established exclusive residential zones for whites and Negroes. None of these decisions helped the Negroes very much in practice, however: separate facilities were still not in fact equal; Negroes were prevented from voting by a number of legal devices and by social pressure; and in 1926 the Court refused to disturb the right of private persons to enter into restrictive covenants barring the sale or lease of property to Negroes.

The increasing concern of the Supreme Court for civil liberties in the 1930's and 1940's was accompanied by an increasing concern for civil rights, and the latter trend has never waned. The Court has probed ever more deeply beneath the form of government action to its substance. In 1935 it set aside the conviction in the second 'Scottsboro case' because Negroes were systematically excluded from grand and petit juries in the counties where the indictment was found and the trial held. By 1944 it had made it impossible to use any legal device to discriminate clearly against Negro voting in southern Democratic primaries and general elections. In 1948 it held that neither a State nor a national court could enforce a private restrictive racial covenant. By 1954 it had laid down a line of precedents requiring increasingly strong proof that separate educational facilities were really equal.

The last cases had usually involved State facilities for higher education, for the National Association for the Advancement of Colored People, which helped bring many of the cases to the Court, had apparently decided to attack segregated education at that level first, as the best way to lead the Court and southern opinion to the decisive issue. The Court ruled on that issue on

285

17 May 1954: it held unanimously that separate public school facilities 'are inherently unequal' and therefore unconstitutional. It postponed argument on the means it should use to carry out its decision until the 1954-5 term. Although Negro rights in practice still fall short of Negro rights in law, the decisions of the Court in the last twenty years have helped to improve the position of the Negro in the South—in the administration of justice, elections, and educational and other facilities. The decision of 17 May 1954 is an augury of more help to come.

Little need be said about other cases involving civil rights. The Court has protected aliens, particularly Asiatics, from some forms of national and State discrimination. It has not had to protect female voting rights under the Nineteenth Amendment, though it has had occasion to deal with sex discrimination in jury service. In 1927 the Court sustained a State law permitting, under very careful provisions to prevent abuse, the sexual sterilization of mental hospital patients afflicted with hereditary forms of insanity and imbecility; the law had been attacked as a violation of the due process and equal protection clauses. In 1942 in the case of Skinner v. Oklahoma, however, it declared a State law permitting the sterilization of 'habitual criminals' to be contrary to the equal protection clause. The Court objected to the distinctions between the crimes which made a third offender subject to the law and those which did not: 'Sterilization of those who have thrice committed grand larceny with immunity for those who are embezzlers is a clear, pointed, unmistakable discrimination. . . . The equal protection clause would indeed be a formula of empty words if such conspicuously artificial lines could be drawn. . . .' Chief Justice Stone, concurring, thought the decision would rest better on due process grounds.

The vital issue in each case is: is the inequality of treatment reasonable? Again the judges of the Supreme Court are not interpreting the Constitution so much as their own sense of justice. In recent years, on the racial questions that have increasingly held their attention, their sense of justice has been markedly democratic.

Finally, the limits of judicial protection of freedom. Justice

Jackson's argument in the West Virginia flag-salute case that the provisions of the Bill of Rights were to be enforced by the courts 'beyond the reach of majorities' and subject to 'the outcome of no elections' was an assertion of judicial power in a limited field no less arrogant than the assertions of more general application a few years earlier. But Justice Jackson's faith in judicial power was breached a year later. Dissenting in the case that upheld the evacuation of the Nisei, he suggested that, while the Court should not enforce the military order, it should not try to control the action of the military authorities: 'I would not lead people to rely on this Court for a review that seems to me wholly delusive.' Indeed, judicial protection of freedom in critical times has not had an impressive record. The four times when the freedom of white men has been most threatened from within in the United States have been: the period of the enforcement of the Alien and Sedition Acts; the period of the conflict between the North and South, with the suppression of dissent in the South before the Civil War, the suspension of some procedural guarantees during the Civil war, and the infringement of some rights in the South during the 'reconstruction' era after the Civil War; the period of the First World War and Bolshevik scare; and the present period of the Communist scare. The Court has never successfully challenged the main elements of the suppression of freedom during the height of a crisis. It has sometimes challenged minor restrictions; it has sometimes won redress for victims after the crisis has passed; it has sometimes, especially in the 1930's and early 1940's in civil liberty cases and since the 1930's in civil rights cases, led a political trend to greater freedom; but it has not safeguarded freedom at the points and at the times that it has needed safeguarding most.

The truth is that the Court is no less a political institution in interpreting constitutional provisions about private rights than in interpreting constitutional provisions generally. It can lead, but not long set itself against, the main stream of public opinion. The Court must, in its fashion, follow the election returns.

This is not, however, the chief reason for the weakness of judicial protection of freedom. Except at the height of a crisis, national public opinion is rarely strongly insistent on the legal suppression of freedom. The Court soon regains its influence in interpreting civil liberty and civil rights provisions. The chief reason is that the most persistent and pervasive threat to freedom is not amenable to judicial control. It is private or social pressure. Alexis de Tocqueville wrote in the 1830's:

'In America the majority raises formidable barriers around the liberty of opinion; within the barriers an author may write what he pleases, but woe to him if he goes beyond them. Not that he is in danger of an auto-da-fé, but he is exposed to continued obloquy and persecution. His political career is closed forever, since he has offended the only authority that is able to open it. Every sort of compensation, even that of celebrity, is refused to him. Before making public his opinions he thought he had sympathizers; now it seems to him that he has none any more since he has revealed himself to everyone; then those who blame him criticize loudly and those who think as he does keep quiet and move away without courage. He yields at length, overcome by the daily effort which he has to make, and subsides into silence, as if he felt remorse for having spoken the truth.'[1]

If de Tocqueville exaggerated the extent of the limits on free discussion, he at least discerned the cause. The passage is topical to-day.

It is important to keep in mind that the constitutional guarantees define *civil* liberties and rights, that is, liberties and rights against government action. Ordinarily they do not provide in themselves opportunities for challenging the exercise of private power in the courts. In the absence of appropriate legislation, the Supreme Court has had difficulty in finding justiciable issues arising from private or social infringements of freedom. The strange and tortuous legal reasoning it has had to use raises doubts, indeed, whether it ought to try, without legislative support, to control the private exercise of power.

Thus, in 1944 in the case of Steele *v.* Louisville & Nashville R.R. Co. the Court held that a trade union could not discrim-

[1] *Democracy in America* (Phillips Bradley, ed., New York: Alfred A. Knopf, 1945), I, 264. Quoted with permission of the publishers.

inate against Negro workers when engaged in collective bargaining. Since the provisions of the national Constitution apply only to government action and the provisions of national legislation permitting the trade union to act as a bargaining agent were silent on the issue before the Court, the Court justified its decision on the ground that it could be inferred that Congress would not allow a trade union which discriminated to act as a bargaining agent. Chief Justice Stone put it delicately in the Opinion of the Court: 'Congress plainly did not undertake to authorize the bargaining representative to make such discrimination.' Justice Murphy put it more frankly and accurately in his concurring opinion: 'The Act contains no language which directs the manner in which the bargaining representative shall perform its duties. But it cannot be assumed that Congress meant to authorize the representative to act so as to ignore rights guaranteed by the Constitution. Otherwise the Act would bear the stigma of unconstitutionality. . . .' In 1946 the Court held that a company-owned town could not require pedlars of religious literature to apply for permits. In 1948 it held that for a State or national court to uphold a private restrictive racial covenant was unconstitutional government action. The decisions of the Court in the 'white primary' cases have been mentioned in Chapter 4. Similar decisions in segregated education cases are now likely, since some southern States have threatened to turn their public school systems into 'private' school systems in order to evade the anti-segregation decision of 1954.

Even the most determined Court, however, cannot strike at the subtler forms of private pressure. There are still many southern communities where Negroes dare not exercise their legal civil rights. There are still suppressions of freedom of speech the Courts cannot reach. Ironically, the present social pressure against freedom has been largely directed by a man able to take advantage of constitutional provisions and interpretations that are as much a part of the English heritage of constitutional government in America as the Bill of Rights. Senator McCarthy has made statements protected by the constitutional immunity of senatorial speech which even the American law of libel would apply to; he has used the constitu-

T

tional authority of Congress to conduct investigations to further his activities. On the other hand, he has complained of the constitutional provisions that appear to stand in his way, in particular the constitutional guarantee of immunity from self-incrimination. But 'McCarthyism' neither fundamentally depends on nor is seriously hampered by constitutional clauses.

Whether it waxes or wanes is not a question of law but of politics. The preservation of freedom is, in the last analysis, not a task for the American courts but for the American people. At times the issue of the present crisis may seem in doubt. But it should be some comfort, and perhaps a guide, to remember that in past crises the principle of the Declaration of Independence 'that all men are created equal, that they are endowed by their Creator with certain unalienable rights, that among these are life, liberty, and the pursuit of happiness' has prevailed. That assertion, according to Abraham Lincoln,

'was of no practical use in effecting our separation from Great Britain; and it was placed in the Declaration not for that, but for future use. Its authors meant it to be—as, thank God, it is now proving itself—a stumbling-block to all those who in after times might seek to turn a free people back into the hateful paths of despotism. They knew the proneness of prosperity to breed tyrants, and they meant when such should reappear in this fair land and commence their vocation, they should find left for them at least one hard nut to crack.'

It has not been cracked yet.

Appendix

Constitution of the United States of America

PREAMBLE

We the People of the United States, in order to form a more perfect Union, establish justice, insure domestic tranquility, provide for the common defence, promote the general welfare, and secure the blessings of liberty to ourselves and our posterity, do ordain and establish this Constitution for the United States of America.

ARTICLE I

Section 1. All legislative powers herein granted shall be vested in a Congress of the United States, which shall consist of a Senate and House of Representatives.

Section 2. The House of Representatives shall be composed of members chosen every second year by the people of the several States, and the electors in each State shall have the qualifications requisite for electors of the most numerous branch of the State legislature.

No person shall be a Representative who shall not have attained to the age of twenty-five years, and been seven years a citizen of the United States, and who shall not, when elected, be an inhabitant of that State in which he shall be chosen.

Representatives and direct taxes shall be apportioned among the several States which may be included within this Union, according to their respective numbers, which shall be determined by adding to the whole number of free persons, including those bound to service for a term of years, and excluding Indians not taxed, three fifths of all other persons. The actual enumeration shall be made within three years after the first meeting of the Congress of the United States, and within every subsequent term of ten years, in such manner as they shall by law direct. The number of Representatives shall not exceed one for every thirty thousand, but each State shall have at least one Representative; and until such enumeration shall be made, the State of New Hampshire shall be entitled to chuse three, Massachusetts eight, Rhode-Island and Providence Plantations one, Connecticut five, New-York six, New Jersey four, Pennsylvania eight, Delaware one, Maryland six, Virginia ten, North Carolina five, South Carolina five, and Georgia three.

When vacancies happen in the representation from any State, the executive authority thereof shall issue writs of election to fill such vacancies.

The House of Representatives shall chuse their Speaker and other officers; and shall have the sole power of impeachment.

Section 3. The Senate of the United States shall be composed of two Senators from each State, chosen by the legislature thereof, for six years; and each Senator shall have one vote.

Immediately after they shall be assembled in consequence of the first election, they shall be divided as equally as may be into three classes. The seats of the Senators of the first class shall be vacated at the expiration of the second year, of the second class at the expiration of the fourth year, and of the third class at the expiration of the sixth year, so that one third may be chosen every second year; and if vacancies happen by resignation, or otherwise, during the recess of the legislature of any State, the executive thereof may make temporary appointments until the next meeting of the legislature, which shall then fill such vacancies.

No person shall be a Senator who shall not have attained to the age of thirty years, and been nine years a citizen of the United States, and who shall not, when elected, be an inhabitant of that State for which he shall be chosen.

The Vice President of the United States shall be President of the Senate, but shall have no vote, unless they be equally divided.

The Senate shall chuse their other officers, and also a President pro tempore, in the absence of the Vice President, or when he shall exercise the office of President of the United States.

The Senate shall have the sole power to try all impeachments. When sitting for that purpose, they shall be on oath or affirmation. When the President of the United States is tried, the Chief Justice shall preside: And no person shall be convicted without the concurrence of two thirds of the members present.

Judgment in cases of impeachment shall not extend further than to removal from office, and disqualification to hold and enjoy any office of honour, trust or profit under the United States: but the party convicted shall nevertheless be liable and subject to indictment, trial, judgment and punishment, according to law.

Section 4. The times, places and manner of holding elections for senators and representatives, shall be prescribed in each State by the legislature thereof; but the Congress may at any time by law make or alter such regulations, except as to the places of chusing Senators.

The Congress shall assemble at least once in every year, and such meeting shall be on the first Monday in December, unless they shall by law appoint a different day.

Section 5. Each House shall be the judge of the elections, returns and qualifications of its own members, and a majority of each shall constitute a quorum to do business; but a smaller number may adjourn from day to day, and may be authorized to compel the attendance of absent members, in such manner, and under such penalties as each house may provide.

Each House may determine the rules of its proceedings, punish its members for disorderly behaviour, and, with the concurrence of two thirds, expel a member.

Each House shall keep a journal of its proceedings, and from time to time publish the same, excepting such parts as may in their judgment require secrecy; and the yeas and nays of the members of either House on any question shall, at the desire of one fifth of those present, be entered on the journal.

Neither House, during the session of Congress, shall, without the consent of the other, adjourn for more than three days, nor to any other place than that in which the two houses shall be sitting.

Section 6. The Senators and Representatives shall receive a compensation for their services, to be ascertained by law, and paid out of the Treasury of the United States. They shall in all cases, except treason, felony and breach of the peace, be privileged from arrest during their attendance at the session of their respective houses, and in going to and returning from the same; and for any speech or debate in either house, they shall not be questioned in any other place.

No Senator or Representative shall, during the time for which he was elected, be appointed to any civil office under the authority of the United States, which shall have been created, or the emoluments whereof shall have been encreased during such time; and no person holding any office under the United States, shall be a member of either house during his continuance in office.

Section 7. All bills for raising revenue shall originate in the House of Representatives; but the Senate may propose or concur with amendments as on other bills.

Every bill which shall have passed the House of Representatives and the Senate, shall, before it become a law, be presented to the President of the United States; if he approve he shall sign it, but if not he shall return it, with his objections to that house in which it shall have originated, who shall enter the objections at large on their journal, and proceed to reconsider it. If after such reconsideration two thirds of that House shall agree to pass the bill, it shall be sent, together with the objections, to the other House, by which it shall likewise be reconsidered, and if approved by two thirds of that House, it shall become a law. But in all such cases the votes of both Houses shall be determined by yeas and nays, and the names of the persons voting for and against the bill shall be entered on the journal of each House respectively. If any bill shall not be returned by the President within ten days (Sundays excepted) after it shall have been presented to him, the same shall be a law, in like manner as if he had signed it, unless the Congress by their adjournment prevent its return, in which case it shall not be a law.

Every order, resolution, or vote to which the concurrence of the Senate and House of Representatives may be necessary (except on a question of adjournment) shall be presented to the President of the United States; and before the same shall take effect, shall be approved by him, or being disapproved by him, shall be repassed by two thirds of the Senate and House of Representatives, according to the rules and limitations prescribed in the case of a bill.

Section 8. The Congress shall have power to lay and collect taxes, duties, imposts and excises, to pay the debts and provide for the common defence and general welfare of the United States; but all duties, imposts and excises shall be uniform throughout the United States;

To borrow money on the credit of the United States;

To regulate commerce with foreign nations, and among the several States, and with the Indian tribes;

To establish an uniform rule of naturalization, and uniform laws on the subject of bankruptcies throughout the United States;

To coin money, regulate the value thereof, and of foreign coin, and fix the standard of weights and measures;

To provide for the punishment of counterfeiting the securities and current coin of the United States;

To establish post offices and post roads;

To promote the progress of science and useful arts, by securing for limited times to authors and inventors the exclusive right to their respective writings and discoveries;

To constitute tribunals inferior to the Supreme Court;

To define and punish piracies and felonies committed on the high seas, and offences against the law of nations;

To declare war, grant letters of marque and reprisal, and make rules concerning captures on land and water;

To raise and support armies, but no appropriation of money to that use shall be for a longer term than two years;

To provide and maintain a Navy;

To make rules for the government and regulation of the land and naval forces;

To provide for calling forth the militia to execute the laws of the Union, suppress insurrections and repel invasions;

To provide for organizing, arming, and disciplining, the militia, and for governing such part of them as may be employed in the service of the United States, reserving to the States respectively, the appointment of the officers, and the authority of training the militia according to the discipline prescribed by Congress;

To exercise exclusive legislation in all cases whatsoever, over such district (not exceeding ten miles square) as may, by cession of particular States, and the acceptance of Congress, become the seat of the Government of the United States, and to exercise like authority over all places purchased by the consent of the legislature of the State in which the same shall be, for the erection of forts, magazines, arsenals, dock-yards, and other needful buildings;—And

To make all laws which shall be necessary and proper for carrying into execution the foregoing powers, and all other powers vested by this Constitution in the Government of the United States, or in any department or officer thereof.

Section 9. The migration or importation of such persons as any of the States now existing shall think proper to admit, shall not be prohibited by the Congress prior to the year one thousand eight hundred and eight, but a tax or duty may be imposed on such importation, not exceeding ten dollars for each person.

The privilege of the writ of habeas corpus shall not be suspended, unless when in cases of rebellion or invasion the public safety may require it.

No bill of attainder or ex post facto law shall be passed.

No capitation, or other direct, tax shall be laid, unless in proportion to the census or enumeration herein before directed to be taken.

No tax or duty shall be laid on articles exported from any State.

No preference shall be given by any regulation of commerce or revenue to the ports of one State over those of another; nor shall vessels bound to, or from, one State, be obliged to enter, clear, or pay duties in another.

No money shall be drawn from the Treasury, but in consequence of appropriations made by law; and a regular statement and account of the receipts and expenditures of all public money shall be published from time to time.

No title of nobility shall be granted by the United States: And no person holding any office of profit or trust under them, shall, without the consent of the Congress, accept of any present, moleument, office, or title, of any kind whatever, from any King, Prince, or foreign State.

Section 10. No State shall enter into any treaty, alliance, or confederation; grant letters of marque and reprisal; coin money; emit bills of credit; make any thing but gold and silver coin a tender in payment of debts; pass any bill of attainder, ex post facto law, or law impairing the obligations of contract, or grant any title of nobility.

No State shall, without the consent of the Congress, lay any imposts or duties on imports or exports, except what may be absolutely necessary for executing its inspection laws: and the net produce of all duties and imposts, laid by any State on imports or exports, shall be for the use of the Treasury of the United States; and all such laws shall be subject to the revision and controul of the Congress.

No State shall, without the consent of Congress, lay any duty of tonnage, keep troops, or ships of war in time of peace, enter into any agreement or compact with another State, or with a foreign power, or engage in war, unless actually invaded, or in such imminent danger as will not admit of delay.

ARTICLE II

Section 1. The executive power shall be vested in a President of the United States of America. He shall hold his office during the term of four years, and, together with the Vice President, chosen for the same term, be elected, as follows

Each State shall appoint, in such manner as the legislature thereof may direct, a number of electors, equal to the whole number of senators and representatives to which the State may be entitled in the Congress: but no senator or representative, or person holding an office of trust or profit under the United States, shall be appointed an elector.

The electors shall meet in their respective States, and vote by ballot for two persons, of whom one at least shall not be an inhabitant of the same State with themselves. And they shall make a list of all the persons voted for, and of the number of votes for each; which list they shall sign and certify, and transmit sealed to the seat of the Government of the United States, directed to the President of the Senate. The President of the Senate shall, in the presence of the Senate and House of Representatives, open all the certificates, and the votes shall then be counted. The person having the greatest number of votes shall be the President, if such number be a majority of the whole number of electors appointed; and if there be more than one who have such majority, and have an equal number of votes, then the House of Representatives shall immediately chuse by ballot one of them for President; and if no person have a majority, then from the five highest on the list the said House shall in like manner chuse the President. But in chusing the President, the votes shall be taken by States, the representation from each State having one vote; a quorum for this purpose shall consist of a member or members from two thirds of the States, and a majority of all the

States shall be necessary to a choice. In every case, after the choice of the President, the person having the greatest number of votes of the electors shall be the Vice President. But if there should remain two or more who have equal votes, the Senate shall chuse from them by ballot the Vice President.

The Congress may determine the time of chusing the electors, and the day on which they shall give their votes; which day shall be the same throughout the United States.

No person except a natural born citizen, or a citizen of the United States, at the time of the adoption of this Constitution, shall be eligible to the office of President; neither shall any person be eligible to that office who shall not have attained to the age of thirty five years, and been fourteen years a resident within the United States.

In case of the removal of the President from office, or of his death, resignation, or inability to discharge the powers and duties of the said office, the same shall devolve on the Vice President, and the Congress may by law provide for the case of removal, death, resignation or inability, both of the President and Vice President, declaring what officer shall then act as President, and such officer shall act accordingly, until the disability be removed, or a President shall be elected.

The President shall, at stated times, receive for his services, a compensation, which shall neither be encreased nor diminished during the period for which he shall have been elected, and he shall not receive within that period any other emolument from the United States, or any of them.

Before he enter on the execution of his office, he shall take the following oath or affirmation:—'I do solemnly swear (or affirm) that I will faithfully execute the office of President of the United States, and will to the best of my ability, preserve, protect and defend the Constitution of the United States.'

Section 2. The President shall be Commander in Chief of the Army and Navy of the United States, and of the militia of the several States, when called into the actual service of the United States; he may require the opinion, in writing, of the principal officer in each of the executive departments, upon any subject relating to the duties of their respective offices, and he shall have power to grant reprieves and pardons for offences against the United States, except in cases of impeachment.

He shall have power, by and with the advice and consent of the Senate, to make treaties, provided two thirds of the Senators present concur; and he shall nominate, and by and with the advice and consent of the Senate, shall appoint ambassadors, other public ministers and consuls, judges of the Supreme Court, and all other officers of the United States, whose appointments are not herein otherwise provided for, and which shall be established by law: but the Congress may by law vest the appointment of such inferior officers, as they think proper, in the President alone, in the courts of law, or in the heads of departments.

The President shall have power to fill up all vacancies that may happen during the recess of the Senate, by granting commissions which shall expire at the end of their next session.

Section 3. He shall from time to time give to the Congress information of the state of the Union, and recommend to their consideration such measures as he shall judge necessary and expedient; he may, on extraordinary occasions, convene both houses, or either of them, and in case of disagreement between them, with respect to the time of adjournment, he may adjourn them to such time as he shall think proper; he shall receive ambassadors and other public ministers; he shall take care that the laws be faithfully executed, and shall commission all the officers of the United States.

Section 4. The President, Vice President and all civil officers of the United States, shall be removed from office on impeachment for, and conviction of, treason, bribery, or other high crimes and misdemeanours.

ARTICLE III

Section 1. The judicial power of the United States, shall be vested in one Supreme Court, and in such inferior courts as the Congress may from time to time ordain and establish. The judges, both of the supreme and inferior courts, shall hold their offices during good behaviour, and shall, at stated times, receive for their services, a compensation, which shall not be diminished during their continuance in office.

Section 2. The judicial power shall extend to all cases, in law and equity, arising under this Constitution, the laws of the United States, and treaties made, or which shall be made, under their authority;—to all cases affecting ambassadors, other public ministers and consuls;—to all cases of admiralty and maritime jurisdiction;—to controversies to which the United States shall be a party;—to controversies between two or more States;—between a State and citizens of another State;—between citizens of different States;—between citizens of the same State claiming lands under grants of different States, and between a State, or the citizens thereof, and foreign States, citizens or subjects.

In all cases affecting ambassadors, other public ministers and consuls, and those in which a State shall be party, the Supreme Court shall have original jurisdiction. In all the other cases before mentioned, the Supreme Court shall have appellate jurisdiction, both as to law and fact, which such exceptions, and under such regulations as the Congress shall make.

The trial of all crimes, except in cases of impeachment, shall be by jury; and such trial shall be held in the State where the said crimes shall have been committed; but when not committed within any State, the trial shall be at such place or places as the Congress may by law have directed.

Section 3. Treason against the United States, shall consist only in levying war against them, or in adhering to their enemies, giving them aid and comfort. No person shall be convicted of treason unless on the testimony of two witnesses to the same overt act, or on confession in open court.

The Congress shall have power to declare the punishment of treason, but no attainder of treason shall work corruption of blood, or forfeiture except during the life of the person attainted.

ARTICLE IV

Section 1. Full faith and credit shall be given in each State to the public acts, records, and judicial proceedings of every other State. And the Congress may by general laws prescribe the manner in which such acts, records and proceedings shall be proved, and the effect thereof.

Section 2. The citizens of each State shall be entitled to all privileges and immunities of citizens in the several States.

A person charged in any State with treason, felony, or other crime, who shall flee from justice, and be found in another State, shall on demand of the executive authority of the State from which he fled, be delivered up, to be removed to the State having jurisdiction of the crime.

No person held to service or labour in one State, under the laws thereof, escaping into another, shall, in consequence of any law or regulation therein, be discharged from such service or labour, but shall be delivered up on claim of the party to whom such service or labour may be due.

Section 3. New States may be admitted by the Congress into this Union; but no new State shall be formed or erected within the jurisdiction of any other State; nor any State be formed by the junction of two or more States, or parts of States, without the consent of the legislatures of the States concerned as well as of the Congress.

The Congress shall have power to dispose of and make all needful rules and regulations respecting the Territory or other property belonging to the United States; and nothing in this Constitution shall be so construed as to prejudice any claims of the United States, or of any particular State.

Section 4. The United States shall guarantee to every State in this Union a republican form of Government, and shall protect each of them against invasion; and on application of the legislature, or of the executive (when the legislature cannot be convened) against domestic violence.

ARTICLE V

The Congress, whenever two thirds of both Houses shall deem it necessary, shall propose amendments to this Constitution, or, on the application of the legislatures of two thirds of the several States, shall call a convention for proposing amendments, which, in either case, shall be valid to all intents and purposes, as part of this Constitution, when ratified by the legislatures of three fourths of the several States, or by conventions in three fourths thereof, as the one or the other mode of ratification may be proposed by the Congress; provided that no amendment which may be made prior to the year one thousand eight hundred and eight shall in any manner affect the first and fourth clauses in the Ninth Section of the First Article; and that no State, without its consent, shall be deprived of its equal suffrage in the Senate.

ARTICLE VI

All debts contracted and engagements entered into, before the adoption of this Constitution, shall be as valid against the United States under this Constitution, as under the Confederation.

This Constitution, and the laws of the United States which shall be made in pursuance thereof; and all treaties made, or which shall be made, under the authority of the United States, shall be the supreme law of the land; and the judges in every State shall be bound thereby, anything in the Constitution or laws of any State to the contrary notwithstanding.

The Senators and Representatives before mentioned, and the members of the several State legislatures, and all executive and judicial officers, both of the United States and of the several States, shall be bound by oath or affirmation, to support this Constitution; but no religious test shall ever be required as a qualification to any office or public trust under the United States.

ARTICLE VII

The ratification of the conventions of nine States, shall be sufficient for the establishment of this Constitution between the States so ratifying the same. . . .

Amendments

ARTICLE I

Congress shall make no law respecting an establishment of religion, or prohibiting the free exercise thereof; or abridging the freedom of speech, or of the press; or the right of the people peaceably to assemble, and to petition the Government for a redress of grievances.

ARTICLE II

A well regulated militia, being necessary to the security of a free State, the right of the people to keep and bear arms, shall not be infringed.

ARTICLE III

No soldier shall, in time of peace be quartered in any house, without the consent of the owner, nor in time of war, but in a manner to be prescribed by law.

ARTICLE IV

The right of the people to be secure in their persons, houses, papers, and effects, against unreasonable searches and seizures, shall not be violated, and no warrants shall issue, but upon probable cause, supported by oath or affirmation, and particularly describing the place to be searched, and the persons or things to be seized.

ARTICLE V

No person shall be held to answer for a capital, or otherwise infamous crime, unless on a presentment or indictment of a grand jury, except in cases arising in the land or naval forces, or in the militia, when in actual service in time of war or public danger; nor shall any person be subject for the same offence to be twice put in jeopardy of life or limb; nor shall be compelled in any criminal case to be a witness against himself, nor be deprived of life, liberty, or property, without due process of law; nor shall private property be taken for public use, without just compensation.

ARTICLE VI

In all criminal prosecutions, the accused shall enjoy the right to a speedy and public trial, by an impartial jury of the State and district wherein the crime shall have been committed, which district shall have been previously ascertained by law, and to be informed of the nature and cause of the accusation; to be confronted with the witnesses against him; to have compulsory process for obtaining witnesses in his favour, and to have the assistance of counsel for his defence.

ARTICLE VII

In suits at common law, where the value in controversy shall exceed twenty dollars, the right of trial by jury shall be preserved, and no fact tried by a jury, shall be otherwise re-examined in any court of the United States, than according to the rules of the common law.

ARTICLE VIII

Excessive bail shall not be required, nor excessive fines imposed, nor cruel and unusual punishments inflicted.

ARTICLE IX

The enumeration in the Constitution, of certain rights, shall not be construed to deny or disparage others retained by the people.

ARTICLE X

The powers not delegated to the United States by the Constitution, nor prohibited by it to the States, are reserved to the States respectively, or to the people.

ARTICLE XI

The judicial power of the United States shall not be construed to extend to any suit in law or equity, commenced or prosecuted against one of the United States by citizens of another State, or by citizens or subjects of any foreign State.

ARTICLE XII

The electors shall meet in their respective States, and vote by ballot for President and Vice President, one of whom, at least, shall not be an inhabitant of the same State with themselves; they shall name in their ballots the person voted for as President, and in distinct ballots the person voted for as Vice President, and they shall make distinct lists of all persons voted for as President, and of all persons voted for as Vice President, and of the number of votes for each, which lists they shall sign and certify, and transmit sealed to the seat of the government of the United States, directed to the President of the Senate;—The President of the Senate shall, in the presence of the Senate and House of Representatives, open all the certificates and the votes shall then be counted;—The person having the greatest number of votes for President, shall be the President, if such number be a majority of the whole number of electors appointed; and if no person have such majority, then from the persons having the highest numbers not exceeding three on the list of those voted for as President, the House of Representatives shall choose immediately, by ballot, the President. But in choosing the President, the votes shall be taken by States, the representation from each State having one vote; a quorum for this purpose shall consist of a member or members from two-thirds of the States, and a majority of all the States shall be necessary to a choice. And if the House of Representatives shall not choose a President whenever the right of choice shall devolve upon them, before the fourth day of March next following, then the Vice President shall act as President, as in the case of the death or other constitutional disability of the President.—The person having the greatest number of votes as Vice President, shall be the Vice President, if such number be a majority of the whole number of electors appointed, and if no person have a majority, then from the two highest numbers on the list, the Senate shall choose the Vice President; a quorum for the purpose shall consist of two-thirds of the whole number of Senators, and a majority of the whole number shall be necessary to a choice. But no person constitutionally ineligible to the office of President shall be eligible to that of Vice President of the United States.

ARTICLE XIII

Section 1. Neither slavery nor involuntary servitude, except as a punishment for crime whereof the party shall have been duly convicted, shall exist within the United States, or any place subject to their jurisdiction.

Section 2. Congress shall have power to enforce this article by appropriate legislation.

ARTICLE XIV

Section 1. All persons born or naturalized in the United States, and subject to the jurisdiction thereof, are citizens of the United States and of the State wherein they reside. No State shall make or enforce any law which shall abridge the privileges or immunities of citizens of the United States; nor shall any State deprive any person of life, liberty, or property, without due process of law; nor deny to any person within its jurisdiction the equal protection of the laws.

Section 2. Representatives shall be apportioned among the several States according to their respective numbers, counting the whole number of persons in each State, excluding Indians not taxed. But when the right to vote at any election for the choice of electors for President and Vice President of the United States, Representatives in Congress, the executive and judicial officers of a State, or the members of the legislature thereof, is denied to any of the male inhabitants of such State, being twenty-one years of age, and citizens of the United States, or in any way abridged, except for participation in rebellion, or other crime, the basis of representation therein shall be reduced in the proportion which the number of such male citizens shall bear to the whole number of male citizens twenty-one years of age in such State.

Section 3. No person shall be a Senator or Representative in Congress, or elector of President and Vice President, or hold any office, civil or military, under the United States, or under any State, who, having previously taken an oath, as a member of Congress, or as an officer of the United States, or as a member of any State legislature, or as an executive or judicial officer of any State, to support the Constitution of the United States, shall have engaged in insurrection or rebellion against the same, or given aid or comfort to the enemies thereof. But Congress may by a vote of two-thirds of each House, remove such disability.

Section 4. The validity of the public debt of the United States, authorized by law, including debts incurred for payment of pensions and bounties for services in suppressing insurrection or rebellion, shall not be questioned. But neither the United States nor any State shall assume or pay any debt or obligation incurred in aid of insurrection or rebellion against the United States, or any claim for the loss or emancipation of any slave; but all such debts, obligations and claims shall be held illegal and void.

Section 5. The Congress shall have power to enforce, by appropriate legislation, the provisions of this article.

ARTICLE XV

Section 1. The right of citizens of the United States to vote shall not be denied or abridged by the United States or by any State on account of race, color, or previous condition of servitude—

Section 2. The Congress shall have power to enforce this article by appropriate legislation—

ARTICLE XVI

The Congress shall have power to lay and collect taxes on incomes, from whatever source derived, without apportionment among the several States, and without regard to any census or enumeration.

ARTICLE XVII

Section 1. The Senate of the United States shall be composed of two Senators from each State, elected by the people thereof, for six years; and each Senator shall have one vote. The electors in each State shall have the qualifications requisite for electors of the most numerous branch of the State legislatures.

Section 2. When vacancies happen in the representation of any State in the Senate, the executive authority of such State shall issue writs of election to fill such vacancies: *Provided,* That the legislature of any State may empower the executive thereof to make temporary appointments until the people fill the vacancies by election as the legislature may direct.

Section 3. This amendment shall not be so construed as to affect the election or term of any Senator chosen before it becomes valid as part of the Constitution.

ARTICLE XVIII

Section 1. After one year from the ratification of this article the manufacture, sale, or transportation of intoxicating liquors within, the importation thereof into, or the exportation thereof from the United States and all territory subject to the jurisdiction thereof for beverage purposes is hereby prohibited.

Section 2. The Congress and the several States shall have concurrent power to enforce this article by appropriate legislation.

Section 3. This article shall be inoperative unless it shall have been ratified as an amendment to the Constitution by the legislatures of the several States, as provided in the Constitution, within seven years from the date of the submission hereof to the States by the Congress.

ARTICLE XIX

Section 1. The right of citizens of the United States to vote shall not be denied or abridged by the United States or by any State on account of sex.

Section 2. Congress shall have power to enforce this article by appropriate legislation.

ARTICLE XX

Section 1. The terms of the President and Vice President shall end at noon on the 20th day of January, and the terms of Senators and Representatives at noon on the 3d day of January, of the years in which such terms would have ended if this article had not been ratified; and the terms of their successors shall then begin.

Section 2. The Congress shall assemble at least once in every year, and such meeting shall begin at noon on the 3d day of January, unless they shall by law appoint a different day.

Section 3. If, at the time fixed for the beginning of the term of the President, the President elect shall have died, the Vice President elect shall become President. If a President shall not have been chosen before the time fixed for the beginning of his term, or if the President elect shall have failed to qualify, then the Vice President elect shall act as President until a President shall have qualified; and the Congress may by law provide for the case wherein neither a President elect nor a Vice President elect shall have qualified, declaring who shall then act as President, or the manner in which one who is to act shall be selected, and such person shall act accordingly until a President or Vice President shall have qualified.

Section 4. The Congress may by law provide for the case of the death of any of the persons from whom the House of Representatives may choose a President whenever the right of choice shall have devolved upon them, and for the case of the death of any of the persons from whom the Senate may choose a Vice President whenever the right of choice shall have devolved upon them.

Section 5. Sections 1 and 2 shall take effect on the 15th day of October following the ratification of this article.

Section 6. This article shall be inoperative unless it shall have been ratified as an amendment to the Constitution by the legislatures of three-fourths of the several States within seven years from the date of its submission.

ARTICLE XXI

Section 1. The eighteenth article of amendment to the Constitution of the United States is hereby repealed.

Section 2. The transportation or importation into any State, Territory, or possession of the United States for delivery or use therein of intoxicating liquors, in violation of the laws thereof, is hereby prohibited.

Section 3. This article shall be inoperative unless it shall have been ratified as an amendment to the Constitution by conventions in the several States, as provided in the Constitution, within seven years from the date of the submission hereof to the States by the Congress.

ARTICLE XXII

Section 1. No person shall be elected to the office of the President more than twice, and no person who has held the office of President, or acted as President, for more than two years of a term to which some other person was elected President shall be elected to the office of the President more than once. But this Article shall not apply to any person holding the office of President when this Article was proposed by the Congress, and shall not prevent any person who may be holding the office of President, or acting as President during the term within which this Article becomes operative from holding the office of President or acting as President during the remainder of such term.

Section 2. This article shall be inoperative unless it shall have been ratified as an amendment to the Constitution by the legislatures of three-fourths of the several States within seven years from the date of its submission to the States by the Congress.

Index